SEMEIA 33

RENÉ GIRARD AND BIBLICAL STUDIES

Guest Editor of this Issue:

Andrew J. McKenna

© 1985

by the Society of Biblical Literature

SEMEIA 33

Copyright © 1985 by the Society of Biblical Literature

All rights reserved. No part of this work may be reproduced or transmitt
in any form or by any means, electronic or mechanical, including photo-
copying and recording, or by means of any information storage or retriev
system, except as may be expressly permitted by the 1976 Copyright Act
in writing from the publisher. Requests for permission should be address
in writing to the Rights and Permissions Office, Society of Biblical Liter
ture, 825 Houston Mill Road, Atlanta, GA 30329, USA.

ISSN 0095-571X
ISBN 978-1-58983-588-7

Printed in the United States of America
on acid-free paper

CONTENTS

I. Introduction
   Andrew J. McKenna 1

II. "The Ancient Trail Trodden by the Wicked": Job as Scapegoat
   René Girard 13

III. Applications
   Prophecy, Sacrifice and Repentance in the Story of Jonah
      Sandor Goodhart 43
   A Girardian Interpretation of Paul: Rivalry, Mimesis and Victimage in the Corinthian Correspondence
      Robert Hamerton-Kelly 65
   Community—Its Unity, Diversity and Universality
      Thomas Wieser 83
   Christian Morality and the Pauline Revelation
      Eric Gans...................................... 97

IV. Evaluations
   Christ's Death and the Prophetic Critique of Sacrifice
      Raymund Schwager, SJ 109
   René Girard on Job: The Question of the Scapegoat
      Baruch Levine.................................. 125
   The Innocent Transgressor: Jesus in Early Christian Myth and History
      Burton L. Mack 135

V. Bibliographical Note, Works Consulted 167

CONTRIBUTORS TO THIS ISSUE

Andrew J. McKenna
Department of Modern Languages
Loyola University of Chicago
Chicago, Illinois 60626

René Girard
Department of French
Stanford University
Stanford, California 94305

Sandor Goodhart
Department of English
University of Michigan
Ann Arbor, Michigan 48109

Robert Hamerton-Kelly
Dean of Chapel
Stanford University
Stanford, California 94305

Thomas Wieser
World Council of Churches
P.O. Box 66
150 Route de Ferney
1211 Geneva 20
Switzerland

Eric Gans
Department of French
University of California-Los Angeles
Los Angeles, California 90024

Raymund Schwager, SJ
Jesuitenkolleg Innsbruck
Sillgasse 6, Postfach 569
A 6021 Innsbruck
Austria

Baruch Levine
Department of Near Eastern Languages and Literature
New York University
50 Washington Square South
New York, New York 10012

Burton L. Mack
The Institute for Antiquity and Christianity
Claremont Graduate School
831 Dartmouth Avenue
Claremont, California 91711

I
INTRODUCTION

INTRODUCTION

Andrew J. McKenna
Loyola University of Chicago

René Girard's research spans the fields of literature, anthropology and Scripture, and somewhat in that order. *Deceit, Desire and the Novel* focuses on the first, articulating the dialectics of mimetic desire informing human relations as revealed in the novels of Cervantes, Stendhal, Dostoevsky, Flaubert and Proust. *Violence and the Sacred* uncovers this same dialectic in Greek tragedy, which serves in turn to reveal the fundamental motivations of ritual sacrifice as reported in anthropological literature. *Des Choses cachées depuis la fondation du monde* recapitulates the anthropological theory by way of formulating a genetic hypothesis of human culture, but it stands out as well by its central focus on Scripture, to which it accords a foundational role in the revelation of this dialectic and of its mortal consequences. In *Le Bouc émissaire* Girard responds to critics of his theory by differentiating rigorously between the role of the victim as it is disguised in myth on the one hand and as it is revealed in Scripture on the other. A fourth major work, on Job as scapegoat *(La Route antique des hommes pervers: Essais sur Job)*, has just appeared; a specimen of its opening chapters is offered here, along with Baruch Levine's dissenting response. All the fundamentals of Girard's theory are presented in these pages: mimetic rivalry in the community, the efficacy of sacrificial substitution which emerges to resolve it, the role of Scripture in revealing the mystified agency of the victim, in denouncing the efficacy of the scapegoat. In what follows, I shall briefly review these fundamentals across the books which focus on them in order to stress their unifying logic. And I will suggest in passing the import of the essays contained in this volume.

What Emma desires in *Madame Bovary* is a Great Passion. Such a desire does not originate with this farmer's daughter; it is insinuated to her by the books and stories surreptitiously consumed during her convent education. Her desire is mediated by the desires of others, rather like Dante's Paolo and Francesca, whose first kiss, as Girard reminds us elsewhere (1978b: 1–8), is inspired by a simultaneous reading of *Tristan and Iseult*. This is the case too for Don Quijote, whose delusion of knight errancy originates in his massive readings in medieval romance. Dostoevsky's protagonist in *Crime and Punishment* kills an old pawnbroker woman: not out of any personal emnity towards her, nor for monetary gain, but out of a desire to be Napoleon, to be a conquering hero, to live beyond conventional norms of good and evil. Stendhal's protagonist in *The Red and the Black* undertakes the comically awkward seduction of Madame de Rênal in provincial Verrières, and later of Mathilde de la Mole in Paris, in pursuit of his goal of heroic social conquest; it is a dream born of his admiration of Napoleon induced by a cashiered army surgeon in the early years of the Bourbon Restoration. Marcel Proust's narrator desires to see a play, to write a book, to possess a woman, to go to a party, always because some magical prestige has been attached to these objects by another. What is common to these antiheros, because it is constitutive of our species, is mimetic desire, desire which is mediated by another, desire whose object is designated by another who serves as a model to the desiring subject.

A summary paragraph towards the beginning of *Deceit, Desire and the Novel* states the case succinctly:

> The great novelists reveal the imitative nature of desire. In our day its nature is hard to perceive because the most fervent imitation is the most vigorously denied. Don Quijote proclaimed himself the disciple of Amadis de Gaule and the writers of his time proclaimed themselves the disciples of the Ancients. The Romantic *vaniteux* does not want to be anyone's disciple. He convinces himself that he is thoroughly original. In the nineteenth century spontaneity becomes a universal dogma, succeeding imitation. Stendhal warns us at every step that we must not be fooled by these individualisms professed with fanfare, for they merely hide a new form of imitation. Romantic revulsion, hatred of society, nostalgia for the desert, just as gregariousness, usually conceal a morbid concern for the Other. (1966: 15)

The Other is capitalized here for its generality, its universality, as the arbitrary, ubiquitous, non-localizable, non-specific and somewhat sacred origin of desire; as the structural origin of desire. The simple fact is that desire does not originate in us, nor in the object, but in others, who, be they parents, peers or subordinates, serve as a model for the selection of the object. Social relations precede object relations and determine them. This is perfectly obvious to anyone who attends to the quarrels among children, who only want what another has, or to the dynamics of high fashion, which depends entirely upon mimetic desire to generate attraction to objects of no intrinsic value whatsoever. Desire for such commodities is utterly metaphysical, being mediated by the image of cold satisfaction, of god-like self-possession radiating from those cadaveresque mannequins who are projected as their possessors.

It is because our desire imitates the desire of others in the selection of its objects that the other serves a rival and obstacle to the fulfillment of desire. This is a structural necessity which accounts for the way that concern with the Other is often literally morbid, or mortal. A brief statement from *"To Double Business Bound,"* a collection of essays, formulates the violent implications of mimesis: "To imitate the desires of someone else is to turn this someone else into a rival as well as a model. From the convergence of two or more desires on the same object, conflict must necessarily arise" (140). Because desire is mimetic, its ultime consequence, its logical destiny, is conflict. If we are to understand human behavior, we must distinguish between the logic of ideas and the logic of desire: if we all think the same thing, we will of course agree and there will be harmony among us; if we all desire the same thing, which we are bound to do if our desires imitate each other, there will be competition and conflict among us—not in spite of our resemblance but because of it. This dialectic is as simple in its structure as it is broad in its implications.

It is the structural inevitability of conflict as induced by mimetic desire that leads to the theory formulated in *Violence and the Sacred*. In the selection of a single victim or host of victims, it is the function of sacrifice to deflect violence away from the human community. In the violent rivalry of all against all, no community can exist. It is in the violent unanimity of all against one that the community is born, and periodically reborn through ritual sacrifice. For the destruction of the victim effectively unifies the community at the same time that it alienates its own self-destructive violence. The scapegoat truly represents the community in that it is a surrogate or substitute victim for all its otherwise self-destructive violence. The substitution of animal victim for man follows the logic of this original substitution, while assuring against virtually endless reprisals from friends or relatives of the victim within the community.

The efficacy of sacrifice depends on a fundamental misunderstanding as to the origin of violence, which is attributed to the scapegoat victim by a sort of retrospective illusion; for its destruction brings peace to the community. The victim is hallowed, sanctified, sacralized for being deemed the savior of the community; in a sense he is indeed its origin, its foundation, the telos of any community being to sustain itself by channeling its violence in a direction which will not engender self-destructive reprisals. The sacralization of violence in the form of the victim, in the divine metamorphosis of the victim, is described concisely in this passage from a central chapter on Dionysus:

Men would not be able to shake loose the violence between them, to make of it a separate entity both sovereign and redemptory, without the surrogate victim. Also, violence itself offers a sort of respite, the fresh beginning of a cycle of ritual after a cycle of violence. Violence will come to an end only after it has had the last word and that word has been accepted as divine. The meaning of this word must remain hidden, the mechanism of unanimity remain concealed. For religion protects man as long as its ultimate foundations are not revealed. To drive the monster from its secret lair is to risk loosing it on mankind. To remove men's ignorance is only to risk exposing them to an even greater peril. The only barrier against human violence is raised on misconception. In fact, the sacrificial crisis is simply another form of that knowledge which grows greater as the reciprocal violence grows more intense but which never leads to the whole truth. It is the knowledge of violence, along with violence itself, that the act of expulsion succeeds in shunting outside the realm of consciousness. (1977: 135)

Violence is the sacred, being a signifier of intensely mimetic desire which is miraculously diverted from the community in the unanimous destruction of the victim. The violation of taboo—from Saturnalian gluttony and promiscuity to royal incest—in ritual sacrifice finds its explanation in the necessity to renew the crisis of difference, the mimetic crisis, from which the difference of divinity subsequently preserves the community. The fundamental ambivalence of the sacred, as holy and accursed, as beneficial and terrible, is the consequence of the paradoxical role of the victim in the foundation of culture, and of sacrificial violence in the preservation of culture.

The whole truth of this matter, according to Girard, is reserved for Scripture, which consists in the representation of this process from the perspective, not of the community, which depends upon a misunderstanding of its violence, but of the victim, whose epistemological privilege is paramount. But we do not learn this from *Violence and the Sacred*, which concerns itself almost exclusively with the interpretation of pagan cultures. The active role of Scripture as an agent of interpretation of pagan culture is the central focus of *Des Choses cachées depuis la fondation du monde*, which had the bizarre fate, by American standards of literary consumption, of being a best-seller for months in France.

What is doubtless most distinctive about Girard's thinking, when viewed against the background of most of the theoretical activity emanating from France over the past twenty years, is its insistence on origins, on foundations. Such notions have become taboo for most structuralist and post-structuralist thinking, which, with Claude Lévi-Strauss, goes so far as to contest the possibility of a science of myth which would not itself be mythic (1964: 22). Yet a genetic hypothesis appears necessary if we are to avoid the self-referential impasses of a literary formalism which is characteristic of so much of such thinking. As Eric Gans has remarked in support of Girard's hypothesis, "Logic can no doubt do without the genetic, at the sacrifice of the ontological" (1981: 2). Girard does not concern us with the origin of being, a purely speculative question whose inspiration, as deconstructionists love to remind us, is "always already" theological, but with the origin of our species. This is the anthropological question par excellence, which no unified theory of culture, no properly scientific reflection on man, can ignore.

Like any hypothesis, Darwin's or Galileo's for that matter, Girard's is to be evaluated according to its explanatory power, both for present and past experience. Like Freud's hypothesis in *Totem and Taboo*, it postulates a foundational murder at the origin of cultural prohibitions; but unlike Freud, for whom an already human community precedes the murder of the father, it argues that our species originates in the consequences of the foundational murder. The passage from nature to culture hinges on mimesis, which animals, as even Aristotle could not fail to see (*Poetics*, IV,2), have in common with humans. But mimetic violence among humans knows no bounds, by contrast with animal behavior, as the data of ethologists testifies fairly conclusively. Among animals, mimesis serves appetitive needs; among humans it generates desires, from the discrete and familial to the fantastical and, as we know, fantastically homocidal. Violence is not instinctual; it reigns in the absence of instinctual brakes to mimesis, an absence possibly resulting from the disposition, at a certain stage of evolution, of projectiles or prosthetic devices to implement a kill. What is at any rate distinctive to *homo necans*, as Walter Burkert identifies our species, is this absence of instinctual breaks to intraspecific violence, breaks which continue to characterize the animal world, as the study of dominance patterns among animals demonstrates. That man disposes of language in the absence of instinct, that language is what breaches, or "supplements," our instinctual fault line suggests the necessity of a theory of violence which is likewise a theory of representation. For representation too, however, skewed and indirect as current research shows it to be, is mimetic. That linguistic symbols stand in for things and represent them stems from the originary role of the victim as a surrogate for the violence of the community.

In the beginning, then, was the victim. Around the victim is poised a circle of violent predators, each bent on appropriation; whence the victim in the first place, the product of a mêlée of violent appropriation which has centered on a single figure whose vulnerability has marked it out for destruction. The impulse to seize the victim is natural to all, but it is no less natural, at a certain stage of evolution, to hesitate, for fear of falling victim in turn to the unanimous violence which produced it. Appropriation of the victim by any one of the group surrounding it now spells danger from each and every one of its number, membership in the group and the group as a whole being defined, constituted, by the relation, a literally a-prehensive relation, to the victim. This apprehension is shared by all, as each communicates it to each other, so that there is a moment of non-instinctual attention bent on seizing the prey, but refraining from it out of self-preservation. In this moment of abstention, of deferred appropriation, desire for the object, towards which each and all are at once rival, model and obstacle, is indissociable from its interdiction; for desire and taboo are but two sides of the same mimetic contagion. (Though Girard never alludes to it, it occurs to me that that paradox informs the Eden narrative, where expulsion issues from mimetic appropriation of divinity inspired by taboo.) The sacred as an absence, as that which is never fully present to human subjects, as a being whose approach or appropriation is fatal to human subjects, stems from this abstinence from the object of mimetic desire, which constitutes the first sign:

> The signifier, that is the victim. The signified is all of the real and potential meaning that the community confers on that victim, and through its mediation, on all things.
> The sign is the reconciling victim. Because we understand without difficulty that men wish to remain reconciled once the crisis is over, we can also understand that they desire to reproduce the sign; that is, to employ the language of the sacred, substituting for the original victim in ritual new victims in order to insure the maintenance of this miraculous peace. The ritual imperative is one with the manipulation of the signs, with their multiplication, and thus new possibilities of differentiation and cultural enrichment constantly present themselves. (1978a: 112)

This is the scenario which provides Eric Gans with an anthropological basis upon which he constructs his "formal theory of representation" (1981: esp. 8–67). In the essay he provides for this volume, he focuses upon this "scene of representation" in order to distinguish between a communal ethic and a personal morality as it emerges from Pauline revelation.

Ritual sacrifice, as the propitiation of a violent divinity, is in fact the reconstitution of the community in and as the alienation of human violence wrought by mimetic desire. It is not, of course, peace among men that is the object of desire, not by any stretch of the historical, political or sociological imagination. We know that nothing unites a community better, with all the good fellowship and cooperation imaginable, than the external threat of a common enemy. But the threat is originally internal; it is the violent threat of all against all. Peace, then, is not the object of desire, but its by-product, being the calm to which the deferred appropriation of the victim gives rise. This calm is attributed to the victim, it is in fact produced by the victim, whose sacralization is the consequence.

It is in a sense true, then, as the myths aver, that man is born of the sacred; but the converse, which the myths conceal, is also true: the sacred is born of man, being the mystified consequence of mimetic desire, that is of man's horror of a violence which he always sees as coming outside himself—as indeed it does, since it is a mimetic response to another's violence. This is what the immolation of the scapegoat resolves.

Thus misunderstanding is essential to the efficacy of sacrifice: it re-presents the violence of origins in the destruction and consequent sacralization of the victim, which bears away the violence of all; it also erases the violence of communal origins, the communal violence which produces the victim, by tracing it to the agency of the victim alone, by erasing traces of its own originary violence, which it invests in or transfers to the victim. Sacralization is just that effort to erase or eliminate any trace between the human community and its victim, to eliminate any mark of community, or communality, of common status or origin, between the victim and its destroyers. Sacrifice, like the original founding event, expels violence, making it other; indeed Wholly Other, which is Rudolph Otto's notorious definition of the sacred, for which Girard alone offers a genetic rather than a merely generic explanation. As this scenario is repeated throughout history, Girard's theory suggests too, on a structural plane, why warring communities regularly sacralize the enemy, dehumanize him and totemize him, making him a monster, allegorizing him as The Force of Evil, as the very Devil, white, black, yellow or red, Himself. The sacrificial dynamic of war, even as we anticipate it on a global scale, comes to the fore, as just that alienation of violence, in which the enemy fills the role of the scapegoat. There is, in this regard, scarcely a page of Robert Jewett's superbly incisive review of American history as a quest of "redemption through violence" which would not draw theoretical rigor from Girard's hypothesis. Girard's theory of the religious is likewise a religious theory of history, and it draws strength, alas, from the very real and all-too-human prospect of apocalyptic closure we read about every day in the newspapers.

For all his reliance on the data and speculations of the human and life sciences, Girard's hypothesis does not claim to originate in them uniquely, but in the Scriptural critique of violence, of victimage, as well. That is something with which contemporary man is experimenting on a scale previously accorded only to celestial divinities. Godlike terror is ours as never before. According to Girard's "fundamental anthropology," the experiment, the hypothesis and its Scriptural revelation are all one from beginning to end, as he argues that survival of the human species depends as never before upon knowing the truth of its violent origin (1977: 240; 1978a: 278; 1982: 295; cf. also Gans, 1981: 22–23).

The unique role of Scripture in Girard's theory is therefore paramount, for he reads it as the progressive revelation of the mimetic crisis in which culture originates and to which culture persistently returns. What Scripture constitutes, from the story of Cain and Abel, of Jacob and Esau, of Joseph and his brothers, through the great prophetic imprecations against sacrifice (1978a: 165–181), is nothing less than a theory of human violence, as opposed to the foundational myths of paganism in which violence is divinized because its uniquely human origins are obscured. In his reading of the Book of Jonah, drawn from a book-length study of Hebrew Scripture according to a Girardian hermeneutic, Sandor Goodhart links this theory to Israel's anti-idolatrous vocation. Violence is accessible to theory, to structural representation, indeed to "deconstruction" (1978a: 70), because its effects are narrated from the perspective of the victim, who must needs challenge the efficacy of sacrifice.

With the passion of Jesus, as recorded in the gospels, the theory of violence attains its summit according to Girard. Repeated insistence on the innocence of the victim functions to confirm the Old Testament critique of sacrifice: "For I tell you that this Scripture must be fulfilled in me, 'And he was reckoned with the transgressors'; for what is written about me has its fulfillment" (Lk 22:37; Is 53:12); "It is to fulfill the word that is written in their law, 'They hated me without a cause'" (Jn 15:15; Ps 35:19). It is on this issue, the innocence of the victim, that Burton Mack focuses his critique of Girard, by pursuing what is an avowedly Girardian reading of early Christian social formation, which for Mack continues to be sacrificial, mythical.

The passion, for all its juridical trappings, is a failed sacrifice for Girard. The uniquely human and mimetic character of violence, which has been "hidden since the foundation of the world" (Mt 13:34-5; cf. 2 Chr 29:30, Ps 78:2), is fully revealed. It is this "non-sacrificial interpretation" of the gospels which Raymund Schwager pursues in depth, exegetically and theologically. Luke's gospel explicitly connects the "foundation" (*kataboles*) with "the blood of all the prophets" (11:50), which Matthew generalizes, universalizes, as "all the righteous blood shed on earth" (23:35); both gospels offer the comprehensive, encyclopedic formula, "from the blood of [innocent, Mt 23:35] Abel to the blood of Zachariah," the last murder victim mentioned in the Old Testament. What is denounced in Jesus' reproach to the Pharisees is not homocide only, but the principle by which murder is justified; what is uncovered is the dissociation from the victim by which homocide and persecution are perpetuated, and furthermore dissociation from the persecutors:

> Woe to you Scribes and Pharisees, hypocrites! For you build the tombs of the prophets and adorn the monuments of the righteous, saying "If we had lived in the days of our fathers, we would not have taken part with them in shedding the blood of the prophets." Thus you witness against yourselves, that you are sons of those who murdered the prophets. (Mt 23:29–32)

"It is not a question," Girard comments, "of a hereditary transmission but of a spiritual and intellectual solidarity which is accomplished remarkably by the intermediary of a ringing repudiation, analogous to the repudiation of Judaism by 'Christians.' The *sons* think to dissociate themselves from the *fathers* by condemning them. By this very fact, they imitate and repeat their fathers without knowing it. They do not comprehend that in the murder of the prophets it is already a question of rejecting one's own violence far from oneself. The sons remain therefore governed by the mental structure engendered by the founding murder" (1978a: 183).

"Without knowing it": this is a crucial epistemological as well as moral dimension. The complicity in violence is universal, foundational; it is endemic to the species rooted in mimesis, born of a sacrificial (re)solution to mimetic violence. This is the species of "symbol-using animals" (Burke, 1966: 3–22, esp. 18–19 on "unification by scapegoat") whose representations, differentiations and hierarchies disguise violent origins in the expulsion of scapegoats. Ceremonial, liturgized, hieratic victimization and mob violence ultimately reflect the same dynamics, but so does our intellectualist quest for new scapegoats of a more modern, impersonal cast: the Law, the Church, the Schools, the Father, Instinct . . . Anything to deny complicity in violence, which is ever held up as the violence of others, or of some hypostasized Other. It is just the legacy of the Judaeo-Christian tradition, according to Girard, to reveal this complicity, whereby it serves as the basis of a "fundamental anthropology," an anthropology which is grounded in the origin of the species and which is uniquely endowed to assure its perpetuation. However tragic in its own persecutions, this tradition is comic, conciliatory, in its kerygma, as it interrogates the words, "Forgive them for they know not what they do." These words enunciate a structuring principle which locates action in mimesis, the hingepin, or more properly speaking, the lynchpin, of Girard's Judaeo-Christian anthropology. They also mandate an alternative to violent mimesis. What is properly salvific for Girard in the crucifixion of Jesus in his examplarily pacific refusal to reciprocate violence with violence, whereby the injustice of the scapegoat mechanism is fully revealed and made inoperative. "What is essential in revelation from an anthropological point of view is the crisis it provokes in any representation which is persecutory" (1982: 166; cf. 166–180).

The interest of Girard's hypothesis for Biblical scholars no less than for others is cognitive, epistemological. In fact it declares itself as an alternative to the cognitive nihilism which these days beguiles as many theologians and philosophers as literary critics. It is not of course purely cognitive, as opposed to being purely moral, the purity of any such binary opposition being as liable to deconstruction as any other neat dichotomy. Following Girard's thinking, the only irreducible dichotomy is the one between victim and persecutor, and no critique of origin or difference, however bent on "undecidability," is proof against it. For indifference to that difference sanctions the persecution of all. In *Le Bouc émissaire*, Girard insists that it is that difference which informs our Western cognitive impulse:

The scientific spirit cannot come first. It supposes a renunciation of the old preference for causality which is magical and persecutory and which has been so well defined by our ethnologists. To natural causes, distant and inaccessible, humanity has always preferred causes which are *significant in terms of social relations and which admit corrective intervention*, that is to say: victims.

To orient men towards the patient exploration of natural causes, it is first of all necessary to divert their attention away from their victims; how can this be done except by showing them that the persecutors hate without a cause and without appreciable results thereafter? To perform this miracle, not with some exceptional individuals as in Greece, but on the scale of vast populations, what is necessary is the extraordinary combination of intellectual, moral and religious factors which the Gospel text brings to bear. (284–85)

In sum, the cause-effect relationship, as to the origin of scientific causality, is stood on its head:

> It is not because men invented science that they ceased to hunt witches, it is because they ceased to hunt witches that they invented science. The scientific spirit, like the spirit of free enterprise in economy, is a by-product of the actions in depth exercised by the evangelical text. Modern Western culture forgets the revelation in order to interest itself only in the by-products. It has made arms of it, instruments of power and behold today the process is turning around against it. The West believed itself a liberator and it discovers itself a persecutor. The sons curse their fathers and make themselves their judge. (285)

Girard's reading of Scripture may be described as structural to the extent that it views Scripture as a structural reading of history and of culture as a whole.

Ever since Saussure in linguistics—but we already find this operation in Nietzsche's "perspectivism"—attention to entities has been displaced by attention to relations in human affairs, which for Girard are fundamentally and primordially relations of desire. Advanced research in the social sciences has shown how these relations govern entire economies, national and global (Radkowski, 1980; Dumouchel and Dupuy, 1979; Dupuy, 1982). These relations are structurally destined to misunderstanding, just because they are relations of desire, just because human reality is structured by desire, which cannot know itself for being the copy of another desire. The victim is necessarily the key to this misunderstanding, for being an effect whose reality does not brook contradiction, not by any stretch, derealizing, surrealizing or otherwise demystifying, of the imagination. And so, as Girard argues of the Johanine vision of the Last Judgement—"I was hungry and you gave me to eat, I was thirsty and you . . ."—it is only through identification with the victim, or a genuine *imitatio Christi* as it has been called, that all sacrificial practices, all persecutions and injustices, are definitively renounced. In his close linguistic analysis of the Corinthian correspondence, Robert Hamerton-Kelly develops the implications of this positive mimesis, showing how Paul struggled against sacrificial practices in the early Christian community. Thomas Wieser analyzes still other New Testament texts in order to pursue the import of a Girardian reading of Scripture for current ecumenical concerns.

Girard's religious interpretation of history, of culture, allies itself with the Judaeo-Christian tradition against its sacrificial interpretation by institutional Christianity. But Girard is no less opposed to the scientifico-humanist interpretation which contrasts our Western cognitive impulse to Scripture and glories in its triumph over the sacred, to whose violent sway we are only the more prey as a consequence. Girard returns our attention to the mythic in a way which is neither reverent nor fanciful. For the mythic is neither the place where the truth is to be located, as Jungian scholars are wont to argue, nor is it the place where the debunking of origins is to be gratuitously celebrated. The mythic is not where the truth of origins is revealed but just where that truth is disguised, mystified, misrepresented, in an effort to cover up the traces of the victim, of his foundational role in culture. Scripture is just the place were that mystification is revealed, from Abel to Zachariah as if from A to Z. "From the moment that we try to understand myths, we can no longer take the Gospel for another myth, for it is the Gospel which makes us understand myths" (1982: 286). What is revealed is the victim: as the alpha and omega upon which all representations, cultural deferrals, social hierarchies, all Principalities and Powers, Thrones and Dominions, are founded; as the stone which has been rejected by the builders and which has become the cornerstone. For weal or woe, it remains the cornerstone of the entire cultural edifice: we either build upon it, the Scriptural hypothesis, towards a New Jerusalem, or ignore its revelation, consign it to oblivion, and the entire edifice is blown, as we say, to kingdom come. Confronted as we are by a Last Judgement of our own manufacture, from which it is unlikely according to most prognostications that human culture should ever survive, Girard's reading of Scripture makes compelling claims as a reading of the text of history and as a science of man.

* * *

II
"THE ANCIENT TRAIL TRODDEN BY THE WICKED": JOB AS SCAPEGOAT

"THE ANCIENT TRAIL TRODDEN BY THE WICKED": JOB AS SCAPEGOAT

René Girard
Stanford University

What do we know about the book of Job? Not very much. The protagonist bemoans his fate interminably. He has just lost his sons and all his cattle. He scratches his ulcers. The misfortunes which cause him to moan are duly enumerated in the prologue. It is the wickedness which Satan has just done to him, with God's permission.

So we think we know but do we really? Not once in the course of the dialogues does Job mention Satan nor anything about his wickedness. Many will say that all this is too present to his mind and to the mind of his friends so he doesn't have to allude to it.

Perhaps so, but there is something else altogether that Job does talk about, and more than just allusively. He does not remain silent about the cause of his misfortune; he insists strenuously. And it is none of the causes that the prologue talks about. It is a cause which is neither divine, nor satanic, nor material but human, only human.

The strange thing is that across the centuries commentators have never taken that cause the least bit into account. Doubtless I do not know them all but those whom I do know pass over that cause in silence, systematically. It appears that they don't see it. Whether they are ancient or modern, atheist, Protestant, Catholic or Jew, they never ask themselves about the object of Job's complaints. The question appears resolved for them once and for all by the prologue. Everyone sticks religiously to the ulcers, the lost cattle, etc.

And yet, for some time, the exegetes have been warning their readers against this prologue. Its little story, we are told, is not up to the level of the dialogues. We must not take it too seriously. That is all very well, but unfortunately the exegetes do not always follow their own advice. They do not understand what it is in the dialogues that manifestly contradicts the prologue.

In order to contest the traditional vision of the work, do we absolutely have to know Hebrew, do we have to plunge ourselves into the numerous enignmas of this formidable text, do we have to emerge with ever more original solutions? Absolutely not. It is enough to read the translations. If scientific erudition were necessary, I would not allow myself to utter a word, because I am not a Hebraist. The novelty which I am proposing is not hidden in some obscure recess of the book of Job. It is very explicit; it is spread out over numerous and lengthy passages which contain nothing ambiguous or obscure.

Job tells us clearly what he suffers from: he finds himself ostracized, persecuted by those around him. He hasn't done any evil, and everyone turns away from him, everyone has become very harsh towards him. He is the scapegoat of the community.

> My brothers stand aloof from me,
> and my relations take care to avoid me.
> My kindred and my friends have all gone away,
> and the guests in my house have forgotten me.
> Their serving maids look on me as a foreigner,
> a stranger, never seen before.
> My servant does not answer when I call him,
> and I am reduced to entreating him.
> To my wife my breath is unbearable,
> And for my own brothers I am a thing corrupt.
> Even the children look down on me,
> ever ready with a jibe when I appear.
> All my dearest friends recoil from me in horror:
> Those I loved best have turned against me. (19:13–19)

Job reminds us of the scapegoat down to that fetid odor which his wife reproaches him for spreading and which reappears, in significant ways, in a number of primitive myths.

We mustn't allow the allusion to a real goat arouse any misunderstanding. When I speak of the scapegoat, I am not thinking about the animal used in sacrifices, about the famous rite in Leviticus. I am using the expression in the sense in which we all use it without thinking, in connection with what happens around us in politics, in professional life, in family life. This usage is modern and of course does not show up in the book of Job. But the phenomenon shows up, with something more savage. The scapegoat is the innocent person who polarizes universal hatred around him. That is exactly what Job is complaining about:

> And now ill will drives me to distraction,
> and a whole host molests me,
> rising, like some witness for the prosecution,
> to utter slander to my very face.
> In tearing fury it pursues me,
> with gnashing teeths.
> My enemies whet their eyes on me,
> and open gaping jaws.

> Their insults strike like slaps in the face
> and all set on me together. (16:7–10)

Revealing passages such as this are superabundant. As I cannot multiply quotations forever, I choose what seems to me a rather striking passage where the scapegoat is concerned. Chapter 30 (1–12) brings into the picture a subgroup which in Job's society plays the role of permanent scapegoat.

> And now I am the laughing stock
> of my juniors, the young people,
> whose fathers I did not consider fit
> to put with the dogs that looked after my flock.
> ....
> That brood of theirs rises to right of me,
> stones are their weapons, . . . (30:1, 12)

Historians do not know if it is a question here of a racial or religious minority, or perhaps of a kind of sub-proletariat which is subjected to the same sort of regime as the lowest castes in India. It doesn't matter. These people do not interest the author in themselves; they are only there to allow Job to situate himself in relation to them, to define himself as the scapegoat of these scapegoats, the one who is persecuted by those very people who can least offer themselves the luxury of persecution: Job is the victim of all without exception, the goat of the goats and the victim of the victims.

Job complains of physical ills, certainly, but that particular complaint relates clearly to the fundamental source of his woe. He is the victim of innumerable brutalities; the psychological pressure which weighs down on him is not to be born. Job thinks that even his life is begrudged him, especially his life perhaps. He thinks that he is going to die a violent death: he imagines the shedding of his own blood:

> Cover not my blood, O earth,
> afford my cry no place to rest. (16:18)

Am I carried away by my desire to find everywhere my own theses? Here is the explanatory note of the Jerusalem Bible on these two verses: "Blood, if not covered with earth, cries to heaven to vengeance (...) Job, mortally wounded, wishes to leave behind a lasting appeal for vindication: on earth, his blood; with God, the sound of his prayer . . ."

The translation of the two verses and the note are in complete conformity with what we find in the other great translations, the French ones as well as those in other languages. The language of the note remains ambiguous, of course. By whom is Job mortally wounded? It could be by God alone rather than by men, but it is certainly not against God that the blood of the victim cries out for vengeance; it cries out for vengeance before God, just like the blood of Abel, that first great victim exhumed by the Bible. Yahweh says to Cain: "What have you done? Listen to the sound of your brother's blood, crying out to me from the ground" (Gen 4:10).

But against whom does the blood which has been shed cry out for vengeance, who could seek to smother Job's cry, to efface his words, in order to prevent them from reaching God? It is strange that these elementary and decisive questions are never asked.

Job comes back tirelessly to the role of the community in what is happening to him but, and here is the mystery, he no more succeeds in making himself heard by commentators outside the text than by his interlocutors in the book . . . No one takes the least account of what he says.

The revelation of the scapegoat has as little existence for posterity as for his friends. And yet we wish to be very attentive to what Job says; we pity him for not being understood. But we are so concerned with making God responsible for man's misfortunes, especially if we don't believe in Him, that the final result remains the same. We are only a little more hypocritical than Job's friends. For all those who pretend that they have always been listening to Job but who basically have not been listening at all, his words are only wind. The only difference is that we no longer dare to proclaim our indifference, whereas Job's friends, for their part, still dare to do so:

> Is there no end to these words of yours,
> to your long-winded blustering? (8:2)

* * *

This role of victim which Job attributes to himself is necessarily significant within an ensemble of texts, the Bible, where victims always and everywhere appear in the forefront. It takes but a moment's reflection to realize that we must view from a common perspective, that of the victim surrounded by numerous enemies, the reason for the astonishing resemblance between Job's speeches and what we call the pentitential psalms.

On these tragic psalms, we must consult the book by Raymund Schwager, *Brauchen wir einen Sündenbock?* We find in these texts the situation that Job is complaining about in an extremely condensed form. It is an innocent victim who is speaking. He is always in a situation which we may describe as as a lynching. As Schwager has clearly shown, a scapegoat in the modern sense is describing to us the cruelties which he is being subjected to. There is only one difference but it has great consequences. In the psalms, only the victim speaks. In the dialogues of Job, other voices make themselves heard.

To bring together, as I have done, the most revealing passages on Job as scapegoat is to bring together the texts which are most similar to these psalms, similar to the point of being frequently interchangeable. That is, finally, to put the accent on what, for lack of a better term, we are calling the surrogate victim, that formidable common denominator of many Biblical texts which has been mysteriously neglected by everyone. It has been the object of an intellectual expulsion that we must not, I think, hesitate to regard as continuous with the physical violence of antiquity.

To counter the harmful influence of the prologue, and so to finally understand what is at issue in Job, a rereading of a few psalms is a very healthy exercise.

> To every one of my oppressors
> I am contemptible, [un scandale]
> loathsome to my neighbors,
> and to my friends a thing of fear. (31:11)

* * *

Why has Job become the *bête noire* of the community? No direct answer is given. Perhaps it is better that way. If the author gave us something too solid to chew on, if he mentioned any incident, a possible origin of any sort, we would immediately think we understood, we would stop asking questions. Actually we would know less than ever.

Let us not imagine, however, that the Dialogues maintain an absolute silence. They are full of information, but we have to know where to look for it. On the choice of Job as scapegoat, you cannot just go and ask anyone. The "friends," for example, say nothing very interesting about this. They want to make Job responsable for the cruelties that he is subjected to. They suggest that his avarice has ruined him; perhaps he has shown himself to be harsh towards the people; he took advantage of his position to exploit the weak and the poor.

Job passes for virtuous but, just like Oedipus perhaps, he has succeeded in committing a quite invisible crime. If not he, his son then, or another member of his family. A man condemned by the voice of the public could not be innocent. But Job defends himself with vigor, though no accusation is witheld. The indictments do not hold up.

Job does not say that he has never sinned, he says that he has done nothing to deserve his extreme disgrace; just yesterday he was thought to be infallible, he was treated like a saint; today everyone condemns him. It is not he who has changed, it is the men around him. The Job whom everyone execrates cannot be very different than the Job whom everyone venerated.

The Job of the dialogues is not a vulgar nouveau riche who has lost all his money. He is not simply a particular individual who succeeded at first, then "had some problems" and decided to meditate with his friends on the attributes of God and the metaphysics of evil. The Job of the dialogues is not the Job of the prologue. He is a great leader whom public opinion once exalted then brusquely repudiated. Consider Chapter 29 (2–25), which closes:

> If I smiled at them, it was too good to be true,
> they watched my face for the least sign of favor.
> In a lordly style, I told them which course to take,
> and like a king amid his armies,
> I lead them where I chose.

The contrast between the present and the past is not a contrast between wealth and poverty, between health and illness, it is a contrast between the favor and the disfavor of one and the same public. The dialogues are not dealing with a purely personal drama, with a human interest story, but with the behavior of all the people towards a sort of "statesman" whose career has been shattered.

As fanciful as they are, the accusations against Job are revealing. The fallen potentate is especially reproached for abuses of power, and of the sort that could not be the work of a simple landowner, however rich we may suppose him to be. Job makes us think rather of the *tyrant* of the Greek cities. Why, Eliphaz asks him, has Shaddai turned against you?

> Would he punish you for your piety,
> and haul you off to judgement?
> No, rather for your manifold wickedness,
> for your unending iniquities!
> You have exacted needless pledges from your brothers,
> and men go naked now through your despoiling;
> you have grudged water to the thirsty man,
> and refused bread to the hungry;
> and you have narrowed the lands of the poor man down to nothing
> to set your crony in his place,
> sent widows away empty handed
> and crushed the arms of orphans. (22:4–9)

The modern reader gladly adopts the vision of the prologue because it reminds us of our world, or at least the idea that we make of it. Happiness consists in possessing most everything possible without ever falling sick, in an eternal frenzy of joyous consumerism. In the dialogues, on the other hand, the only thing that counts is the relation between Job and the community.

Job presents his triumphal period as the autumn of his life, that is to say: the season which precedes the glacial winter of persecution. It is probable that the disgrace is recent and that it was sudden. Up to the last moment, Job suspected nothing of the reversal which was being prepared:

> My praises echoed in every ear,
> and never an eye but smiled on me; (29:11)

The mystery of Job is presented in a context which does not explain it but which allows us all the better to situate it in causal terms. The scapegoat is a broken idol. The rise and fall of Job are bound up with each other; we have the feeling that these extremes touch each other. We cannot interpret them separately and yet we cannot say that the first is the cause of the second. We sense a social phenomenon which is poorly defined but quite real, a phenomenon whose unfolding is not certain but probable.

The only common point between the two periods is the unanimity of the community, first in its adoration, then in its detestation. Job is the victim of the massive and sudden reversal of a public opinion which is necessarily unstable, capricious, a stranger to any moderation. He hardly appears any more responsible for the change in this crowd than is Jesus for a very similar change, between Palm Sunday and the Passion of the following Friday.

In order for there to be unanimity in both directions, there must be a mimetic contagion at work in each case. The members of the community influence each other reciprocally, they imitate each other in their fanatical adulation and then in their still more fanatical hostility. We will return to this issue later on.

In the last of his three speeches, one of the three friends, Eliphaz of Teman, clearly alludes to Job's predecessors in the double career of all powerful upstart and of scapegoat:

> And will you still follow the ancient trail
> trodden by the wicked?
> Those men who were borne off before their time,
> with rivers swamping their foundations,
> because they said to God, "Go away,
> What could Shaddai do to us?"
> Yet he himself had filled their houses with good things,
> while these wicked men shut him out of their counsels.
> At the sight of their ruin, good men rejoice,

and the innocent deride them:
"See how their greatness is brought to nothing!
See how their wealth has perished in the flames!" (22:15–20)

The "ancient trail trodden by the wicked" begins with greatness, wealth, power, but it ends in a stunning disaster. These are the same two phases which we have just discovered in Job's adventure. It is exactly the same scenario.

As I myself have done, Eliphaz opposes and, as a consequence, makes a connection between the two phases. He sees that they form a whole and that we cannot interpret them separately. There is something about the rise of these men which prepares their downfall. Our basic intuition, in short, is found in these words by Eliphaz. Job has already covered a good part of the way on the "ancient trail trodden by the wicked." He is at the beginning of the last stage.

The events which Eliphaz evokes appear distant, therefore exceptional; but not so exceptional as to prevent the observer from seeing their connection with Job and recognizing in them a recurrent phenomenon. A whole route is quite laid out here: many men have already taken it and now it is Job's turn. All these tragic destinies have the characteristic traits of the broken idol. Their destiny, like Job's, is necessarily determined by the metamorphosis of an adoring crowd into a persecuting crowd.

Eliphaz would not be able to make allusions to events which he situates in the *past*, if the disasters affecting the "wicked" were imaginary. He must be evoking an experience known to all, because it is the experience of the entire community. The violent defeat of the "wicked" remains present in everyone's memory. This sort of affair impresses men too strongly to fall into oblivion. Its stereotyped character helps one to remember it.

It is the same story, it happens again and again, and the warning given by Eliphaz is very reasonable. This is a wise man. Job would do well to take stock of his words. But how can he do so without repudiating his very own self, without admitting that he is guilty.

Is it certain that the "wicked" men are all victims of popular violence? What else could it be a question of? Reread the last four verses of the quote. They allude to a kind lynching:

> At the sight of their ruin, good men rejoice
> and the innocent deride them:
> "See how their greatness is brought to nothing!
> See how their wealth has perished in the flames!"

In the context of a village society, the rejoicing of "good men" and the mockery of the "innocent" cannot be without consequences. We have to reflect here on the formidable efficacity of unanimous reprobation in such a milieu. In order to bring about all the disasters that are ascribed to him, God has only to give a free hand to these good men who call upon the authority of His vengeance.

The disaster which awaits the "wicked" at the term of their career, at the end of the "ancient trail," probably resembles those primitive Feasts whose activities, however attenuated and ritualized, makes us think of a crowd phenomenon. Everything always ends with some form of scapegoat who is burned or drowned. In former times, ethnologists caught the scent of more extreme violence behind the ritual forms they observed. Many contemporary researchers regard them as victims of their romantic and colonialist imagination. I think on the contrary that they were right. To discover in the dialogues the kind of violence we have discovered there owes nothing to colonialism and constitutes, it seems to me, an argument in favor of their thesis.

Many other passages suggest that the central event of the work, the terrible adventure which has just begun for the hero, is a recurrent phenomenon of collective violence which especially strikes the "great," the "tyrants," but not them exclusively; it is always interpreted as divine vengeance, the punitive intervention of the divinity.

I will cite but one example of it here. It is part of the speech of Elihu, the fourth of Job's lecturers. According to general opinion this character does not belong to the original dialogues. He is probably the work of a reader who was scandalized by the impotence of the first three guardians of public order. Elihu scorns the entrenchment of the three in tradition. He presents himself as a man who is "up to date," as a "modern," and he is confident of succeeding where the three others have failed.

He thinks he is more capable simply because he is younger and because he despises the past. We are all quite familiar with this sort of hollow contestation. He doesn't get to the bottom of things. He too seeks to reduce Job to silence but he just repeats in a less savory style what the three others have already recited. He belongs to a stage in which the ancient tradition is more feeble. He nonetheless says things which render the hidden subject of the dialogues more obvious than ever.

The theme of Job as "oppressor of the people" already shows up with the three friends, but Elihu makes still greater use of it. Behind his politico-religious formulae, it is popular violence that shows through.

In an instant, God

> smashes great men's power without enquiry
> and sets up others in their places.
> He knows well enough what they are about,
> and one fine night he throws them down for me to trample on.

He strikes men down for their wickedness,
and makes them prisoners for all to see. (34:24-26)

I am quoting from the Jerusalem Bible: its translation suggests admirably the identity of the god and of the crowd. It is the god who overturns the great but it is the crowd which *tramples* on them. It is the god who puts the victims in chains, but his intervention is public. It is effected in the presence of that same crowd which has perhaps not remained completely passive before such an interesting spectacle. The great are broken "without enquiry," as we might have guessed. The crowd is always ready to lend a hand to the divinity when the latter decides to deal ruthlessly with the wicked. And right away other great people are found to replace those who have fallen. It is god himself who enthrones them, but it is the crowd who adores them, in order to discover a little later, of course, that they are a false elect, and that they are worth no more than their predecessors.

Vox populi, vox dei. As in Greek tragedy, the rise and fall of the great constitutes a *mystery* whose conclusion is what is most appreciated. Although it never changes, it is always impatiently awaited.

***

What do the three "friends" do with the scapegoat. The prologue tells us that they are there to "have pity" on Job and to "console" him. For all their verbosity, their speeches have nothing comforting about them. Critics have recognized this but they attribute the asperities of the friends to their clumsiness. They never really question the quality of these speakers as friends. They persist in believing that their intentions are good.

We don't look closely enough, I think, at what these alleged "friends" say. The first thing that strikes the reader who is not in any way predisposed towards them is the prodigious violence of their speech. Listen to Eliphaz:

> The life of the wicked is unceasing torment,
> the years allotted to the tyrant are numbered.
> The danger signal ever echoes in his ear,
> in the midst of peace the marauder swoops on him.
> He has no hope of fleeing from the darkness,
> but knows that he is destined for the sword,
> marked down as meat for the vulture. (15: 20-23)

Passages of this kind are superabundant. There is always some wicked person, an oppressor of the people. He was all-powerful but he is no more so. God has cursed him. The vengeance of the celestial armies pursues him. One of the three friends, Cophar of Naamat (20:22-29) describes to us the destiny which awaits this mysterious tyrant in especially bloodthirsty terms: "On him God looses all his burning wrath, . . . An arsenal of terrors falls on him,/And all that is dark lies in ambush for him," etc.

The menacing tirades of Cophar find no justification from the perspective of the prologue. Why would a poor wretch, who is downtrodden by inexplicable accidents as Job passes for being, find himself being pursued on top of that by innumerable executioners of a mysterious "divine vengeance"? Why would someone who has just lost his health, his children, his fortune, arouse on top of that the formidable gathering of hostility which is described by the "friends"?

Could it be a question of someone else besides Job in these vociferations? Job is under no such illusion. On three occasions, at point blank, in the same military order, the three friends fire off their superb and sinister imprecations. Whom else could they be aimed at? Job is not yet completely that enemy of God who is always evoked in such language but that is what he could become; that is what he certainly will become if he persists in rebelling against the unanimous voice which condemns him.

That, in short, is the entire message of Eliphaz. The man who is called at times "the enemy of God," at times the "accursed," or more simply "the wicked man," is one and the same as "the wicked" identified by Eliphaz in Chapter 22. For this kind of black sheep there are five or six interchangeable labels. It is always the same threat which these speeches make to Job, that of collective violence, always more collective violence.

Job often has recourse to very realistic language in the passages concerning his experience as a victim; it is even crudely realistic, in conformity with the abasement which is his theme. In contrary fashion, the three friends adopt the style which is appropriate to the grandeur of their theme. Concrete details abound, to be sure, but everything is dressed up in the style of religious epic.

We have to distinguish therefore between two types of discourse, that of the friends and that of Job. We shall see later on that this distinction is not *always* valid but it certainly is for the passages which I have cited thus far. Between the complaints of the underdog and the epic style of the friends the distance is so great as to discourage at first any comparison between them. The celestial armies seem to have nothing in common with the petty persecutions that Job is complaining about.

But if Job and those friends of his were not speaking of the same thing, the dialogues would have no object, there would not properly speaking be dialogue. And that in fact is somewhat the impression of the reader who does not see the key role of the surrogate victim. The reader is struck by a certain incoherence affecting the text as a whole. The characters are not really speaking to one another. This is especially true of the friends. One might say they don't hear Job's complaints, Job's arguments.

Contemporary criticism concerns itself above all with the rhetorical differences between discourses. It takes less interest in what is being talked about than in the way it is talked about. The concern with what it blithely calls the referent is increasingly regarded as alien to literary phenomena, an attitude which is ultimately responsable for all the misunderstandings which poison our intelligence of great texts.

The exegetes of Job have never been able to discover the object which is common to the two types of discourse which we have just distinguished. But not until recently have they stopped looking for it, at least in theory. What characterizes contemporary criticism, on the other hand, is the temptation to abandon that search.

That must not happen. In the vituperations of the friends, the principle theme is the gigantic mobilization aroused by the god, decreed by him, organized by him, against his particular enemies, the enemies of this god. Innumerable hordes converge on the wretch. Where do they come from? Why do powerful armies gather for the sole purpose of destroying an isolated adversary who is incapable of defending himself? Why such a waste of military power?

Let us recall the passages where Job describes his situation in the community. He is alone, surrounded by enemies. It is the same *all against one* that we find here but it is not the same style. Faced with the formidable celestial armies we do not think of Job's ignoble persecutors but it's the same numerical disproportion and it's the same enemy. We are dealing with one and the same phenomenon in both cases.

All these forces converge *simultaneously* on god's enemy. Plausibility is not always satisfied but the *all against one* of the scapegoat only stands out more clearly as a result. It is the only principal of organization but it controls everything. Whoever the adversaries may be, the relation of forces does not change. Behind the strangest, the most monstrous, the least human combatants, what always shows through is the gathering of modest villagers against a single adversary; this poor wretch whom they hold in their grasp is doubtless one of their own.

Consider the animals who fight for god: bulls, dogs, birds of prey, especially vultures. We find all these beasts in myths, and yet still more. They are of course the most ferocious; they are also the species which live in herds, and which hunt or charge collectively, or which feed together from corpses; they are the species which behave, or appear to behave, in the same way as men when they gather against a common adversary, when they go on a manhunt.

We always find allusions to the same fundamental motif, the

destruction of a solitary victim by a host of enemies. It is the same violence in both cases. That is what we must examine to understand the relation of the two styles. Violence is the true "referent," which is poorly disguised in the threats of his friends, and not disguised at all in the words uttered by Job. As far apart as they appear from each other, these two kinds of discourse each deal in their own way with the same phenomenon: the hero's becoming a scapegoat, the lynching that Job feels is building up—towards him.

In sacred discourse, transcendence transfigures everything; we have the impression that everything is happening outside of human history. But we also have the contrary impression. Look at the victim sweat with anguish, look at the arrow going through his liver. This is the impression that Job's more realistic description makes on us. A cross check between the two kinds of discourse is easily made.

The host of enemies always derives from one and the same model, the human crowd. When divine vengeance is in the offing, there is nothing in the universe which does not begin to swirl, to turbulate in the sense of *turba*, the crowd, as illuminated by Michel Serres (1977), and woe betide the being around whom that irresistible turbulence gathers, woe betide the one who is swept up in it. The swirling pack is the mode of existence par excellence for divine vengeance. It throws itself on its victim and tears him to tiny pieces; the terrible appetite for violence is the same for all participants. None of them wishes to miss striking the decisive blow. The images of laceration and of fragmentation remind us of the innumerable dismemberments we find in mythology and ritual, of the innumerable variants of the Dionysiac *diasparagmos*.

The *all against one* of collective violence shows through even in the gathering of three, then of four persons around Job, even in the structure of their discourses. The three, then the four, constitute a small crowd in the midst of a great crowd. The awkward reinforcement of Elihu underlines the structure of the botched kill which dominates the book from one end to the other.

Around the victim at bay, the innumerable troop of words gathers for the *coup de grâce*. The three series of speeches resemble those flights of arrows aimed at the enemy of god. The hostile speeches are not merely an image of collective violence; they are a form of active participation. Job sees this clearly when he denounces the verbal laceration inflicted upon him. The three friends crush him with their speeches, they pulverize him with words (19:2).

Is it not an exaggeration to liken these words to a lynching? The friends do not indulge in gross insults or in physical brutality. They do not spit on Job. They belong to the elite. Do we not catch Job red-handed here in a flight of exaggeration, of "dramatization"?

Absolutely not. By translating all the violence directed against

Job as so much service rendered to god, these speeches justify past brutalities and they incite to new ones. They are more dreadful than the abuse heaped on him by the wretched. Their *performative* value is obvious.

***

The god of the friends always fights three against one, four against one, a thousand against one. He doesn't worry about chivalry, as no one fails to remark. But how pointless and antiquated is the irony which aims at the religious in the abstract, *in toto*, without ever wondering about what is behind these visions. For three centuries, every one takes these visions to be simply imaginary. They are regarded as inventions which are inessential, which come after the invention of this god whose force resides in the number of combattants lined up beneath his banner.

It is believed that the metaphysical god is the fruit of a properly metaphysical imagination and that the celestial armies are secondary fabrications of relatively minor scope. I have always thought that we must reverse the direction of this genesis. We must begin with these armies, which are not at all celestial but which are nonetheless real. We must begin with collective violence. And, for once, we do not have to postulate that violence, to regard it as a simple hypothesis. The author holds it up before our eyes at every moment. It is one with that persecution that Job is complaining about and of which he is the victim.

The speeches of the friends reflect the sacred fury which takes hold of lynchers at the onset of the lynching. From Dionysiac *mania* to Polynesian *amok*, there are many diverse names to designate the collective trance which we also find in Greek tragedy. These inflamed tirades resemble those of the tragic choir in the moments preceding the destruction of the victim, the murder of Pentheus in *The Bacchae*, the discovery of the "culprit" in *Oedipus Rex*.

Before our very eyes the three friends sacralize violence with all their might. The insults and the petty brutalities are transformed into the grandiose accomplishments of a supernatural mission. All the participants become celestial warriors, the closest neighbors as well as the most distant, the respectable citizens as well as the tramps, the young as well as the old, even long time friends, even the closest relative, even his old wife who says to Job: "curse God and die."

How can we deny the relevance of collective persecution in primitive religion for the understanding of these great texts in which we see the tireless alternation of the complaints of the persecuted victim with frenetic calls to murder, couched in the language of the sacred, a language which recalls that of the most savage rituals, the preparations for the collective dismemberment of the victim?

What the community reads automatically in every backfire against leaders elevated by popular favor is the intervention of absolute Justice. What is deployed in the speeches of the three friends is a veritable mythology of divine vengeance.

Because they participate in his lynching, the friends do not understand the role of scapegoat played by Job. The paradox of foundational violence is revealed here in spectacular fashion. Those who manufacture the sacred with their own violence are incapable of seeing the truth. That is just what makes the friends totally deaf to the appeals that Job makes unceasingly. The more they participate in the violence against the unfortunate wretch, the more they are carried away by their barbarous lyricism and the less they understand what they are doing.

The three friends know very well what the social order demands of them but this knowledge does not in any way contradict their fundamental ignorance concerning the scapegoat, their incapacity to conceive of Job's point of view. They have no suspicion of the moral reprobation which this phenomenon inspires in Job, and, beyond Job, in all of us, by the sole grace of the biblical text.

As the Gospels will later say of a similar affair, the three friends "know not what they do" on the moral and religious level. They know very well, on the other hand, what it is they have to do and not to do on the level of a certain victimary cuisine whose meaning tends to elude us though it is by no means beyond reach.

***

When we finally get to the true themes of the work and discover their coherence, we rediscover the "theory" proposed in *Violence and the Sacred* and the works which follow it.

What does that theory say? That the unanimous violence of the group is transfigured as an epiphany of the sacred. In *The Bacchae* the lynching of Pentheus is one with the epiphany of an avenging Dionysus. In the dialogues the lynching of Job and that of all the "wicked" is one with the intervention of divine vengeance.

In order for a human group to perceive its own violence as sacred, it must exercise that violence against a victim whose innocence leaves no trace—by the very fact of that unanimity. That is what I say in *Violence and the Sacred* and that is exactly what we have just seen.

Of the three friends, Bildad of Shuah appears to me as the one most prone to mythology. With him the theme of the celestial armies is building up to a mythology similar to that of the Greek Erynnies or of the German Walkyries. We see clearly here that the religion of Bildad and of his world has not much to do even with those manifestations of the biblical Yahweh which remain most contaminated by mythological violence.

>Disease devours his flesh (of the wicked)
>Death's First Born gnaws his limbs.
>He is torn from the shelter of his tent,
>and dragged before the King of Terrors.
>The Lilith makes her home under his roof,
>while people scatter brimstone on his holding. (18:13–15)

I now read the note of the Jerusalem Bible:

>The "King of Terrors," a figure from oriental and Greek mythology (Nergal, Pluto, etc.), seems here to have infernal spirits (Furies) at command to plague the wicked man even during his lifetime. (. . .) Lilith, another figure of popular legend, is a female demon. (. . .) Brimstone produces, or is symbolic of, sterility and is possibly (in this passage) a precaution against infection.

All the great mythological systems, and not only the Indo-European ones, contain these bands of killers, male or female, who act together, unanimously, and who, by so doing, produce the sacred, sometimes even divinizing their victims. That is the fully mythological version of the celestial armies, that is to say Job's persecutors.

It is easy to criticize the activity of theorists from the outside and in the abstract, but when we are dealing with the book of Job the only real choice, I am convinced, is between the old moralizing cliches on the one hand, the problem of evil and its metaphysical aftermath bequeathed to us by the Prologue, and, on the other hand, the fearful equivalence between violence and the sacred, an equivalence which is not consciously affirmed by the friends, but which is consciously repudiated by the scapegoat.

Far from imprisoning texts within any sort of interpretive yoke, the thesis of the foundational victim allows them to re-emerge from the silence surrounding them. It frees them from the metaphysical and moral trap which has been working so marvelously for millennia. The interpreters fall into this trap all the more willingly because in so doing they elude the double subversion of the received ideas, the religious and antireligious ones alike, with which the attentive reader of the dialogues is necessarily confronted.

An undertaking like mine can have no other goal than to "reduce" a considerable mass of givens to a certain number of principles, as few and as simple as possible. Far from being reprehensible, the quest for universally valid principles appears to me to be alone worthy of pursuit.

It is often said that the victimary thesis is not truly demonstrable because it is never directly legible in a text. It describes a structuring process; it cannot be deduced directly from a single text. It is essentially comparative and hypothetical. I have said all of this myself. The reason is that, with respect to the victimary mechanism, all texts appear necessarily to belong to one or the other of the two following categories:

1. Myths whose structuring by the victimary mechanism cannot be directly shown: from the very fact that myths are structured by the victimary mechanism, the latter can nowhere appear. That is just what we observe once again in all the speeches which are not by Job. We cannot expect of the friends that they recognize their injustice. As with all those who make scapegoats, they take their victim to be guilty. For them, there isn't any scapegoat.

2. Texts in which this same mechanism appears in the light of day. The innocence of the victim is proclaimed; the scapegoat is manifest as such but the persecutors, for the same reason, are no longer around exulting in visions about divine vengeance and celestial armies. They are no longer there to reveal to us the structuring effect which the process exercises on their language, on their vision, on their behavior.

There is nothing more difficult than to detect the structuring mechanism which is at work in a text, to see it in action. It is rather like looking for depth on a two dimensional surface, the written text.

To the extent that that impossibility can be overcome, the dialogues overcome it. They are dialogues precisely in the sense that they present the two visions in counterpoint. The true revelations of the persecuted alternate with the lying and sacralized speeches of the persecutors.

Sometimes we do not even need this counterpoint. In certain statements I have quoted, those of Eliphaz, for example, on the "ancient trail trodden by the wicked," those of Elihu on the god who crushes the great "without enquiry" and on the crowd who tramples, the victimary process shows so clearly through the sacralization process that we no longer need to confront the two kinds of discourse.

But the book of Job gives us so much more than that. What is most extraordinary, I find, is still the counterpoint of the two perspectives, which is made possible by the dialogue form; it is close to a theatrical "mise en scène" which would no longer have carthasis as its object but the disappearance of all catharsis.

We cannot take the correspondences between the two kinds of texts as mere coincidence. Even if he cannot speak in our own language, even if he is sometimes out of his depths and nonplussed by his own daring, the author manipulates these correspondences too powerfully to be unaware of them. The difference in perspective on one and the same collective violence constitutes the true subject of the dialogues. Opposed to the sacred lie of the friends is the true realism of Job.

***

There is an essential dimension of the victimary thesis that remains to be uncovered and that is mimesis. I think that all the conditions of its presence are found together here. Job's lost prestige must have been a personal acquisition. It does not seem that he could have owed it to some function that he performed, nor that it was inherited. Judging by the pleasure he drew from it, we sense that he did not always possess this prestige. This is a man promoted from the ranks.

In order to be as wildly praised and venerated as Job was before becoming a scapegoat, it doubtless sufficed in such a fickle society that initial success make of him the *primus inter pares*. The desires of the people of his class, that of the three "friends," Eliphaz of Teman, Bildad of Shuah and Cophar of Naamat, and still others, focused on that first difference and magnified it disproportionately. It is the elite, at first, who took Job as a model, who flattered him, venerated him, slavishly imitated him. The rest of the people followed, imitating the first imitators.

The absence of social distance favors the reciprocal imitation of equals. Job is identified with his success and to desire this success is to desire Job himself, to desire Job's incomparable being. This identification is emminently competitive, therefore ambivalent from the very start. In his own class, Job only has rivals who try to catch up to him. They all wish to become that sort of uncrowned king that he represents to them.

But royalty, by definition, is not shared. Job cannot succeed as he does without provoking formidable jealousy in his own milieu. He is the *model-obstacle* of the mimetic theory. He arouses Nietzschean resentment; admiration has a backwash, an undertow which never fails—this is the scandal!—to bruise the admirer on the barrier which the model becomes for him. From the very fact that it is based on mimetic desire, the fascination exercised by the rival who is too successful tends to turn into implacable hatred; it is always already mingled with that hatred. It is among people who are socially close that a kind of hateful fascination flourishes; that is the kind that shows through in almost every word of the "friends."

Job's friends evoke his past glory, as does Job himself, but not for the same reasons; they do it in order to lecture him, spitefully and ironically. They feast on the contrast between the present and the past. Their envy must have been powerful indeed to survive the discrediting of their idol. With somewhat obscene haste, they recall to Job the change in his fortune; they verify in a sense their own good fortune:

> If one should address a word to you, will you endure it?
> Yet who can keep silent?
> Many another, once, you schooled,
> giving strength to feeble hands;

your words set right whoever wavered,
and strengthened every failing knee.
And now your turn has come, and you lose patience too;
and it touches you, and you are overwhelmed. (4:2–5)

The envy of the "friends" and of the people of their milieu is essential to the passage from the first mimetic unanimity to the second. Equality of conditions sharpens the fundamental duplicity of mimetic reactions inspired by the "great man." The mimesis of envy and of hatred spreads as rapidly as the mimesis of admiration. It is the same mimesis which is transmuted once the model has become an obstacle, for mimesis is scandalized by that metamorphosis.

The spectacular downfall of Job in public opinion must have begun in Job's social circle and thereafter spread downwards. The untouchables of chapter 30 would never dare to attack Job as they do without encouragement from the upper class. This is scarcely a conjectural matter: the speeches of the friends are an incitement to popular violence.

There must exist therefore a certain temporal interval between the reactions of the elite and those of the crowd. This interval allows us to interpret an important theme, which I have not yet developed, although it figures in the speech of Eliphaz on "the ancient trail trodden by the wicked." It is the theme of divine vengeance *delayed*.

Even when they are already the declared enemies of God, the wicked appear still laden with His blessings. Why this long mansuetude on the part of the divinity? The classic response offered by religious thinking which is victimary is that, far from being fooled, the god resorts to a strategy. He encourages on their part the arrogance which will some day prove fatal to them. The god delays his intervention in order to make the fall of the wicked as spectacular and as cruel as possible.

If we reject the sadistic conception of the divine which is implied by all this, we will have to interpret this idea of vengeance *delayed* in terms of the envious feelings which we sense among the friends of Job.

Job sees perfectly well that the scapegoat is interchangeable with those who persecute him with the greatest ferocity, the so-called friends. He imagines this reversal of the situation, in order to show that the only true difference is in the suffering he undergoes:

I too could talk like you,
were your soul in the plight of mine,
I too could overwhelm you with sermons,
I could shake my head over you,
and speak words of encouragement,
until my lips grew tired.
But, while I am speaking, my suffering remains: (16:4–6)

Great men are too popular to succumb all at once to plots that proliferate around them. Mimetic jealousy smoulders for a long time in the shade. That, I think, is what is signified by the "delay" of divine vengeance. But opinion tires of idols; it ends up by burning what it once adored, having forgotten its own adoration. That is the triumph of the "friends" and that is the moment at which the dialogues are situated.

My reasoning retains a conjectural character inasmuchas the envy concerning Job is not explicit. The friends themselves say nothing about it, of course. Job only makes allusions to it. The text which would tie mimetic envy directly to the phenomenon of the sacralized scapegoat is not to be found in the book of Job. But we do find it elsewhere in the Bible, in Psalm 73, which is at once very like and very unlike those from which I have already quoted; it is very similar in its subject and very different in its perspective.

The narrator presents himself as one of the Righetous, one faithful to the true God, and long discouraged by the apparent inertia of divine Justice. He insists explicitly on the envy inspired by the too brilliant career of those whom he presents, of course, as impious. Fortunately, God has finally decided to intervene.

Contrary to the other tragic psalms, which are all written from the point of view of the victim, this is one of the very rare psalms which reflects the other perspective, that of the friends. In fact it is the only one of which we can say without hesitation that it reflects the perspective of the persecutors:

> My feet were on the point of stumbling,
> a little further and I should have slipped,
> envying the arrogant as I did,
> and watching the wicked get rich.

What he took for the inertia of the god was a canny temporization:

> This is why my people turn to them
> and lap up all they say,
> ....
> until the day I pierced the mystery
> and saw the end in store for them;
> they are on a slippery slope, you put them there,
> you urge them on to ruin,
> untill suddenly they fall,
> done for, terrified to death.

The individual who is speaking to us has long been chomping at the bit before a man, or a group of men, who have long been popular but whose noisy success has abruptly ended in their "fall," in their being "terrified to death." It is the "ancient trail" once again. The people in question here have followed it up to the final precipice and if there existed a list of the "wicked," their names would be found on it next to that of Job.

In short, the narrator is the approving accomplice of a collective violence which he takes for divine. He allows us to imagine the intimate reflections of Job's enemies, those reflections which the three friends keep to themselves.

For proof that the essential here is the infatuation of the people, we have the sentence: "The people turn to them." From the viewpoint of the narrator, the people assure the success of those who ought not to succeed but who nonetheless do so and whose abuses of power last as long as their enjoyment of popular favor.

The Righteous one can very well identify the still moderate envy of his positive imitation; but let that envy become more intense, as a consequence of the obstacle, of the scandal, of the triumph of the "wicked," and it will turn to hatred; now the Righteous one no longer recognizes it. And yet if there is an envy worthy of the name, that is certainly it. The Righteous one interprets his counter-imitation, his most intense resentment, as foreign to envy, whereas it is the paroxysm of envy. What he sees is the epitome of right sentiments, he sees religious fervor in its purest state. There remains but a certain element of mystification, but it is capital—whereby he resembles the friends whose exceeding envy is transformed into religious hysteria.

Psalm 73 does not follow biblical inspiration at its highest register, where what we hear is the voice of the victim. It is very close to the inspiration of the friends in the book of Job. The highest register of inspiration is that of Job, which alone is specifically biblical; it has no equivalent in the Greek world or anywhere else.

Psalm 73 nonetheless has its place in the ensemble constituted by the psalms dealing with the collective victim. We can see this quite well if we compare its role to the role of Job's interlocutors. If the Bible were simply to transfer the monopoly of speech from the persecutors to the victims, if it substituted a "slave morality" for a "master morality," as Nietzsche claims, the revelation would not be as powerful as it is, neither on the moral nor on the intellectual level, which in fact are one and the same level. We would not be called upon to confront perpetually the two perspectives. The Bible would only amount to the revenge, symbolic or real, to which Nietzsche reduces the biblical process. It would boil down to a process of mimetic doubles, an inversion of signs having no essential signification. It is, as we see, something altogether else.

Like Greek tragedy, the Prophets, the dialogues of Job and the psalms visibly reflect great crises; they are political and social crises to be sure, but they are also religious, and they are one with the decadence of sacrificial systems which are still functioning in the two societies. We find ourselves at a junction between a religious phenomenon which is still sacrificial in the strict sense and a political phenomenon which is *sacrificial* in the broad sense. On certain points it is already possible to translate the religious discourse into political discourse and vice versa. Thanks to the work of the people in CREA (Centre de Recherches anthropologiques et épistémologiques) and still others, these possibilities are rapidly growing, but their development is going to be so upsetting for the social sciences that we can expect strong resistance to it.

***

In the dialogues, the conditions which I have shown to be favorable to all mimetic phenomena are visibly found together. The combination of imitation that is positive at first, then "negative," this combination of imitative resentment spread by the friends and by people of their kind is what clearly accounts for the two successive unanimities and for the order of their succession. This double mimesis is revealed in the splendid metaphor of the torrent.

> My brothers have been fickle as a torrent,
> as the course of a seasonal stream.
> Ice is the food of their dark waters,
> they well with the thawing of the snow;
> but in the hot season they dry up,
> with summer's heat they vanish.
> Caravans leave the trail to find them,
> go deep into the desert, and are lost.
> The caravans of Tema look to them,
> and on them Sheba's convoys build their hopes.
> Their trust proves vain,
> they reach them only to be thwarted. (6:15-20)

Job says "my brothers have been fickle as a torrent." To whom, precisely, does the metaphor apply? If the word "brothers" only designates the three friends, Job's direct interlocutors, the metaphor would not be relevant. It must apply to the entire community which is hardly to be distinguished from the friends. Today it rains and friends are drops of water among other drops of water. If the sun shines tomorrow, we shall see them again—as grains of sand in the burning desert . . .

The two unanimities which make of Job an idol and a scapegoat in turn correspond to the springtime flood and to the absolute drought which succeeds it. If the three friends were not always "plugged in" to the fashion of the moment, like every one else, there would be no unanimity. Their mimesis makes them perfectly *representative* of a community which is itself mimetic. If all the citizens were present in person around Job, we would learn nothing that we do not already know. The three comarades suffice for all, just like the choir in Greek tragedy.

Let us look carefully at the metaphor of the torrent. It expresses not only the absence of what is most desirable, whatever that may be, but also the presence, overabundant, stifling, of what is undesirable, whatever that may be as well. This accursed stream always ends up by bringing the thing it holds back from us and which it makes us desire, but precisely when it brings us that thing, we don't desire it any more; indeed, we flee it like the plague and that very thing is the plague from now on.

What is diabolical about the torrent is its cyclical nature, the way its always finally keeps its promise, but always too late, to provide men with what it holds back from them all year round. As it periodically reverses what it gives and refuses, it always revives desires which it never satisfies. The waters which the caravans need badly were so abundant the day before as to render inconceivable their complete disappearance at the precise instant that this need arises.

Without any breaks in its articulation, the metaphor draws from the torrent alone the behavior of normal desire and that of a desire which is ultimately deadly. It dismisses with elegance and simplicity the false common sense which demands at least two causes to account for effects which appear to be so contrary, the duality, for example, of a "pleasure principle" and of a "death instinct." A single principle suffices for everything. Such is mimetic desire.

Those who rightly apprehend desire are so alarmed that they attribute it to the hostile machinations of a devil. The demon has but one goal, it appears, and that is to harm humanity. The Satan of the prologue plays the role that is played by God according to the three friends; it is the role of the torrent in Job's metaphor; it is ever the role of the community in the thrall of mimesis.

Desire takes its projections for reality. The image of the torrent describes the world not as it is at first but as it appears to men when their desire is exasperated, when the prohibitions crumble which protected them from implacable rivalries.

Immense regions of the planet have been transformed into deserts, it appears, because of the uses that men have made of it, because of their desire. The more the desert spreads, inside and outside us, the more we are tempted to blame reality, or God himself, or, worse still, our neighbor, the first Job who comes along . . .

***

By focussing all at once all antagonism on one and the same adversary, the scapegoat causes all other conflicts to disappear, and when he disappears, so do all conflicts without exception, at least temporarily. He reestablishes peace in a way that appears properly miraculous, that reinforces a suddenly restored unity, and that presents itself as the intervention of some supernatural power, of a divinity.

This is a crucial point of the theory. The psychological, moral and social *efficacity* of the scapegoat is one with its religious function for it is this efficacity that makes of the scapegoat mechanism the source par excellence of all social transcendence. It is Job himself who defines his efficacity as a scapegoat, and in a way that is far superior to what we have been able to observe among ourselves. But it is certainly in order to weaken rather than to reinforce the system that the victim speaks of it; he does not speak to celebrate its merits, to provide it with any moral guarantee, to boast its advantages or to advise it as a method of government.

That is what the persecutors do, without even realizing it. Those who use scapegoats do not speak about them. These days, of course, they do speak of them; but they only speak of their own scapegoats in order to view them as something quite the opposite:

> I have become a byword among the people,
> and a creature on whose face to spit.
> My eyes grow dim with grief,
> and my limbs wear away like a shadow.
> At this honest men are shocked,
> and the guiltless man rails agains the godless;
> just men grow more settled in their ways,
> those whose hands are clean add strength to strength. (17: 6–9)

If our translation is correct, what Job is describing here is the beneficial effect on his own community that is produced by unjust persecution. I know of no other text where that effect stands out so boldly. It is the same thing as the *tragic effect*, the Aristotelian catharsis; but we are not dealing here with a theatrical representation, and Job does not try to embellish the truth of the operation with esthetic flourishes.

The translation of this passage is not the same everywhere. The one I have chosen is, as usual, from the Jerusalem Bible, which I recognize as being particularly favorable to my thesis, and as being singularly different from many others. For many ancient and modern translators alike, the second part of this text says some vague things which tend to reverse its meaning. In the New English Bible this reversal is realized maximally and here is the result:

> Honest men are bewildered at this
> and the innocent are indignant at my plight.
> In spite of all, the righteous man maintains his course
> And he whose hands are clean grows strong again.

The man whose hands are clean adds strength to strength here not *because* but *in spite* of the unjust persecution. This interpretation appears to me to be erroneous in view of the context. What the English Bible wants Job to be saying is contradicted by all the texts which we have read. If Job still enjoyed the esteem of the pure and the virtuous, he would not be abandoned by all without exception, he would not be the scapegoat which he describes in so many text which everyone translates in the same way.

The book of Job goes so far in its revelation of the scapegoat as the foundation of the sacred, of ethics, of aesthetics and of culture in general that I am not surprised to find such startling formulations as we have just read. If the Jerusalem Bible is right, the other translations bear witness to the resistance which our minds oppose to this revelation.

The Jerusalem Bible translates the second verse of this passage as "a creature on whose fact to spit." According to Etienne Dhorme (Old Testament: Pléiade edition), a literal translation would give us: "I will be a public Tophet." Dhorme points out in a note that, for the commentator Ibn Ezar, the word Tophet is made up of two terms:

> . . . the valley of Taphet, a place of shame according to Jeremiah, since it is where the Judeans practiced human sacrifice; their sons and daughters were offered up in flames. Taphet may also signify altar or hearth. The Jews read this word with the vowels of the word *boshet* which means shame.

Telescope the two terms, combine the vowels of the first and the consonants of the second and you get *Tophet*. The *public Tophet*, in the form of a man here, is the object of unanimous execration. That is to say: a scapegoat; I do not see any difference from one language to the other. There is no possible ambiguity. In spite of the innumerable tricks that language plays on us, I see no reason to moan about its impotence to communicate unambiguous meaning.

***

Only the real efficacity of the surrogate process can explain the existence of ritual behavior. Amazed by this process, its participants try to reproduce it by imitating it scrupulously. A new victim becomes necessary since the preceding one is no longer around. The principle of substitution is implicit in the observations made by Eliphaz. If Job shows any wickedness, any perversity, he will become the substitute for "the wicked" who preceded him, and he will not be spared his itinerary on "the ancient trail."

Job is the substitute of the wicked men who preceded him. He must therefore be wicked in the same way and that is what everyone is trying to show. The effort is made all the more strenuous by Job who struggles against it like the very devil. He throws every sort of wrench into the sacrificial works but to no avail; for the demonstration of his guilt is secondary with respect to the spontaneous choice of the community.

Society has a good thing, an efficacious purge of its bad humours. It is therefore natural to try to regularize it, to stabilize it in a way that is most advantageous for everyone. That rational and prudent conduct is what inspires ritual. It is the metamorphosis of the surrogate mechanism into a periodic rite.

In certain of its aspects, the phenomenon which concerns us in the dialogues is already ritualized. Everything suggests that the friends are hardly improvising in their behavior towards Job but that they are resorting instead to well tried formulas. They have to conform to some kind of model. Their speeches give off a strong scent of sacrificial liturgy.

The quite rhythmic clamor of the three series of speeches reminds us of the tragic choir, and, beyond that, of the ritual recitations which in preparation for sacrifice are intended to excite the participants against the victim. By their incantatory, repetitive character, these vociferations mime the movement and the cries of a crowd which is polarized around a victim.

The victim is already designated; what must be done now is to focus on the scapegoat all the stray violence that is so dangerous to the community. That is what the three friends are doing with Job. They don't travel "the ancient trail of the wicked" themselves, thank god, but they control the traffic. They know all its detours. They exercise a properly ritual function, just like the choir in Greek tragedy. They assure the proper functioning of the victimary mechanism.

We can count on Job to make that sacrificial recipe explicit. The recalcitrant scapegoat has some observations of incomparable force. Rare, unfortunately, are the readers who are capable of appreciating their soundness. Job resorts to a strange metaphor, one that is unintelligible for all the disciplines which persist in their blindness about the true nature of sacrifice:

> Soon you will be casting lots for an orphan,
> and selling your friend at bargain prices! (6:27)

Job compares himself explicitly to the ideal victim, who has neither relatives, nor servants, nor neighbors, nor even a friend to defend him. He can be chosen without fear of reviving the divisions which sacrifice is intended to cure. In short, Job restates in sacrificial terms everything else we have heard him say. He is abandoned by all; a void opens up around him. His alleged friends make the situation worse by their suggestion that he is the latest edition of the "wicked," of the "enemies of God."

The tone adopted by Job is somberly ironic. If his remark has any weight, it is because we are in the context of a world in which human sacrifice is officially abolished, religiously discredited, but not so completely forgotten that the allusion to the orphan drawn by lot ceases to be intelligible. Perhaps the immolation of children is still practiced secretly in some reactionary quarters.

For many specialists, the understanding of sacrifice consists in properly determining the classifications of the particular system in question. They regard any theory as false, *a priori*, if it is based on distinctions or comparisons which do not figure in the language of that system.

To argue as I do that the matrix of all sacrifice is the collective process of victimization, the scapegoat in the ordinary sense, strikes some people as unjustifiable. The thesis shortcircuits distinctions which the liturgical systems never abolish. It is therefore easy to maintain that I do not respect the facts.

But fortunately for me, here is Job who does the same thing. He too indulges in unseemly comparisons. His metaphors constantly compare things which theoreticians who are respectful of the institutional letter never allow themselves to compare.

We can of course turn a deaf ear, we can always follow the example of the "friends," while modernizing their arguments. The book of Job belongs indubitably to "literature," and the orphan drawn by lot is only a metaphor. I agree, but are we so convinced that nothing true is ever to be learned from literature and its metaphors? Is that metaphor of the orphan drawn by lots really incongruous, or is it on the contrary very well placed and perfectly justified? Is it one of those ultra-modern metaphors which aims at comparing two radically different things only for the sake of the gratuitous shock effect it produces, or is it a metaphor which juxtaposes two things whose comparison is otherwise surprising: not because of the intrinsic distance between two things but because on the contrary their extreme proximity had eluded us up to that point? Is it perhaps a metaphor which, if we permit it, could teach us things which it knows and which we do not?

I choose the second solution. The apparent neutrality of non-literary sources is less rich and, in the final analysis, less trustworthy than great literature. Job is far better situated than we are to make sense out of sacrifice. His metaphors are only meaningful in terms of the generative link between collective persecution and ritualized sacrifice which I have proposed in *Violence and the Sacred*. The existence or nonexistence of this link cannot be made to depend upon whether such indications are given or not given by the systems of liturgical codification. It is quite obvious that these systems never trumpet their own entrenchment in violence. To give the last word to their explicit testimony where a theory of sacrifice is concerned is about as sensible as asking Job's community if the violence committed against him is real and as arbitrarily cruel as he claims it is.

Must we deny the status of victim to Job under the pretext that he is the only one to point it out to us and that neither the three friends nor anyone else in the community acknowledges him as a victim?

In a sense that is what is denied him by all the traditional interpretations. The most efficacious objections are never the most explicit ones. We gladly recognize in Job the victim of God, of the devil, of bad luck, of destiny, of "the human condition," of clericalism and anything else you wish, as long as it is never a question of Job's neighbor, that is to say, of ourselves.

What is this refusal to recognize the victim as such, what is this eternal claim of innocence on the part of humanity, if it is not the incomprehension which the dialogues have as their object to reveal? Secretly we always agree with the three friends who make a show, though not much of one, of pity for Job, but who treat him as guilty; they do this not only to make him their scapegoat but also to deny that such a thing is possible. The two always go together.

What Job says will always elude a mind which is bent on making classifications, whether it is structuralist or not. For this bent itself is the direct descendant of forms of intellectual discrimination which originate in the victimary mechanism and it will never break completely with it.

True anthropological knowledge cannot limit itself to reusing classifications which belong to the systems under study. It must account for them in a theory which is genetic and structural at once. Not any more than Job himself does the victimary theory grossly confuse spontaneous persecution with ritual sacrifice, but it does allow us to determine a relationship between spontaneous persecution and all sacrifice, a relationship which is both metaphorical and real: it is metaphorical in that all ritual activity consists in the substitution of a victim; it is real in that the substituted victim is nonetheless immolated.

Behind the apparent incoherence of the themes, a higher coherence is revealed, but only on one condition. We must interpret the difference in perspective to Job's benefit. We must prefer Job's discourse to what the others say: we must take the revelation of the scapegoat seriously. In a word, we must take it as being *true*.

It is in the light of what Job says that we can interpret the speeches of the friends as well as the whole of the dialogues, but we cannot do the reverse. What the friends say sheds absolutely no light on what Job says. There are two truths in the relative sense, in the sense of a "relativism" or a "perspectivism," but there is only one where knowledge is concerned, and that is the truth of the victim.

It is not enough for us to recognize the object of the debate, the collective violence which is preparing to descend on Job and which has already singed him; we must recognize the two perspectives on that violence and above all we must chose between them. Any avoidance of taking sides is a deception. Any affectation of *impassivity*, whatever its pretext, stoical, philosophical or scientific, perpetuates the status quo, prolongs the occultation of the scapegoat, and effectively makes us accomplice to the persecutors. Job is the opposite of that impassivity. Far from being a source of ignorance, the passionate identification with the victim is the only authentic source of knowledge as of everything else. The true science of man is not impassive.

***

Translated by Andrew J. McKenna

III
APPLICATIONS

PROPHECY, SACRIFICE AND REPENTANCE IN THE STORY OF JONAH

Sandor Goodhart
University of Michigan

ABSTRACT

A careful reading of the final parable of the gourd reveals that Jonah's reluctance to prophesy to Ninevah is not simply lacking in compassion, as modern readings argue. It is also anti-Jewish. The Jews are those who have departed, who have given up the sacrificial or Ninevitian ways of their surroundings to live by the Torah, the Law of anti-idolatry. Jonah makes an idol of this law itself. This diachronic identity between Israel and Ninevah helps us to explain the scriptural and liturgical contexts in which the story is read. As an account of the nature of the prophetic spirit itself, the Jonah story reveals the motor force of Judaism as a collection of rituals in which the substitutive, arbitrary, and expulsive nature of sacrificial gestures are made progressively overt on the social level. On the individual level, the condition of Jewish life is revealed as *teshuvah* or repentance, the abandonment of sin and return to the ways of God.

The Book of Jonah seems at first glance something of a misfit in each of the contexts in which it has traditionally been read. It is scripturally one of the Books of the Prophets but it clearly lacks the monumentalism associated with so many of the others—for example, the Book of Isaiah, or of Jeremiah. The story seems in fact, in style and setting, more akin to the wisdom literature that grew up around the court of King Solomon—for example, the Book of Job. And perhaps it is this personal quality that we reflect when we choose to memorialize it in popular imagination—and to the scorn of most commentators—as the story of a man who was swallowed by a whale, a kind of Biblical Pinocchio.

The details of the plot, even for a wisdom tale, are somewhat odd. The whole first half is spent just in getting Jonah to prophesy at all. And when he does, and is successful beyond his wildest expectations, he is strangely angered by that success, so much so in fact that God Himself is impelled to intervene to teach him an "object lesson" with the gourd (or kikayon plant) in a parabolic final scene that is itself set apart, in a manner not unlike the story in which it is contained.

What kind of prophetic instruction are we to gain from this tale? Neither of the two major interpretive traditions in which it has been read seem to have satisfactorily replied to the question without neglecting some part of the story. The most familiar reading—represented, for example, within the Jewish community, by a thinker like Abraham Heschel—focuses upon the final moments which seem expressive of "the mystery of compassion," largely to the exclusion of the narrative to that point.[1] And the older tradition, which is probably less familiar (and less palatable) to modern readers, concerns with almost equal exclusivity Jonah's refusal to prophesy to the Ninevites, a reluctance which it reads, moreover, within a strictly historical framework, as redemptive.[2]

Jonah knows, this reading asserts, that if Ninevah repents (which undoubtedly it will), then things will look bad for Israel who in the other Prophetic Books has stubbornly refused to repent. Scoffers, moreover, will then denounce Jonah as a false prophet (since his prophecy has not come true) and cast aspersions upon the institution of prophecy itself. And finally, since in the far distant future, Ninevah is destined to become the "rod of God's wrath" against Israel, Jonah knows that such an action is now aiding and abetting that future event.

The older reading, in short, seems as trapped by its literalism and historicism as the newer is by its formal abstractions. In context of the final debate between Jonah and God, each interpretation would seem to have aligned itself with one or another position—to the exclusion identically of the narrative context in which that exchange occurs.

Nor does the story seem any less out of place within the liturgical context within which it is customarily read. Recited on the afternoon of Yom Kippur, the holiest day of the Jewish calendar, the day of repentance and of the scapegoat ritual (cf. Gaster), the story has been linked to cultic and spiritual traditions that seem equally remote from its homespun wisdom. What has the story to do with ritual sacrifice? The only sacrifices performed in the story are those of the sailors after Jonah has been expelled from the ship and those pagan sacrifices performed just before Jonah enters Ninevah.

And if we accept the notion of repentance or *teshuvah* in its traditional understanding as the abandonment of sin and the return to the ways of God (Zlotowitz: xxxviii–lxvi), then the only enduringly repentant figures within the story are non-Jews and God Himself. The sailors on the ship bound for Tarshish repent after Jonah requests to be tossed overboard and the sea is strangely calmed. The Ninevites repent once Jonah has begun his mission—so completely, in fact, that some commentators have wondered whether some of the sailors slipped into the city before him. And, of course, God Himself, upon seeing the true repentance of the Ninevites, relents of His planned destruction of them.

But Jonah seems constitutionally bent upon pursuing one path from beginning to end. However repentant he becomes within the belly of the great fish, his spiritual condition seems to have altered decisively by the time he sits upon the hill to brood over the salvation of Ninevah. "Was not this my contention when I was still on mine own soil?" he remarks (IV.2). "I therefore had hastened to flee to Tarshish".[3] His position seems to have come full circle to the point from which he began.

Is the Jonah story an anomaly within these traditional contexts, a kind of freak of scriptural and liturgical history? Or are these frameworks critical to its truths in ways that we have yet to perceive? In answering this question we may be in a better position to engage certain others which are often raised in these discussions. These are larger questions concerning Jewish and non-Jewish relations, as well as questions concerning the one Biblical theme in which each of the above contextual frameworks—prophecy, interpretation, sacrifice, and repentance—converge: the coming of the Messiah.

II.

That the story of Jonah is dominated by Jonah's reluctance to prophesy to the Ninevites is acknowledged by even the most casual of readers.[4] That this reluctance structures the story systematically—setting up an intricate pattern of repetitions and transformations—is less commonly acknowledged.

The story is divided into two major parts, the second of which is a development and repetition of the first. The first part in particular is patterned as a version of the Oedipus story. The very efforts Jonah makes to avoid undertaking the mission God requires of him are the efforts which bring it about, although in the Hebrew context that fulfillment is regarded as positive. The prophetic call comes and Jonah flees to Tarshish. But his presence on the ship only intensifies his difficulties and he arranges to be removed from the scene once again, the sailors on the ship, as a kind of narrative aside, converting to the religion of the Hebrews in the process. Now he finds himself within the tempest tossed sea itself and is straightaway swallowed by a large fish. Miraculously preserved in tact after several days within the belly of the fish, he thanks God for all He has done for him and is suddenly expelled from the fish onto dry land, the same land in fact from which he began, only to face the prospect of the same divine command. As if in echo of the sailors, the rabbinical commentators themselves, this time, convert Jonah's prayer of thanksgiving into a prayer of repentance, citing his words as an instance of "the prophetic past" (Zlotowitz: 107).

The second part of the narrative continues the same ironic conjunction of cause and effect. But now it is his fulfillment of the divine mission that renders him increasingly unhappy. The call comes to Jonah a second time and this time—as if in negative imitation of his initial flight—he goes. He preaches to the Ninevites and is successful beyond all measure. But that success is repellent to him and he retires to a hill to await the outcome. A gourd grows to shelter him from the heat and he rejoices over it and when on the next day it withers, he is even more upset than before. Finally, God speaks to him about his experiences and, once he has expressed his anger at the salvation of the Ninevites and the loss of the gourd, God delivers His final speech in which He puts into perspective all that has occurred.

At the same time, and independent of this forward diachronic progression, there is a clear pattern of repetition and intensification that we have already in part suggested. Each scene reflects in some fashion all that has preceded it. Jonah flees God's prophetic call and the elements of that initial scene—the word of God, the tempestuous conditions of Ninevah and its fruitless religious appeals, the expulsion of Jonah from the scene—are repeated in scene two—once before he arrives, and then again during his presence on the ship. The breath of God creates the storm in which the sailors fruitlessly call upon their Gods, offer sacrifices, and expel cargo. The word of the commander to "arise" comes to Jonah (who has fallen asleep in the innermost hold of the ship) and after a process of ritual selection (the questions and the casting of lots) he is thrown overboard. Similarly, the scene within the water reproduces in significant measure the same elements. God designates a sacrificial monster from the tempestuous depths to engulf Jonah who offers a religious prayer of thanksgiving for past salvation which results in his expulsion from those depths. From religious and pagan encounters we have moved to environmental encounters of the most intense kind.

Part Two plays off of this pattern with opposed narrative effect. The opening scene echoes the opening of the story. The word of God comes regarding conditions in Ninevah, appeals to Jonah's sense of religious duty, and Jonah removes himself from the premises—this time to fulfill his mission. The second scene of part two similarly echoes its counterpart in part one. The word of God comes (through Jonah) to a tempestuous city, the city is responsive to his words and engage the appropriate religious behavior, and Jonah leaves—although as before the religious response and his departure are appropriate. And the third scene on the hill recalls the conclusion of part one within the depths. God exchanges words with Jonah. The heat of the day oppresses him. The gourd arises to protect him and quickly withers, an event which induces Jonah's anger once again. And God's final speech, recapitulating all that has occurred, and closing off the narrative, becomes the touchstone for rabbinical commentary upon the tale.

What is the function of this curious narrative structure in which an unmistakable and continuous forward movement results in diametrically opposed encounters, or, to put it the other way around, in which decisively contrasted sequences turn out to be continuous with each other? Moreover, what is the function of the final exchange between God and Jonah upon the hill which at once continues this narrative development and yet seems at the same time to include within it all that has occurred?

To situate that final encounter in something of its narrative context, let us turn to the opening of Part Two.

III.

"And the word of Hashem came to Jonah a second time saying: 'Arise! Go to Ninevah, that great city, and cry out to her the proclamation which I tell you.' " The opening words of Part Two echo unmistakably the opening words of Part One (I.1–2). The word of *Hashem* came to Jonah and this time he goes. Why? Jonah had achieved repentance in the belly of the fish, the sages tell us, and in order for repentance to be complete, the penitent must be tried in circumstances similar to those in which he previously failed (cf. Zlotowitz:118). The word of God comes and this time he goes without a moment's hesitation—like Abraham to the sacrifice of Isaac. His repentance would seem just about complete.

And as if for a kind of bonus, his efforts are successful beyond his wildest expectations. Barely has he stepped foot in Ninevah—which was "enormously large" we are told and "a three day journey" across (III. 3)— and barely has he offered his proclamation—"Forty days more and Ninevah shall be overturned" (III. 4)—than his appearance occasions a repentance of unprecedented proportions. "The people of Ninevah had faith in God, so they proclaimed a fast and donned sackcloth" (III. 5).

And no sooner does the word of Jonah's appearance in the city reach the king than he decrees repentance into state law. "He rose from his throne and removed his robe . . . he covered himself with sackcloth and sat on ashes" and issued a city-wide proclamation: no one—neither men nor cattle—shall eat or drink, but rather they shall "cover themselves with sackcloth" and pray to God (III. 6–8).

> Everyone is to turn back from his evil way and from the robbery which is in his hands. He who knows—let him repent and God will be relentful; He will turn away from His burning wrath so that we perish not. (III. 8–9)

So intense and deeply felt are these penitential gestures that even the cattle are kept in a fast. If ever Jonah contemplated the fears to which the commentators allude, his experience in Ninevah should have dispelled them completely. Their repentance is massive and genuine. Moreover, they repent without in way challenging either Jonah in particular or the institutions of prophecy of which he is representative. They are fully aware, it seems, that God sometimes turns from the destruction He plans when He sees that Man turns from his evil ways (Zlotowttz: 82). It is a gesture more expected of Israel than Ninevah—which has been compared in the commentaries to the cities of Sodom and Gomorrah (Zlotowitz: 82, 122). Jonah seems, in fact, to have very little to do with what occurs. It is as if all that was needed was the prophet's appearance in the city for a movement of staggering proportions to begin—which may be in part why commentators sometimes suggest that sailors from the ship from which Jonah was expelled had made their way to Ninevah before him (Zlotowitz: 123).

And the response of God? He sees the depth and breadth of their repentance and calls off the disaster He had in store for them. He relents from destroying them. Jonah's success, in short, would seem the completion and reversal of all that has occurred in Part One. All that would be left to include—as a kind of parallel to the end of Part One—would be some kind of prayer on Jonah's part to God, thanking him for all He has done for mankind, declaring His greatness—His universal glory, mercy, and justice—the kind of prayer, in fact, which the liturgists saw fit to tack on to the reading of the Book of Jonah on the afternoon of Yom Kippur from the Book of Micah:

> Who is a God like You, Who pardons iniquity, and forgives the transgression of the remnant of His heritage? He does not maintain His anger forever, because He delights in mercy. He will again have compassion on us; He will suppress our iniquities; and You will cast all their sins into the depth of the sea. (VII. 18–19)

It is as if the liturgists of Yom Kippur are mindful of the developments we have been suggesting and draw them to their natural conclusion.

But all of this makes what in fact follows the repentance of the Ninevites and God's relenting of His planned destruction so strange:

> This displeased Jonah greatly and it grieved him. He prayed to Hashem, and said: "Please, Hashem, was not this my contention when I was still on my own soil? I therefore had hastened to flee to Tarshish for I knew that You are a gracious and compassionate God, slow to anger, abounding in kindness, and relentful of punishment. So now, Hashem, please take my life from me, for better is my death than my life. (IV. 1–3)

The very qualities for which the prayer from Micah praises God—compassion, slow to anger, kindness, mercy, etc.—which are, moreover, the very qualities Jonah anticipated that God would display, are the very reasons Jonah cites for his anger against what has occurred and, moreover, for his flight initially from *eretz Israel* to Tarshish.

Why is Jonah angry at his success? Moreover, why is he so intensely angry that he asks God to take his life, that he asserts "better is my death than my life"?

What is strange about Jonah's anger in the first place is that it seems to cast doubts upon his entire history to this point. Either he was not fully repentant in the belly of the great fish—as the Rabbis claimed—or his condition of true repentance has lapsed and he is in need of it again. Secondly, the issue of his flight seems raised now once and for all. Since the story concludes with this exchange, we must assume that somewhere along the way this issue has been resolved in a fashion that remains to be elucidated. And since the final scene takes up his initial reluctance to prophesy to the Ninevites as its central concern it would seem natural to suppose that it is here that the story in its entirety becomes readable.

There is also something else. In the way in which the last scene stands apart from the others it reproduces to some extent—in miniature as it were—the whole of the Jonah story thus far. It restages the Jonah story from a certain distance so that its contours can become clear. It operates much the same way, for example, as the episode within the belly of the great fish does (with its series of thoughts and cries within remembered prayers): it is a reflection of both the narrative to that point and the narrative to come and thus a staging of the relations between the "insides" of the story and the multiplicity of engulfing conceptual frameworks within which those entrails reside—the fish, the sea, the Jonah story, the Books of the Prophets, Hebrew scripture, Judaic culture, the world, etc. It stages those relations from without as the former does from the depths. It provides a "Part Two" to the Jonah story which is not disimilar to the "Part Two" in which it is contained. And thus it parallels certain other scriptural texts in which a "Part One" is followed by a "Part Two" which restages the earlier sequence in such a way that its salient features become apparent—both to readers of the story and to the characters within it (who are thus rendered like those readers). I have tried elsewhere to suggest how the Joseph story is structured in such a fashion (Goodhart).

Let us turn, then, to this Jonah story within the Jonah story upon which everything seems to converge.

* * * * *

The Ninevites repent. God relents from the disaster He has planned. And Jonah is greatly displeased and retires to the hill to watch what will become of the city: ". . . was not this my contention when I was still on my native soil? . . . So, now, Hashem, please take my life from me, for better is my death than my life."

The first part of the exchange draws into the fore the central movement of the narrative so far. The envisioning of just this conclusion was what led him to flee God's request initially, Jonah relates. And his offering of the ultimate sacrifice ("Better is my death than my life") reflects what was already present to his thoughts when he was aboard the tempest-tossed vessel and asked that he be thrown overboard. It is in fact this offer which redeems him in the eyes of most traditional commentators since in the face of a perceived embarrassment to Israel (the suppression of a prophecy, the Talmudic authorities tell us, was a crime punishable by death) he does what all major leaders of Israel have done—Abraham, Moses, David, etc. (Zlotowitz: 86, 99).

Moreover, it puts to rest any speculation that Jonah fled because he feared God would not be compassionate or that the Ninevites would not repent of their ways since in function of a logic that remains to be elucidated he flees precisely because of God's compassion and because he knows that Ninevites will repent.

And the second part of the narrative stages in turn the first part. God draws Jonah's attention to what he has said, to his own words, registering Jonah's response. "And Hashem said: 'Art thou that deeply grieved?'" There may even be something slightly ironic about God's response, perhaps even sardonic, given that fact that Jonah is angry that he has just saved a city full of people from disaster. "Does that, indeed, bother you?" God seems to be saying. "Let Me get clear on exactly what it is you are telling me," as if there is more to follow.

In fact, there is. The first exchange having set the stage for what is to come, God will now make his own move: He will deconstruct Jonah's anger and reluctance to prophesy in a gesture calculated to inspire in Jonah (and perhaps us as well) a profound repentance.

> Jonah had left the city and stationed himself at the east of the city. He made himself a booth there and sat under it in the shade until he would see what would occur in the city.
>
> Then Hashem, God, designated a kikayon which rose up above Jonah to form a shade over his head and relieve him from his discomfort. And Jonah rejoiced greatly over the kikayon.
>
> Then God designated a worm at the dawn of the morrow and it attacked the kikayon so that it withered. And it happened when the sun rose that God designated a stifling east wind; the sun beat upon Jonah's head and he felt faint. He asked for death saying: "Better my death than my life!"
>
> And God said to Jonah: "Are you so deeply grieved over the kikayon?"
>
> And he said: "I am greatly grieved to the point of death."

Hashem said, "You took pity on the kikayon for which you did not labor nor did you make to grow; which materialized overnight and perished overnight. And I—shall I not take pity upon Ninevah that great city, in which there are more than a hundred and twenty thousand persons who do not know their right hand from their left, and many beasts as well. (IV.5-11)

These final verses of the Jonah story have puzzled readers for as long as they have read it. The scene seems clearly to be of climactic importance in the narrative to this point. And yet it is so parabolic and oblique in its reference to the details of the story we have witnessed that it has given rise to a variety of partial and (for that reason) insufficient readings.

The most common reading (which we cited earlier) is that God teaches Jonah an "object lesson" in compassion. God sets the scene by generating in Jonah the same response that he felt for the impending salvation of the Ninevites and then pointing out, "You felt compassion for a gourd for which you did not work, which is not your handiwork, and which is as transitory as the wind. How much more compassion should I feel for the people of the great city of Ninevah—who *are* My handiwork, for whom I *have* worked, and whose repentance may sow seeds for the repentance of others in the future?" The rhetorical form, of course, is that of a *kal vachomer* or *a fortiori* argument which is used commonly in scripture and so lends an added familiarity and strength to the words.

There may, however, be another reading, a more subtle and complex strategy on God's part, in function of which, in fact, the more common reading is itself implicated.

What is striking above all in the context in which the verses appear is the repetition of Jonah's response, a repetition which draws our attention to what has changed. "Are you so deeply grieved over the kikayon?" God asks, at once in repetition of the sentiment on Jonah's part that God registered earlier and in a kind of amazement, offering Jonah as it were a way out of the corner in which he has lodged himself. But Jonah will not take that exit and repeats himself with an emphasis that can leave no doubt about his intentions. "I am greatly grieved to the point of death."

What God is showing Jonah, in other words, in the first instance is that what has troubled him—"to the point of death" as he says—is nothing more terrible than a matter of personal discomfort. What "grieves" him, in one case as in the other, is the loss of his own personal protection from the heat of the sun, the fear of his own exposure in the light of day. What has angered him in the salvation of the Ninevites is the loss in some way of his own security, the threatened exposure of his own weaknesses and failings, the loss of his "kikayon". The traditional reading of Jonah's reluctance to prophesy—for fear of exposing Israel who will not repent in the other books of the Prophets—gains validity in this light if we substitute for the threat to Israel at large the more immediate danger to Jonah in particular.

But why has God chosen to reveal the real object of Jonah's concern in this particular way? Why a "kikayon" plant? What in the first place is a "kikayon"? There are many conjectures among the commentators as to the particular plant being referred to. Some identify it as a kind of gourd, others as a castor oil plant. Rashi, the foremost medieval commentator within the rabbinical tradition, identifies it only as a "plant containing many leaves, which provides shade," presumably agreeing with those who feel it is unnecessary to identify it more specifically, since such "speculation diverts from the lesson of the narrative" (Zlotowitz: 136). It is not the salvation of Ninevah at all that draws Jonah's attention, God seems to be saying, but something else: let us call it a "kikayon." Perhaps our difficulty in knowing how to translate this word reflects the more profound difficulty of identifying the nature of the substitute.

The function of the "kikayon," that is, may be at least in part to signify that Jonah has invested his energies precisely in an object, a thing of this world, an idol. And as God elicits from Jonah the intensity of his investment ("better my death than my life," Jonah says; "I am greatly grieved . . . to the point of death"), the status of that object becomes clear for us: it has become for Jonah a kind of divinity. Quite apart from a perceived threat to his own exposure, what describes Jonah's relationship to Ninevah is a form of idolatry.

In what way? Rabbi J. H. Hertz, in his excellent commentary to this story in a widely used conservative liturgical text, draws our attention to this aspect of Jonah's relation to Ninevah. "The Book of Jonah is the most ill-used and least understood of all the Books of the Bible," Hertz writes.

> The purpose of Jonah's adventures is to teach him by experience, and through him Israel and mankind, a lesson which had to be learned. The lesson cannot be only, as some have maintained, that God accepts repentance; if that were all, chapter four would be irrelevant and unnecessary. Nor can it be the only lesson that the Gentiles too are God's creatures, and worthy of pardon if sincerely repentant. Jonah knew and understood that lesson; his very reluctance to deliver his message was based on the fear that the Ninevites might repent, if warned, and be forgiven, and that he would therefore be the agent of their salvation. (964)

Dismissing the traditional accounts, Hertz shrewdly draws our attention to the absolute difference upon which Jonah's view is founded.

> The essential teaching is that the Gentiles *should not be grudged* God's love, care, and forgiveness. It is this grudging which is so superbly rebuked

throughout the Book, and most of all in the final chapter, which must rightly be considered the climax of the story. [964]

Jonah has refused to prophesy to the Ninevites, in other words, because he would reserve salvation for the Israelites alone. He would make an idol, ironically, of the law of anti-idolatry itself. But what God would teach him, what the Book of Jonah would teach us, is that to begrudge salvation to the Ninevites is not simply snobbish: it is anti-Jewish. For who are the Jews? They are not some people indigenous to the region in which they live, who have been given some kind of special handling by God. They are, precisely, those who have left, those who have given up the sacrificial ways of the lands from which they come in order to be Jews in the first place.

The Jews, in other words, are ex-Ninevites and by this same understanding, as those who have given up their sacrificial and idolatrous ways and turned in repentance to the religion of the Hebrew God, the Ninevites are the new Jews. To turn against the Ninevites therefore is to turn against the Jews. And likewise either to justify Jonah's flight (on the basis that it saves Israel) or to criticize it (on the basis that he must have compassion for the non-Jews)—these two positions traditionally adopted participate equally in Jonah's own misunderstanding. It is to preserve in either case the difference between the two, between the Israelites and the Ninevites, the very difference that the story is working prophetically to undo. It is to make an idol of the law of anti-idolatry once again—just as Jonah himself did.

And if we can identify this new idolatry—which is given in the face of the revelation of the law of anti-idolatry—as itself "Ninevitian," a new form of sacrificial thinking which founds itself once more on the very distinctions Judaism founded itself upon rejecting, then we may say that Israel and Ninevah (or Judaism and sacrificial modes of thinking) are distributed along an axis which is neither historical nor parabolic, neither diachronic nor synchronic, but rather which occupy two apparent "sides" of a Moëbius strip in which there is really only one side, one continuous and twisting path between them. The Ninevites are the "other" of the Jews at every point if and only if they are at the same time the future or the past of the Jews, the future or the past of where the Jews already are.

But there is a third understanding of the final scene that needs to be made explicit, one that in fact combines each of the first two. And this understanding derives from God's final words to Jonah. The scene with the gourd reveals to Jonah in the dreamlike language of parable the source of his anger at the salvation of the Ninevites—the fear of his own exposure. And the particularity of that language helps us to specify the nature of that relationship from a Biblical perspective: Jonah is reenacting the very idolatry whose rejection enabled the Jews to give up their sacrificial origins and become Jews in the first place. To turn against the Ninevites is to turn against the Jews. It is to fall into a Ninevitian sacrificial mode of a new and more dangerous order since it is to do so in the wake of the revelation of anti-idolatry. It is to make an idol of the law of anti-idolatry itself.

But why the particularity of the kikayon with regard to Jonah individually? God's final words give us the clue: "You took pity on the kikayon . . . shall I not take pity upon Ninevah." But Jonah never "took pity" on the kikayon in the narrative we have. He "rejoiced" over it when it offered him shade, and "grieved" over it—even to the point of wishing for his own death—when it was lost but never "pitied" it (the Hebrew word for "pity" is *choos*) in the narrative we have. Why has God seemingly altered this description?

In a sense, in substituting the kikayon for Ninevah as the object of Jonah's concern God has acted somewhat in the manner of a primitive shaman with him. The object has functioned both to clarify and delineate Jonah's relation to Ninevah prior to this scene. But lest this object in itself gain undue attention in Jonah's eyes, God is about to snatch that away as well. Having shown him what his anger is (viz. a "kikayon," an excuse, an idolatrous substitute for his own fears of exposure), He will now show him what this kikayon is: namely, a substitute, in turn, for his own self-condemnation and self-judgment.

"Better is my death than my life" is the clue. The intensity with which Jonah greeted the loss of the gourd reflects a depth of personal involvement that far exceeds either an onerous prophetic task he perceives God as giving him or an idolatrous perspective with regard to non-Jews. And it is that depth of internal involvement which God reflects when He characterizes Jonah's relationship to the kikayon retrospectively as one of "pity." You have seen yourself in the kikayon, God tells him implicitly, your own transitory nature, and your own impending demise, and it is that which you have pitied—the "kikayon" with the "kikayon."

Behind Ninevah, in other words, behind the kikayon, is the real object of Jonah's fascination which is himself—which he has not created, for which he has not labored, and which will perish overnight. "Better is my death than my life" is a resonant judgement not of Ninevah but above all of himself. And it is in these terms that Jonah's response to Ninevah finds its greatest source of power. At root Jonah has made an idol not only of Ninevah but of himself. Why is taking himself as an idol bad? Because it is that, above all, which is "Ninevitian." It is that which Jews left in order to be Jews. You are angry at saving the Ninevites, God tells Jonah implicitly, because you are in danger of being embarrassed, in danger of being exposed as a Ninevitian yourself, a new Ninevitian, one who has made an idol of the law of anti-idolatry, but a Ninevitian nonetheless. And in fleeing My prophetic task, you do that once again.

And yet, having characterized Jonah's relation to the kikayon as one of pity (and thereby a revelation of Jonah's self-indictment and its consequences), God will now make the boldest stroke of all: He will offer Jonah (and those for whom the story of Jonah is their "kikayon") the way out of that dilemma. Leave the pitying to Me, He tells Jonah. Don't take over My position. Let Me decide who is worthy of pity and who is not. Let Me alone make human beings in My image. The rejoicing over kikayons and the grieving over their loss is My job, not yours. And you do yourself and Me a disservice by usurping My role in these matters, in creating idols of earthly concerns, in fashioning human kikayons after your own image.

"And I—shall I not take pity upon Ninevah that great city?" God's final pronouncement, in other words, completes the deconstruction begun at the outset of this final scene. By your own argument, God in essence is telling Jonah, should I not do what you would rather I refrain from doing, namely, save the city of Ninevah? Should I not save them precisely by imitation of your example, by thinking of them as *My* kikayons, pityable in the same way in which you would take yourself as an object of pity? And is it not better, after all, that I should make kikayons rather than you? And that you render back unto Me what was Mine to begin with, what you appropriated idolatrously from Me—ironically in your manner of defining yourself as anti-idolatrous? For in appropriating my role from Me it is you who now reside in Ninevah, in "that great city, in which there are more than a hundred and twenty thousand persons who do not know their right hand from their left, and many beasts as well." In cutting Me off from Ninevah, you are cutting Me off, in the same gesture, from yourself. ". . . shall I not take pity upon Ninevah?"

IV.

The profound diachronic continuity between Israel and Ninevah, and the radical difference between idolatry and divinity that at every point sustains that continuity will explain for us the entire narrative. The story of Jonah is among the Prophetic Books not because it relates (or fails to relate) the historical or cultural circumstances of Israel's relation to its prophets but because it demystifies for us the prophetic spirit itself, the spirit which in the sixth century before our era canonized the Biblical texts and thus in some very real sense "wrote" the Bible.

What is prophetic thinking? We have always had difficulty from within a Platonic perspective imagining as genuine any knowledge issuing from sources other than reason or decision-making. And we have accepted this alternative claim only in those realms where it can be declared to have come from beyond conscious human relations—from the intervention of some outside agency (for example, divine providence) or from the interruption of our everyday lives by some inside unconscious agency that we can attribute to our own desires.

What the prophetic calls upon us to imagine on the other

hand—within both the Pre-Socratic Greek context and within Israel in the centuries during which the Biblical texts were canonized—is the "middle" that has been excluded from these considerations, the matrix of human relations in which we were immersed before invoking this ratio. In particular, it calls upon us recognize the dramas in which human beings are always already engaged and to name in advance the end of those dramas.

To think the relation of Ninevah to Israel prophetically, therefore, is to think in transformational and sequential terms that do not derive from some external synchronic grid against which such developmental changes can be measured. Israel is what Ninevah is becoming as it turns away from the idolatrous sacrificial ways of its past, and, moreover what it is in danger of becoming once again should it make an idol of that transformation itself. To insist upon the difference between the two—even in the wake of the revelation of the law of anti-idolatry—is to make an "object lesson" or kikayon of that very revelation, to participate in a new idolatry, one which is, in a sense, even more dangerous than the first since there is no longer any revelation of which it is not already cognizant. It is to fall into a new sacrificial mode which is identical in kind (if not in detail) with the old sacrificial mode, the one rejected in order to formulate that revelatory difference in the first place.

And it is preeminently this danger, the danger of making a kikayon of the law of anti-kikayons, that the story of Jonah is about. Coming in scripture after the giving of the Law, it concerns less the nature of anti-idolatry *per se* (as do the books of the Torah) than the kinds of idolatrous traps into which we can fall even after we are in possession of that Law. Jonah is the Israelite who would reserve the revelation of the Law of anti-idolatry for himself and God's interaction with him serves to deconstruct that position—to stage its limits—in two distinct ways: in such a way that Jonah can understand it (with the kikayon), and in such a way that through Jonah's recognition we can see it as well, we who have made a kikayon or object lesson of the story of Jonah within the Books of the Prophets no less than he has. The story of Jonah is to the Books of the Prophets what the scene of the kikayon is to the story of Jonah, each in fact functioning the same way that the Biblical scripture does for us.

Moreover, perhaps we now also understand why the story of Jonah "feels like" wisdom literature—for example, like the Book of Job. It may be that the story of Jonah locates itself at the same place in the history of sacrificial thinking as the wisdom texts, at those moments when the wisdom of the Hebraic God and the Law He reveals comes itself under fire. To make an idol of the law of anti-idolatry is to feel in possession of a truth denied to others, denied in particular to non-Jews, and therefore to have subsumed in some fashion divine revelation under the aegis of human history. It is to make a kikayon of ourselves before God, to do, that is, precisely what God chastises Jonah for doing in "pitying" the gourd. And if we have traditionally set up two explanations of Jonah's behavior—that he is acting on behalf of Israel when he rejects his mission to prophesy to non-Jews and that he needs to learn the mystery of God's compassion for all creatures—have we not erected our readings upon the same premises, turning either to the historical situation or the parabolic context of human values in order to found our case, the two grounds, that is to say, whose appropriation the story is primarily challenging?

And perhaps in recognizing the ways in which, within the history of interpretation, we have reproduced the humanistic usurpation already at stake within the narrative, we come to understand as well something of the dynamics of interpretation itself in the Jewish context. In some fundamental way, the traditional exoteric readings of the text do serve to actualize potentials that are already preserved within the narrative itself (and therefore they are true to the text, so to speak) but potentials in particular which the narrative has raised in order to challenge. To view Jonah's behavior as redemptive or lacking in compassion is to construct a view not incompatible finally with Jonah's own view although it is the "Ninevitian" or sacrificial qualities of such a view that God and the narrative have displayed for us (and for Jonah).

At the same time, the construction of such interpretation is as well a break with the text, a refusal to take seriously the radical otherness that the text as text would demand of us, a making accessible of its intricacies (and thereby extension of it) to the present hour and to everyday life. It is in this way preeminently that the Jewish conception of interpretation (Fishbane) differs from the Platonic conception—for which there are always true and false readings and the contractual preservation of a difference between the inside and the outside of the text. For Judaism there are no true or false readings (in the sense of transcontextual truths), not because all readings are partial and the puzzle remains to be solved, but rather because there are always new puzzles, because the function of interpretation is to make the text accessible to the present hour and the present hour is always changing. In this way, therefore, many interpretations (which are mutually exclusive) may come to be regarded as equally "true" readings (those of Rashi, Maimonides, and so forth) and interpretation may be construed necessarily as endless. Interpretation, in this regard, has become a version of the practice of anti-idolatry itself.

Idolatrous, therefore, and anti-idolatrous, sacrificial and anti-sacrificial, interpretation within Judaism is a kind of coded communication, a communication which at once offers us the domain in which an anti-idolatrous reading is to be found and yet necessarily "gets it wrong" so to speak. Breaking with the text, it recreates the text in interpretation. The strength of the traditional reading which takes Jonah's reluctance as redemptive, for example, is that it recognizes that it is Israel that is really at stake in "Ninevah" although it reads this identity as historical rather than developmental, and social rather than individual. In the same way, the real strength of the more modern view which reads Jonah's anger as lacking in compassion is to have recognized in Ninevah a certain profound identity with Israel although it postulates that identity within the very humanistic framework the story is challenging, in terms of the very "pity" or making of kikayons that the final speech of God reveals as so dangerous.

And perhaps within this understanding of the doubleness of interpretation, we understand the wisdom of the liturgists who saw in the story of Jonah a text which is appropriate to both traditional legal practices of Yom Kippur and the notion of repentance or *teshuvah* which is taken as the central theme of that day. Like the ancient halachic practices of ritual scapegoating, for example, the story must be understood as profoundly anti-sacrificial.

Theories of sacrifice and sacrificial structuration depend upon a distinction between violence, expulsion, and crisis on the one hand and sacrifice, sacralization and the difference between the sacred and the profane on the other (Girard: 1977). Yet the story progressively intermixes the two. God calls upon Jonah to prophesy to the Ninevites (a gesture that must be understood as summoning Jonah to his sacred duty) and Jonah responds by expelling himself from the premises. Then, in the second scene, expulsions and sacrifice begin to become confused. There are gestures of expulsion and violence on one side (the tempest, for example, which may be construed as the sea trying to expell the ship, or the tossing of cargo overboard to lighten it) and gestures of sacrifice on the other (the sacrifices to God that the sailors make, for example, after Jonah is removed). But there is also the confusion between the two when Jonah asks them to expell him in order to save them and they first reject (or expell) the idea and then finally carry it out. Then in scene three, the mixture becomes even more apparent. There is the great fish which is undoubtedly an image of sacrificial mechanism on the one hand, and the prayer of Jonah who is caught within that mechanism, a prayer which is equally without doubt a gesture of holiness. And the result is an expulsion (literally, a vomiting) which is also identically a salvation (or rescuing) which makes possible for Jonah a new beginning.

Then, in Part Two, there seems to be both a continuation of this intermixing of sacrificial and expulsive gestures and (by comparison with part one) a new conceptualization. Jonah in the first scene this time refuses to disobey God's command, in a kind of negative imitation of Part One. The Ninevites likewise immediately turn away from their former behavior and towards the ways of the God of Israel. Even God gets into the act as it were and upon seeing the Ninevites give up their sacrificial ways gives up His planned destruction of them. And once this success is achieved, that success is itself rejected. In the third scene, Jonah rejects his success and returns to his old objections: he rejoices in his booth on the hillside and then laments its loss. Whereupon God turns Jonah's attention first from Ninevah to the kikayon and then from the kikayon to himself and finally to divinity.

In short, the story in its entirety seems to reenact the history of Israel itself, from "Ninevah" to "Jerusalem," or from Egypt to the land of Canaan. For it traces the transformation from a sacrificial perspective to an anti-sacrificial one (conceived as a form of turning away from the idolatrous ways of one's past and a turn to the ways of God).

This is just what the day of Yom Kippur reenacts. Interspersed with texts that recall the scapegoat rituals of the High Priests in the Temple of Jerusalem, the services of the day turn more and more focally upon the theme of *teshuvah* or repentance. The very name of the day Yom Kippur refers doubly to the "day of the lots" (those cast during the scapegoat ritual in order to determine which of two identical goats was to be led off the edge of a cliff to "Azazel," and which was to be sacrificed in the ritual slaughter) and the "day of atonement or repentance."

What is *teshuvah?* The notion has been traditionally understood as an abandonment of sin and a return to the ways of God. But if we conceive of this notion broadly enough it may be seen to encompass all that we have identified as the conditions of Judaism itself—both its birth from cultures in which sacrifice no longer works and the ongoing motor force of Judaism at its most individual and personal level. The linkage, therefore, of the story of Jonah with the notion of repentance and the ancient halachic practices of the day of Yom Kippur—the holiest day of the Jewish calendar, the day on which human beings may purify themselves and become as angels—may reproduce for us, in fact, precisely the circumstances within the story. The story of Jonah becomes then our parable of the kikayon through which the dangers of our own idolatrous behavior may be narratively staged in order that we may stop and return to the ways of God.

In what way? Repentance is the abandonment of sin and the return to God, the giving up of those energies devoted to paths that take us away from God and the return of what properly belongs to God. In historical terms, therefore, it is the giving up of the sacrificial ways in which one has lived and turning to the ways of God. Perhaps in this connection we understand why the Midrash lists repentance as one of the seven conditions in which the world was created: without repentance, the Sages say, the world would inevitably perish in the face of God's judgment (Weissman: 1).

But repentance is also the motor force of Judaism. To turn (or more precisely to turn back) is to presuppose that one has stopped, that one has given up—even fleetingly—the path one was on in order to pursue another. The notion of stopping or resting is built into the cycle of Jewish life. It is the notion of the Sabbath or day of rest, a day which reproduces the action of God after the universe was created on the seventh day. It is what one does after a death for a specified period of time. The day of Yom Kippur itself is conceived along these lines as a day of stopping, a day on which one gives up all of the activity that may take us away from God and devotes oneself exclusively to rest, prayer, and study of Torah. The very word *teshuvah* is said to be linked etymologically to the word for sabbath (*shabbat*), for sitting in mourning (*shivah*), for the number seven (*sheva*), and so forth. And the day of Yom Kippur is often described as the "sabbath of sabbaths."

It is, however, and perhaps more significantly, the condition of Jewish spiritual life as well:

They asked Wisdom, "what is the sinner's punishment?" It told them: "Sinners—let them be pursued by their evil." They asked Prophecy, "What is the sinner's punishment?" It told them: "The soul that sins—it shall die!" They asked Torah, "What is the sinner's punishment?" It told them: "Let him bring a guilt-offering and gain atonement!" They asked the Holy One, Blessed Be He, "What is the sinner's punishement?" He told him: "Let him repent and gain atonement!" (Zlotowitz: xx)

Repentance is the regenerative force *par excellence* in Judaism and therefore appropriate to the one day ordained since creation, in the view of the Sages, for purification, for the separation of light from darkness, the sabbath of sabbaths so to speak.

But why the story of Jonah? The thematic correspondence is manifest. The idolatry and pagan sacrifices of the sailors during the storm, the repentance of the sailors after Jonah is tossed overboard, the repentance of the Ninevites and of Jonah within the belly of the great fish—all these sequences reproduce the themes of the day.

And even more significant, perhaps, is the ritual or "performative" context in which the story is introduced. Listening to the story of Jonah within the synogogue service, watching Jonah have his own history staged before him, first with the parable of the kikayon, and then in God's speech to him about the kikayon and about Ninevah (a history in which he turns out to be an extension of the history of those he would consider is bitterest enemies), is a process which reenacts our own history. This history—within Judaism at large, within our individual lives, within our very experiences of the day of Yom Kippur—is staged before us, a history which turns out to be similarly the record of our diachronic continuity with those elements of that history which we might consider to be radically other from our own experiences—Biblical texts, for example. We find ourselves reenacting, in short, the very patterns with which the narrative is already primarily concerned, in the very act, moreover, of engaging that narrative. The story of Jonah comes to instruct us in repentance within the congregation in the same intensely personal way in which the words of God instruct Jonah within the story.

But there is something else. The hearing of the Jonah story in synogogue at the climax of the afternoon service when the most devotional and confessional portions have just been recited focuses the individual encounter with God in such a way that the third reading we have suggested of the final scene is enacted as well. In this setting it is not the historical, nor the universalist, nor the ritualistic character of the story that is foremost but the deeply personal. Repentance in this reading of the Jonah story comes to mean the giving up of self-condemnation and self-judgement.

And once again the traditional interpretative strategies by which we have engaged the story offer us a coded version of this understanding. "Why did Jonah flee?" begins the commentary of Pirkei d'Rabbi Eliezer. "He passed judgement upon himseslf" (Zolowitz: xix). The modern reading observes that judgement is at stake but presupposes the difference between the Ninevites and the Israelites and believes the indictment concerns the non-Jews. In context of the synogogue service we now understand we must have compassion, the story tells us, in the first instance not upon the others but upon ourselves, or, rather, upon others but precisely in so far as we recognize already ourselves in those others. We must give up the judgement of ourselves, the self-condemnation, upon which the fashioning of kikayons is based. We must, in short, engage in self-forgiveness and it is the lack of self-forgiveness (expressing itself first as anger against the salvation of the Ninevites) that is above all finally reflected in Jonah's resonant words "better is my death than my life."

And the traditional historical reading, then, in this same light, instructs us in the potential future of that dangerous self-judgement. The Ninevites will turn to God and we (who maintain the difference between Israel and Ninevah) shall be implicated by their conversion. Moreover, if we continue on this path, we shall soon witness the rise of scoffers who will challenge the very institutions from which we have come. And in the far distant future, the consequences will be even more drastic. Empires shall swallow up Israel and the Temple itself shall be destroyed. The history of Judaism relative to Hellenism, Christianity, and Rome seems already here to have been imagined.

We have come a long way. And there remains more to be said. But it is already clear that the question on the horizon concerns the relation of Judaism to Christianity. Does not this relation turn, finally, upon the same questions of prophetic understanding, of sacrificial behavior, and of repentance in context of which we have examined the story of Jonah? And does not the familiar phrase "until the conversion of the Jews," a phrase used with haunting resonance throughout the middle ages (and well into the seventeenth century in fact) to refer to "the end of time," bear all the mystery? Turning as it does upon the difference between Latin and Hebrew, between *conversio* and *teshuvah*, does not the phrase designate less an historical moment than a metaphysical one, a moment when those who are Jews (and are denying that Judaism) give up that denial and return to Judaism itself, a moment, that is to say, when Jewish anti-Jewishness (either inside or outside of institutional Judaism) begins to take cognizance of itself? Such a moment will no doubt designate the end of historical time as we know it.

Moreover, do not these escatological considerations lead directly to still another one—namely the coming of the Messiah? Is not the debate between Jonah and God, between one who would give up his life for Israel and one who would deconstruct the limits—the conditions and the consequences—of that perspective, the same debate?

Perhaps we have always known all of this. Have we not in fact encapsulated just such an understanding within the least likely of places—within a children's fable about a man who is swallowed by a whale? Is not the very anecdote that we are so fond of telling (and universally repudiating) about the story of Jonah in fact a rebus concerned precisely with prophecy, sacrifice and repentance? Does not the image of the great fish (or *og gadol*) which has swallowed Jonah reproduce in pictoral language the very relationship we have discerned between Ninevah (that great city or *ha'ir hagdola*) and Israel, a prophetic relationship, that is to say, in which Israel has been engulfed by the sacrificial mechanisms of its own Ninevitian ways and can emerge from this idolatrous or kikayonic condition only by a prayer, a Hebrew prayer uttered in genuine repentance and as thanksgiving for a salvation that has either not yet or already occurred and in a verbal construction scholars would readily identify as "the prophetic past" (Zlotowitz: 107).

This misfit, then, within Biblical scripture and Jewish liturgy which is the story of Jonah, would turn out already to have contained that scripture and that liturgy—even the world itself—within its entrails. And the real butt of the joke we tell ourselves may turn out to be less those who take it to be the story of a man swallowed by a whale (or man-eating shark) than those who, from within the sacrificial and idolatrous mechanisms of their own interpretive depths, would dismiss such a fiction as the fable of an uncomprehending child.

NOTES

1. "God's answer to Jonah, stressing the supremacy of compassion, upsets the possibility of looking for a rational coherence of God's ways with the world. . . . beyond justice and anger lies the mystery of compassion" (Heschel: 67).

2. For an account of this traditional view, see the ArtScroll edition of the text (Zlotowitz).

3. The text I have relied upon throughout is that of Zlotowitz. Although the text of J. H. Hertz is more widely used within the liturgy of conservative Judaism, the English translation of Zlotowitz is closer to modern English idiom and more attentive to the subtleties of interpretive problems in translating from the original Hebrew. The only oddity of this translation—to scholarly eyes—is the use of the Hebrew word *hashem* (meaning "the name") in place of more familiar renderings of the Tetragrammaton.

4. The following paragraphs summarize a much longer analysis of the first part of the Jonah story which is part of a forthcoming manuscript on Biblical readings.

A GIRARDIAN INTERPRETATION OF PAUL: RIVALRY, MIMESIS AND VICTIMAGE IN THE CORINTHIAN CORRESPONDENCE

Robert G. Hamerton-Kelly
Stanford University

ABSTRACT

There are four apparent features of the Corinthian correspondence which suggest that a Girardian interpretation would be illuminating: 1) A community split by rivalry into factions; 2) calls by the apostle to his readers to imitate him as he imitates Christ; 3) the self-understanding of the apostle as victim and scapegoat; and 4) the exposition of the nature of the Christian community as the body of the crucified victim. The investigation of each of these features confirms the illuminative power of the Girardian hermeneutical theory. Mimetic rivalry is the cause of the factionalism, and the apostle counters it with the exhortation to imitate Christ the victim rather than each other. He presents himself as such an imitator of Christ, especially in his sufferings and trials *(peristaseis)*; and he presents an understanding of the church as the body of Christ the victim.

Rene Girard's hermeneutical proposal is the most promising opportunity since the advent of the historical-critical method to make sense out of the Biblical texts. It is based on a universal human phenomenon, namely violence, and enables us to understand a very wide range of texts. (cf. James Reston, "The Invisible Wars," *The New York Times*, May 23, '84, p.25: "According to the Center for Defence Information here, over four million people are engaged now in 42 different wars, rebellions and civil uprisings. . . . The interesting thing is that in this 'age of communications,' most of these conflicts are almost invisible beyond the field of battle.") Its detractors object that the theory is imperialistic, claiming to be the one key to the understanding of all ritual, myth, and great literature; they also object to Girard's placing the Gospels above other texts as revealing with special clarity the clandestine process of mimetic rivalry and victimage, (Girard et al. 1978a; Girard 1982).

Girard's method is, however, a fine example of the "hermeneutics of suspicion" (Ricoeur, 1970). Most texts conceal more than they reveal. Mythology, the clearest instance of this concealment, is a fabric of deceit woven to hide our violence from us by transforming it and including it as a component in an edifying story about the fundamentals of culture. In this way we are deceived into regarding culture as an expression of human benignity rather than an accomodation to human hostility, made possible by the victim, who attracts random violence onto himself and thus makes possible the unanimity necessary to culture.

It is more remarkable that there is relative peace within human groups than that there is conflict; and such peace is made possible by the victim. Given this key, the reader, exercising a hermeneutic of suspicion, will find in, with, and under the texts, the strategies of desire, mimetic rivalry and the hapless scapegoat.

There is considerable resistance to this proposal on the part of the academy, for reasons both legitimate and otherwise. We cannot concern ourselves with those other reasons here, having more important things to discuss than the dispiriting effluence of the politics of knowledge; but the legitimate criticisms deserve at least to be mentioned at the outset. The most telling objection to the Girardian thesis is that it is unlikely *a priori* that there is only one explanation for the origin and continued functioning and significance of all of human culture. The unwillingness of the academy to accept such a claim is soundly based on the results of many failures to carry through such an explanation, and the reluctance to consider such a claim seriously, while it may not measure up to the highest standards of the academy, is at least humanly understandable. A second criticism is that his latest claims about the Bible are redolent of a Christian chauvinism, which, if it can be shown to be the case, is clearly unacceptable.

It is not possible to answer these criticisms here; we can only mention them. In the mean time we hope to demonstrate the extraordinary fruitfulness of a Girardian hermeneutic for the Pauline texts. That it bears fruit, enabling us to understand hitherto obscure statements in the texts themselves, and also to understand how the texts are concerned with perennial and vital human issues, how they illumine the human condition and reveal things hidden from the foundation of the world, amounts to a considerable entry on the credit side of the ledger.

Raymund Schwager (1978) points out, at the beginning of his excellent programmatic essay, that Girard's hermeneutic is quite different from the one entailed by the historical-critical method. It is synthetic rather than analytic, and, according to Schwager, bears some resemblance to the typological exegesis of the Fathers (1978: 11). One should be prepared, therefore, to hear something different from what the usual historical-critical method has to say; while the solid results of that method have also to be taken into account.

The basic components of the Girardian hermeneutical theory are mimetic rivalry and the scapegoat mechanism. Human desire is essentially imitative. It copies the other in his desire; objects become desirable because somebody else desires them. Eventually desire becomes competitive and loses sight of the object because of concentration on the rival. The rivalry becomes violent, one tries to kill the other, and such violence makes community impossible, until the group spontaneously discovers the scape-goat mechanism, which transforms random violence into unanimous violence by directing it against one victim. Violence then unites rather than divides the group, making community and cuture possible. The scapegoat victim is sacralized by the process, he/she embodies the sacred which has the two valencies of violence as destructive and as unifying. The process of killing the victim is re-enacted ritually in sacrifice, a good and life-giving activity, thereby concealing from us the originary and persisting violence and giving us a false estimate of human nature and society, as essentially benign. The scapegoat, therefore, is the generator of all culture.

While the broad sweep of the theory makes it vulnerable to legitimate questioning, Schwager has shown that it fits much of the Biblical data with remarkable appropriateness. We intend to show that it illumines critical aspects of the Pauline texts as well, a section of scripture so far only touched on by both Schwager and Girard (1978a).

The Corinthian correspondence, *prima facie*, shows the following signs which suggest that a Girardian interpretation would be appropriate:
1. A community split into factions by rivalry—1 Cor. 1:10 ff; 2 Cor. 10–13.
2. Calls by the apostle to his readers to imitate him as he imitates Christ—1 Cor. 4:16; 11:1; combined with a lively concern with the nature of sacrifice and the proper attitude towards it—1 Cor. 10:14–22.
3. The self-understanding of the apostle as a victim and scapegoat—1 Cor. 2:1–5; 4:9–13; 2 Cor. 12:7–10.
4. Exposition of the nature of Christian community as the body of the crucified victim—1 Cor. 12; cf. 1:18–2:5.

There are, therefore, in the Corinthian letters, four critical Girardian themes, which command our attention: rivalry, mimesis, community and victimage.

1. *Factions in the Community: "Let him who boasts, boast in the Lord" (1 Cor. 1:31).*

Near the beginning of his treatment of the matter of divisions in the church, Paul calls the community, those who have been called into the *koinōnia* of his son Jesus Christ (1 Cor. 1:9). *koinōnos* is an old term for a companion at a sacrificial meal (Eur. El. 637; Pl.Sym. 188B; *TDNT*

III, 799), and maintains this meaning in Paul (1 Cor. 10:18) who calls the partakers of the sacrificial meal "partners of the altar" *(koinōnoi tou thysiastēriou)*. So we are immediately alerted to the sacrificial context within which the apostle thinks when he approaches the question of an understanding of Christian community in this his major letter on the subject. (We are not convinced by Sampley, 1980, who argues that the term *koinōnia* draws its meaning from the context of the *societas* contract in Roman law.) He argues against the possibility that there can be more than one "Christian" group, by bringing the crucified one, the innocent victim, to the center of attention. "Is Christ divided? (there is no sacrificial connotation here; *merizō* is the usual term for being divided into parties or factions) Was Paul crucified for you . . . ?" (1:13). It is precisely the "wisdom of the world," which would ignore, bypass, or cover up the Cross, which leads to the breakup of community (1:18 ff); and it is the *skandalon* (vs. 23) of the cross which makes unity possible and, indeed, mandatory.

How may we construe this in a Girardian manner? Girard argues that the New Testament is consistently anti-sacrificial, by which he means that it never claims that God desired or required the death of Christ, that the murder of Jesus is seen for what it is, the killing of a hapless victim by the human mob, albeit tricked out in the costumes of state and religious legitimacy. Jesus went the way of the many casualties of the Roman/Sadducean establishment, an instance of mob violence against another innocent victim. It is never claimed that God required this death to satisfy some violent need in Himself; rather Paul appeals to the Cross as the basis of communal unity, because by the imaginative identification with the victim, called faith, mimetic rivalry is stilled. The cross is necessary because of human mimetic rivalry and violence, not because of a divine need for sacrifical appeasement. (Schwager: 215 note: "Jesus must die, if only so that men may transfer their hatred of God to the Son of God and of mankind to the Son of Man.") The Cross is a scandal because it reveals what we would conceal by our human wisdom, namely, the scapegoat mechanism, and by revealing it renders it no longer effectual.

In a Girardian reading one may further assume that the rivalries among the groups attached to Paul and Peter and Apollos respectively was caused by mimesis and fueled by suppressed violence. By rejecting the Cross, the Corinthians had no means of transforming the violence; they were in a sacrificial crisis.

The rejection of the Cross was a critical element in the theologies of the Corinthian sects. We may deduce this both from the logic of Girardian hermeneutics and from the evidence of the text—namely the great emphasis Paul lays on the Cross. That rejection of the Cross was also the actual cause of conflict, even though we are not able, despite learned speculation, to know the precise contents of the sectarian theologies. Paul does not attack any one group but rather the fact of sectarianism in general (Conzelmann, 1975:34), and he counters the malaise by exalting the Cross and denigrating "the wisdom of the world" *(hē sophia tou kosmou)* (vs.20). The foolishness of the preaching of the Cross, furthermore, unites both Jews and Greeks (vs. 24), overcoming what a Jew would see as the great division in the world (cf. Gal. 3:28–29).

This puts us in touch with a basic element in the Apostle's self-understanding; he is the apostle to the Gentiles, and so he is God's agent for healing the division in humanity (Gal. 1:15–16). It is significant, therefore, that after placing the crucified one at the center of attention he characterises the community itself as despised, like the Lord (compare *ta exouthenēmena* [vs. 28] and LXX Psalm 21 [22]:7, the great "Passion" Psalm) and emphasizes his own physical and psychological weakness (2:3). He identifies the community and himself with the crucified one, with the victim; they are all victims, and that is the realization which prohibits boasting (1:31), cancels mimetic rivalry, and unites all people.

2. *Be imitators of me, as I am of Christ (1 Cor. 4:16, 11:1).*

As the exposition continues in 1 Corinthians we find this insight confirmed. In 1 Cor. 3:17 the community is called the temple of God *(vaos tou theou)*, the place of the victim's death, and that is followed by a climactic repetition of the essential identity of Paul, and Apollos, and Cephas, and the community, and the crucified Christ, and God (3:22–3), something which the wisdom of the world, which boasts in human status, does not understand (3:18–21).

This leads into a discussion of the status of the apostle as the most reliable representative of the truth of identification with the victim. The apostles are the scapegoats of the world, the very bearers of the dirt to be removed from the world *(hōs perikatharmata tou kosmou egenēthēmen, pantōn peripsēma, heōs arti-* 4:13; Bauer, *ad loc., perikatharmata* = scapegoats for the world; *peripsema* = the dirt removed; cf. 2 Cor. 5:21; Gal. 3:13—Christ himself became "sin," became "the curse," that is, was identified as scapegoat with the dirt to be removed.)

What is this dirt to be removed? It is the violence resulting from mimetic rivalry, from the "puffing up of one over the other," in the community, for which purpose they had used the figures of Paul and Apollos (1 Cor. 4:6). This is a misuse of the Apostles, because they are men sentenced to death and scapegoats; they are "last of all, like men sentenced to death, . . . a spectacle to the world, to angels and to men. . . . fools for Christ's sake . . . weak . . . in disrepute. To the present hour we hunger and thirst, we are ill-clad and buffeted and homeless, working with our own hands" (1 Cor. 4:9–11). And then follows a precise account of the benefits that accrue to the community from the scapegoat: "When reviled we bless; when persecuted we endure; when slandered we comfort *(parakaleō)*. We have become as the scapegoats of the world, the noxious discharge of all, until now" (4:12b-13). The passage begins with the image of the condemned criminal *(epithanatios)* brought into the arena to die fighting gladiators or wild beasts *(theatron . . . tǭ kosmǭ)*, and it ends with the scapegoat image. It is bracketed thus by the images of victimage, for the sake of emphasis; one should view the apostles as condemned criminals and scapegoats, like Jesus.

As the scapegoat, the apostle counteracts mimetic rivalry; this is what the Girardian hermeneutic has enabled us to see. It is, therefore, no surprise when the apostle goes on immediately to use the very word "imitator"—*mimētēs (parakalō oun hymas, mimētai mou ginesthe*-4:16). This suggests that Paul understands the situation in the same way as the Girardian hermeneutic does! It is mimetic rivalry that has caused the members of the church to puff themselves up with reference to one another; mimesis is endemic to human community, so, since the apostle knows this, he urges the right kind of mimesis; not the kind that covers up the mechanism of the victim and enables them spuriously to claim that they are wise and strong and held in honor (4:10), but the kind which enables them to see that their community was brought into being by a victim imitating a victim, a scapegoat imitating a scapegoat (4:15). And the chain of mimesis can be extended; Timothy, whom Paul is sending to them, will remind them of the apostle's "ways in Christ," (4:17; cf. Acts 19:22), so in fact they may imitate Paul by imitating Timothy (cf. Betz, 1967: 156 on the theme of the "ways").

The other context in 1 Cor in which Paul uses the word *mimētēs* is a discussion of pagan sacrifice, in 1 Cor. 10:23–11:1. Is there any significance in this juxtaposition of mimesis and sacrifice? In ch. 4 we have seen the theme of mimesis arise in connexion with the scapegoat idea, as the Giraridan hermeneutic predicted. We should, therefore, expect a similar confirmation of that hermeneutic in the contiguity of sacrifice and mimesis.

Our first clue is in 10:6 where the sin of the fathers in the wilderness is that they "desired" *(epethymēsan)*. This led to idolatry, fornication and the testing of God. Gerhardsson has shown that this congeries of wrong attitudes represents a standard analysis of the etiology of sin amongst the rabbis of that time (B. Gerhardsson, 1966). Craving *(epithymia)* leads to discontent with God's providence, which in turn leads to a tempting of God, and finally to the apostasy of idolatry. Fornication is not included in Gerhardsson's discussion, possibly because the discussion was directed to explaining the three temptations of Jesus according to Q, which fit admirably the progression of sin, from desire through testing to idolatry; and grumbling (1 Cor. 10:10) might be classified as a sub-category of desire or craving.

In choosing idolatry as the summary category (10:14), however, the Apostle is in harmony with the rabbinic viewpoint which sees it as the epitome of sin: what begins as *epithymia* ends as *eidōlolatria*, and idolatry must be avoided at all costs—therefore desire must be dealt with. How? It is at this point that the Girardian hermeneutic enables us to understand a notoriously opaque passage. The apostle says that the unity of the church is constituted by all its members being *koinōnoi* of Christ's blood and body, by sharing the one cup and the one loaf (*hoti heis artos, hen sōma hoi polloi esmen, hoi gar pantes ek tou henos artou metechomen*-10:17).

Then in verse 19 ff. he denies that the food offered to idols is anything sacred, or that the idol itself represents anything divine. Why then should one flee idolatry, if the idol is nothing? Because sacrifices to idols are really demonic, that is, they are made not to the divine but to the demonic (*daimoniois kai ou theō*, 20), and therefore, those who share the sacrificed food are *koinōnoi* with demons. What then is this demonic which is not divine? How shall we understand this passage? Girard suggests that, in the Bible, Satan represents the baleful process of mimetic rivalry. The demonic, therefore, has no metaphysical status apart from the "metaphysic of desire" (Girard, 1965). What Paul is saying here is that participation in idolatrous sacrifice instigates and energizes mimetic rivalry, destroys the community, and is precisely the opposite of the *koinōnia* of the one loaf which makes the Christians one body. The demonic is the hidden power of mimetic desire which seems to strike from without, and is therefore easily mythologized, but in fact strikes from within, in fact is nothing other than our inherent propensity for rivalry arising out of mimetic desire.

The issue of idol worship was a live one in the Corinthian church, and not merely a theoretical problem; apparently some church members understood freedom from legal morality to mean that "all things are permitted" (10:23), presumably because of the utter inwardness and totally spiritual nature of salvation by faith in Christ. Some of these "spirituals," to judge from the discussion in this chapter, considered participation in pagan worship to be one of the things permitted to Christians—because they know that an idol is not divine. Paul argues that such worship is demonic and those Christians who participate in it are, like the fathers in the wilderness, subject to the temptations of craving, grumbling and fornication which are the traditional concomitants of idolatry. Then he specifies another baleful effect of such behavior; it does not profit the community and it does not build it up (vs. 23); because it does not take into account the impact that it might have on others. So Paul propounds a moral principle that is the precise antidote to mimetic rivarly—"Let no one seek his own advantage but rather the advantage of the other" (*mēdeis to heautou zēteitō alla to tou heterou*—24)—and he bases this injunction in the first place on his own behavior ("And be without offense to Jews and Greeks and to the church of God, just as I also please all people in everything, not seeking my own advantage but that of the many, that they may be saved."—10:32-3; cf. 9:19-23), but ultimately on the behavior of Christ himself: "Be imitators of me as I am of Christ!" (*mimētai mou ginesthe, kathōs kagō Christou*—11:1).

The apostle and his church understand themselves to be called to imitate not the day to day conduct of the historical Jesus, but rather the act of self-effacement which the Cross represents, the fact of the divine self-emptying (2 Cor. 8:9). "To imitate Paul and Christ means to be conformed to Christ's suffering and death in the giving of oneself over to the service of others, 2 Cor. 13:4" (Furnish, 1968: 223; cf. Phil. 3:10; 2:1-11; Rom. 15:1-3; Gal. 6:17; Col. 1:24). This is evident not only from the Pauline texts themselves, but also from the historical background of the religious idea of mimesis as it was available to Paul. The *mimos* was originally the agent in a Dionysiac dedication; mimesis therefore is a technical term from the cult of Dionysus (Betz, 1967: 60) designating the cultic representation of the myth on which the cult rests (ibid. 86). Therefore the imitation is not of the details of the god's activity but rather of the main moment in the myth; and this was the concept which Paul employed in calling for mimesis of himself as of Christ, a concept which he received in the Hellenistic Jewish synthesis of which he partook, a fact which we know from the frequent occurrence of the idea in that other well-known first century Jew, Philo of Alexandria (ibid. 135-6).

A glance at the instances of the term *mimētēs* in other parts of the Pauline corpus confirms our reading of it in 1 Corinthians. In 2 Thess. 3:7 and 9 the term is used in a seemingly superficial sense: imitate the fact that we did not sponge off the community, but worked with our own hands. However, working with his own hands is one of the afflictions the apostle includes in the list of sufferings in 1 Cor. 4:12 which qualify him as a scapegoat; so once again mimesis is linked to the apostle's self-understanding as a representative of the crucified one, who "although he was rich became poor for our sake" (2 Cor. 8:9). In 1 Thess. 1:6 mimesis is linked specifically with the suffering of Christ: "And you have become imitators of us and of the Lord, receiving the word amidst much affliction, with joy of the holy spirit, so that you might become an example to all the believers in Macedonia and Asia;" and in Phil. 3:17 those whom the apostle calls to imitate him are contrasted with those who behave "as enemies of the Cross of Christ" in Phil. 3:18. This last passage corroborates our interpretation of Paul's argument in 1 Corinthians: those who are dividing the community are those who spurn the crucified one, by spurning his representative. Because they are "enemies of the Cross," their mimetic rivalry has wrought havoc; therefore the apostle exalts the Cross as an antidote to their rivalry.

The fact that we have found the term *mimētēs* twice in 1 Cor., once in connexion with the apostolic self-identification as scapegoat and once in connexion with pagan sacrifice, is a significant testimony to the hermeneutical accuracy of the Girardian hypothesis. The hypothesis has also enabled us to understand at a hitherto unparallelled level of depth the logic of the argument against factionalism in the church. It also enables us to comprehend the whole self-understanding of the Apostle more clearly than hitherto.

3. *The Apostle as victim.*

We have seen already that the apostle can refer to himself explicitly as a scapegoat (1 Cor. 4:13). At this point we may profitably consider his self-presentation at greater length, in order to confirm the impression that he considers apostolic existence to be essentially identification with Christ as victim.

According to Girard an essential aspect of the victim is the mark, some abnormality that singles him/her out. In women, for instance, it is menstruation; with Jews it is their religious and cultural oddness; and the sick and disfigured of all kinds bear their afflictions as invitations to victimage. The more obvious the disfigurement the more effective the incitement; ugly old women are, for instance, more often identified as witches . . . or the spectacularly beautiful . . . anyone whose extraordinariness awakens atavistic fears.

There was something about Paul which made him publicly contemptible from time to time. It may be that he suffered from an affliction of the eyes which made his appearance repulsive at times. In our opinion, the evidence in Gal. 4:12–20, and elsewhere in the epistles, suggests an eye affliction, but one cannot be sure; the state of the evidence does not allow for more than a conjecture as to the nature of his much discussed "thorn in the flesh" (2 Cor. 12:7). The fact is, however, that Paul was visibly stricken when first the Galatians saw him, and in such a way as to tempt people to despise him and turn away. In 2 Cor. 10:10 it is his speech that is despicable, which leads Barrett (1973) to suggest that the "thorn" was a speech impediment. In any case, the evidence in Gal. 4:12–20, and in 2 Cor. 10–13, to which we now turn, suggests that there was something about Paul which rendered him contemptible from time to time. Something like a mark of the victim.

Remarkably, from our point of view, the passage, Gal. 4:12–20, begins with an exhortation to imitation, "Become as I am, because I also have become as you are, I beseech you, brothers!" (vs. 12). Betz (1979) thinks the passage is based on the conventional forms of expression about friendship and calls this phrase "an epistolary cliche belonging to the friendship topos." It may be that too, but in its present context it is far more than a mere cliche; it is a statement of the essence of friendship, namely mimesis, and is yet another instance of the apostle's insight into the strategies of desire. Next (vss. 13–14) we read that the Galatians did not scorn (*exoutheneō*; cf. 1 Cor. 1:28; 2 Cor. 10:10) or despise (*ekptyō*) him. As Betz points out, the language here is reminiscent of demon possession, which might, at that time, easily have been assumed to be the cause of his illness. Paul was received not as a demon but as an angel, or, even more telling, as Christ himself (vs. 14). He was received as Christ himself, not in spite of his affliction, but because of it. The willingness of the Galatians to accept and not to despise him, was precisely the force which transformed the demonic into the divine, because it broke the power of mimetic rivalry, transforming it into sympathy with the victim. Rivalry is transformed into sympathy; bad mimesis becomes good mimesis: "I bear you witness that (in imitation of me in my suffering) you would, if it were possible, have torn out your own eyes and given them to me" (vs. 15).

The rivals of the Apostle "pay zealous court to you" (*zēloō*) (vs. 17), a word from the vocabulary of erotic love, describing the efforts of the lover to win the beloved. Thus, once again, we are deep in the realm of mimetic desire and its strategies. Paul's rivals are wooing the Galatians as part of a strategy to gain control over them. By imitating them Paul's converts are playing into their hands; they should rather be imitating him in his weakness, siding with the victim, as they did when first he came to them, representing, in his physical exigency, Christ himself; bearing the mark of the victim.

Thus the themes of imitation and victimage continue in tandem in the letter to the Galatians. The epistle ends with the following: "For the rest, let no one trouble me, for I bear in my body the marks (*stigmata*) of Jesus" (6:17). These *stigmata* are all the wounds he has sustained in his service of the cross, including the physical infirmity which he sustained naturally. They constitute collectively the mark of the victim.

"Nothing made him express so clearly and powerfully his own understanding of apostleship as the mission to Corinth of the false apostles" (Barrett, 1973:42). As in Galatia so in Corinth there were those who argued that Paul was not a genuine apostle of Christ. As we infer from the Galatians passage, part of their argument rested on the fact of his physical infirmity (2 Cor.: 10:10), but it was mostly an argument about status. We turn now to 2 Cor. in order to explore by means of our Girardian hermeneutic this second instance of rivalry within the Corinthian correspondence, the rivalry between Paul and his opponents, which is essentially separate from the rivalry between the factions in the congregation. By observing the way Paul presents himself in this conflict we may see precisely what conduct the apostle is recommending to his congregants when he urges them to imitate him in dealing with one another.

2 Cor. is a conglomerate of shorter letters. Since we cannot discuss its composition here, we follow the consensus as set out by Barrett (1968:11–14), and read chapters 10–13 as the "Tearful letter" (2 Cor. 2:4), chapters 2:14–6:13, & 7:2–4, as the "Triumphal letter" (2 Cor. 2:14), and 1:1–2:13, 7:5–16, 9:1–15 as a travel letter. The rest of the text we may leave aside for our purpose.

Catalogues of adverse circumstances, such as the one we encountered in 1 Cor. 4:9–13, occur once in the "tearful" letter (11:23–29) and twice in the "triumphal" letter (4:7–12, 6:4–10). Such catalogues also occur in Stoic and Cynic sources where they are called *peristaseis* (Conzelmann, 1975:89). In those sources they are used to demonstrate the divine power at work in the missionary by which he is preserved amidst the *peristaseis*. While that theme is present in the Pauline usage, it is nuanced by the situation of rivalry in which he finds himself.

In the "tearful" letter, we see a Paul who has been driven to the limits of endurance. "One must boast . . ." (11:30, 12:1), may have been one of the opponents' catchwords, which Paul takes up, as he does elsewhere (1 Cor. 6:12, 13). With biting irony he asks permission to play the fool (11:1), and immediately confesses his jealousy *(zēlos)* over them, a jealousy that has a sexual component. He wants to present them to God as a pure virgin, but they are in danger of being dazzled by the blandishments of his opponents and thus seduced as Eve was seduced. In order to counteract the seducers he is willing to boast, but they should know that in doing so he is behaving like a man who has taken leave of his senses. In the passage leading up to the *peristaseis*, 11:16–21, the term "fool" occurs five times in six verses, and as he begins his recitation, claiming to be a superior servant of Christ (vs. 23), he interrupts the sentence to insert, "now I'm really talking like an idiot" *(paraphronōn lalō)*. And he ends the performance by telling the humorous story of his escape from Damascus in a basket (vss. 32–33).

We may conclude from this that Paul is parodying the boasting of his opponents. Only as a clown will he enter the arena of mimetic rivalry. Humor, here in the form of irony, sarcasm, and burlesque, is a well known way of dealing with the pomposity of status claims. So although it may appear that Paul has forsaken his principled opposition to all puffery, and, having been driven to the limit, is fighting the opposition with their own weapons, the opposite is the case: he is ridiculing them, clowning with the things that they consider so solemn.

There are, however, notes of seriousness in the recitation of the *peristaseis* in ch. 11; as if he could not entirely play the fool. The *per-*

istaseis played too important a role in his understanding of his ministry for him to present them in pure irony. It is not the sufferings themselves that are to be taken lightly, but the invidious comparisons. He speaks like an utter idiot precisely when he claims to be a *better* servant of Christ than the opponents; and one must agree that on any measure, such a comparison is childish.

The dominant theme of his self-presentation in the "tearful" letter is, "If I must boast, I shall boast of my weakness" (11:30; 12:9–10), because the strength of Christ comes through most effectively at times of weakness. This might be taken to mean that the power of the divine is most effective when human power is least able to interfere, as if there were an essential incongruity between the human and the divine; but that interpretation is really only a reaction to the misinterpretation by the opponents. They make too much of human gifts and accomplishments, and this reaction makes too little. Girard helps us to see that Paul's position is not that all human participation in the work of salvation is best excluded so that the divine might have a clear run, but rather that, since the problem to be solved is mimetic rivalry, the right kind of human participation is one that emphasizes human need and the interdependence that is the opposite of mimetic rivalry. This is done by identifying with each other in our needs and vulnerabilities and, by the imaginative and volitional act of faith, identifying with the sufferings of Christ, by siding with the victim, and therefore with the victims. "Who is sick and I am not sick? Who is made to stumble and I am not furious?" (11:29).

The well-known passage about the thorn in the flesh (12:1–10), which follows immediately upon this list of *peristaseis*, confirms our interpretation. Its main point is that weakness is, paradoxically, an essential element in the effectiveness of the apostolic ministry. In weakness the power of Christ to diffuse mimetic rivalry is most effective; so it is not despite his affliction that Paul is a successful apostle of Christ, but precisely because of it: "Therefore I am content with weakness, contempt, persecution, deprivation and frustration, for Christ's sake; for when I am weak, then am I strong" (12:10).

The "tearful" letter closes with declarations by the apostle that he is not concerned to be personally vindicated, but only that the Corinthians do what is right (13:7), and the clearly anti-mimetic declaration: "We are content, at any time, to be weak, as long as you are strong; and this is my prayer, that all may be right with you" (13:9).

A somewhat different note is sounded in the "triumphal" letter, by means of the *peristaseis* lists, although the fundamental convictions remain the same as in the "tearful" letter. The note of irony has been replaced by a straight-forward exposition of the fact that sufferings are an essential part of the apostolic ministry. The "triumphal" letter comprises the following: 1. The introductory thanksgiving, 2:14–17; 2. Do we need letters of recommendation?—a question which leads to a discussion of the relationship between the letter and the spirit, 3:1–18; 3. This *diakonia*, a treasure in earthern vessels, 4:1–15; 4. A digression on heavenly existence, caused by the reference to "things unseen" in 4:18, 5:1–10; 5. A ministry of reconciliation, 5:11–6:13; 6. Concluding summary statement, 7:2–4.

The gravamen of the letter is in sections 3 and 5, both of which deal with the nature of the apostolic ministry *(diakonia)*, and both of which contain a list of sufferings. If we bracket the digression in section 4, we have, structurally speaking, a sustained presentation of the ministry as a ministry of reconciliation, beginning at 4:1, "Therefore, having this ministry *(diakonia)* . . ." and culminating in 6:3ff, "Giving no offence to anyone, so that the ministry *(diakonia)* might not be harmed . . ." This is a theme one might expect under the circumstances; the apostle and his congregation have just been reconciled; the mimetic rivalry which bedevilled their relations has been dealt with by the antidote of the Cross as represented in the apostolic sufferings. Now, after the heat and intensity of the "tearful" letter, Paul reiterates, twice, the fact that suffering, when understood as identification with Christ the victim, is the solution to rivalry; and not merely the solution to a crisis, as the Corinthians had experienced, but also a general and essential feature of apostolic, and, therefore, of Christian existence.

The Girardian hermeneutic is profoundly illuminating of the logic of the presentation in sections 3 and 5. This *diakonia* is a *diakonia* of reconciliation, firstly, because it is an outburst of the creative energy of God. "We do not proclaim ourselves but Jesus Christ as Lord, and ourselves as your slaves on account of Jesus. Because the God who said, 'Out of darkness let light shine,' has shone in our hearts, to give the light of the knowledge of the glory of God in the face of Christ" (4:6). This ministry brings new creation (5:17), but the way the energy of the new creation is mediated to the world is in "earthen vessels" (7). This means that its power is experienced by those who are willing to imitate, not one another in rivalry, but the crucified Christ in humility: "For the love of Christ constrains us, having concluded this, that one has died for all and therefore, all have died. And he died for all so that those who live may live no longer for themselves, but for him who died for them and was raised" (5:14–15). The only sense that one can make out of the conclusion that all have died if one has died for them, is that the natural mimesis is being interpreted in a special way, as the imitation of Christ in his death. The theme of imitation continues in the hitherto enigmatic statement which occurs a little further on, "He made him to be sin who knew no sin, so that in him we might become the righteousness of God" (5:21).

Having identified these two statements as the keys to the whole exposition, we are in a position to understand the passage that falls between them. What formerly seemed a somewhat random remark about once knowing Christ "after the flesh" (vs. 16) now appears to be an essential part of the logic of the argument. It is generally agreed that what is at stake is a way of knowing Christ, and not a distinction between knowing the earthly Jesus, on the one hand, and the risen Christ, on the other. What is the knowledge according to the flesh? It is the knowledge from within the coils of mimetic rivalry, characterised by the "works of the flesh" which are predominantly ". . . quarrels, a contentious temper, envy, fits of rage, selfish ambitions, dissensions, party intrigues, and jealousies, . . ." (Gal. 5:20–21). The "we" then, who once knew Christ in a mistaken way, includes the apostle in his role as persecutor, and the Corinthians in their factionalism; but now we all know Christ as the mediator of reconciliation, which in truth is what he is, and by accepting him as such we might become in him "the righteousness of God" (vss. 17–21).

We may now look more closely at the *peristaseis* lists which bracket this exposition of reconciliation. The first one, in 4:8–12, contains an explicit statement of the scapegoat function of the apostle, designed, we now see, to deal with mimetic rivalry: "Always bearing in the body the death of Jesus, so that the life of Jesus might be manifest in our body. For while alive we are always being handed over to death on account of Jesus, so that the life of Jesus might be manifest in our mortal flesh. So death is at work in us, but life in you" (vss. 10–12). The apostle separates himself from his converts in as much as he does not demand that they suffer like him—he suffers, like Jesus, on their behalf. He asks, rather, that they acknowledge that the power of the new creation comes through humble self-giving, and be willing to adopt the attitude that is appropriate to the beneficiaries of such a ministry. Paul is content to be a scapegoat on their behalf.

In the second list we find the same scapegoat theme, now directly reminiscent of the central element in the call to mimesis. It is not to be an act by act imitation of the historical Jesus, but rather an imitation of the dominant event in the schema of salvation, stated most succinctly in 2 Cor. 8:9, "For you know the grace of our Lord Jesus Christ, that, being rich, he made himself poor for our sake, so that we might, through the poverty of that man, become rich." The apostle echoes this in the second *peristaseis* list when he says that the apostles are "poor men who make others rich" (6:10). The form of this statement is characteristic of all the items in the list, suggesting that it might indeed have been formulated in the light of the central mimetic theme as set out in 2 Cor. 8:9.

In conclusion we may consider the theme of the apostolic sufferings as it occurs in the Deutero-Pauline Colossians and Ephesians, especially Colossians 1:24, "Now I rejoice in my sufferings on your behalf, and I fill up what is lacking of the persecutions of Christ, in my flesh, for the sake of his body, which is the church." Lohse (1971) represents the consensus when he understands this text to refer to the messianic woes, the sufferings which were expected immediately to precede the eschatological dénouement. For our purposes the important point is the following, to quote Lohse:

> The image of the apostle which was formed by the Christian generation was essentially characterized by the exhibition of his sufferings, much like the image which post-biblical Judaism formed of the prophets. Without exception they were pictured as persecuted and suffering, and martyrdom was the very reason they were raised to their position of honor. According to Acts 9:16 it has been decreed from the beginning that Saul/Paul must suffer for the name of Christ. In Ephesians 3:1 Paul is called a prisoner of Christ Jesus on behalf of the Gentiles. The Pastorals are presented as the testament which the imprisoned apostle entrusts to the church before his end (2 Tim. 1:8, 16ff; 2:9). Exactly in his sufferings did the apostle perform his office for the whole church. (72)

Let this quotation suffice to indicate that the earliest interpreters of Paul understood his *diakonia* aright, and as a corroboration of the interpretation we are proposing.

The fact that his *diakonia* is always for the sake of the church brings us now to a consideration of his understanding of the nature of the Christian community. We have seen Paul combatting threats to its unity, and we must now go on to ask whether our discussion enables us to understand better his more positive teaching on the subject. And that means we must enquire about the meaning of the term "body" as the apostle uses it in this regard.

4. *The church as the body of Christ the victim.*

1 Cor. 12 is a classic locus of the teaching on the church as the body of Christ. It begins with an enigmatic passage about idolatry and the cursing and confessing of Christ. The key to the enigma is that the apostle still has in mind the image of the fathers in the wilderness, which he used in 10(cf. 10:2–4; 12:13), and along with that image the argument made there about the community- destroying propensities of idolatry. Juxtaposed with this is the startling information that somebody thought that cursing Jesus could be a sign that he was speaking by inspiration of the Holy Spirit. Is this merely a juxtaposition, or is there a logic to the passage? We suggest that there is, indeed, a logic, which becomes evident in the light of our argument hitherto.

Pagan enthusiasm leads to the same kind of community-destroying behavior as does "enlightened" participation in pagan feasts. Whatever the circumstances might have been, and there have been many suggestions, it seems clear that Christians actually cursed Jesus. (We find it simply unlikely that Paul would have formulated such a negative counterpart, as Conzelmann argues; and the many other attempts to empty the passage of Christological significance are equally unconvincing.) Why would anyone have done such an odd thing? Schmithals (1972) is essentially correct in seeing an actual occurrence behind this text, and one which was fraught with theological significance. Unfortunately he got the significance wrong, falling victim as he did to the panGnostcism which afflicted German scholarship in the wake of Bultmann. *The cursers were not gnostics who objected to the flesh of Jesus, but mimetic rivals who despised his weakness and his victim status.* It is crucially significant that the name Jesus is used in both the negative and the positive forms of the confession; while the rivals curse Jesus because of his victimage, the truly inspired Christian confesses Jesus for precisely the same reason, because he is the victim who conquers mimetic rivalry.

So the Church is the body of the victim and must take its cue from that fact. The nature of power in the church, while it might be imaged by means of the relatively conventional comparison of the community to a human body in which all the limbs work together harmoniously, is conditioned and controlled by the nature of that body as the body of the victim.

This is corroborated by the fact that an account of the institution of the last supper precedes our passage; the proclamation of the Lord's death, and the worthy participation in that memorial, is the context out of which the image of the church as the body arises (11:17–34). In this instance the argument of chapter 10 is essentially repeated: the participation in the one loaf and the one cup makes the Christians one body (cf. 10:16–22); but it is always the body of Jesus the victim, not the body of the risen, spiritual Christ: ". . . you proclaim the Lord's death until he come" (11:26b).

The famous hymn to love in chapter 13 might be read as a summary of the antidote to mimetic rivalry (Schwager:227). Love is "patient, kind, not jealous *(zēlos)*, not boastful, not puffed up *(physioutai)*, not given to disgraceful behavior, not out for its own advantage, not bad tempered, not thinking the worst, not rejoicing in injustice, but delighting in the truth; bears all things, believes all things, hopes all things, endures all things" (13:4–7). It is surely not necessary to spell out how these attributes of love correlate, with startling precision, to all the features of mimetic rivalry that Girard has analysed in several works, and that have emerged from the Corinthian correspondence as the things plaguing the unity of that Pauline congregation.

Conclusion.

So, we have seen a demonstration of the Girardian hermeneutic in action on the Pauline text; it has been a valuable tool for opening up the meaning of the text. We have merely begun the analysis of the Pauline corpus. When one considers that virtually all of Paul's correspondence deals with conflict and rivalry in various congregations, one can see that the apostle is a prime candidate for a thorough Girardian interpretation. This circumstance probably also favors the hermeneutic, so that one cannot draw too far-reaching a conclusion about its efficacy as a key to all human culture; but be that as it may, it has certainly opened up a fresh and promising avenue of approach to an understanding of the apostle Paul.

Abbreviations

Bauer, *A Greek-English Lexicon of the New Testament and other Early Christian Literature*, trans. Arndt & Gingrich. Chicago: University of Chicago Press, 1957.

TDNT, *Theological Dictionary of the New Testament*, ed. G. Kittel. Vol. III. Grand Rapids: Wm. Eerdmans, 1965.

COMMUNITY—ITS UNITY, DIVERSITY AND UNIVERSALITY

Thomas Wieser
World Council of Churches

ABSTRACT

The essay examines a number of New Testament passages from the perspective of the thesis developed by René Girard, concerning foundational violence. According to this thesis, human communities, prior and outside the Christian revelation, develop out of an act of violence which unites all over-against one. Jesus' message heralds a new community, a new humanity. His message is examined, first with reference to his own ministry as he confronts—and dissolves—established human communities; second, in the Book of Acts which describes the founding of a new community; third, in 1 Corinthians where Paul faces divisions in the community; and fourth, in John 17 which develops the notion of unity and universality. In its conclusion the essay draws some implications for the present-day institutional life of the churches within the context of the ecumenical movement.

In this essay we shall consider some New Testament passages dealing with the notion of community. In doing so we shall use as a hermeneutical key the thesis developed by René Girard concerning foundational violence and its revelation in the New Testament writings.

As Girard has shown, the formation of human communities as part of human cultural development involves at its center the scapegoat mechanism, the choice of a victim to be sacrificed for the benefit of the rest of the community. Community solidarity is based on the principle of all-against-one. Moreover, in order to maintain its unity and to prevent a new outbreak of the crisis that tore it apart, the community imposes upon its members certain rules, especially those prohibiting mimetic behaviour, since the crisis is attributed to rivalry resulting from such behaviour (1978a:33ff.).

The revelation of the scapegoat mechanism, a central focus of the New Testament message according to Girard, renders this mechanism inoperative for the formation of the human community. Not surprisingly, the question of community life and of its origin is therefore of crucial importance in the New Testament, so much so that the creation of

83

a radically new type of community has been hailed by New Testament scholarship as the principal effect and even as the primary intention of Jesus' proclamation of the kingdom of God.

The question is, then, whether a new operating principle for community formation is being introduced in the New Testament. What takes the place of foundational violence and what is proposed as a means for maintaining the peace in the community in the place of suppression of mimetic desire through prohibitions? What are alternative ways of resolving a crisis in the community other than through scapegoating and expulsion?

I. *The gospel as an antidote to established communities*

All four Gospels portray the coming of Jesus and the proclamation of his message of the kingdom of God as a threat to the established community or communities of his time. We shall examine a number of passages in order to understand this threat.

a. *Jesus in the house of Levi* (Mt. 9:9-13 and par.)

Communities function to the degree to which they can create and maintain effective distinctions. One of the chief distinctions is that which separates those forming part of the community from those outside. It is the foundational distinction, and it is inherently violent. For those who find themselves outside are never there by their free will. They are outside because they have been expelled.

The violent origin of the distinction in our passage, between the Pharisees on the one hand and the tax collectors and sinners on the other, is not explicitly mentioned. It is, however, alluded to in Matthew's version when Jesus quotes Hosea 6:6: "I desire mercy, and not sacrifice." The quotation actually interrupts the flow of the narrative. It is an insert. But its insertion highlights the point that the distinction between "righteous" and "sinners" refers to the sacrificial order, the order that has been established through the sacrifice of a victim and is maintained through continual sacrifices and the promulgation of ever more strict and stringent prohibitions.

At the beginning of the story the validity of the distinction is not questioned; it is taken for granted: "Behold, many tax collectors and sinners came and sat down with Jesus and his disciples." Hence the reaction of the Pharisees seems justified: "Why does he eat with tax collectors and sinners?" Even Jesus seems at first to stay within the logic of the distinction: "Those who are well have no need of a physician, but those who are sick." By comparing the tax collectors and sinners to sick people, especially within the cultural context of the time, Jesus seems to agree with the Pharisees' distinction between righteous and sinners.

The reversal occurs in the conclusion of the story: "I came not to call the righteous but the sinners." At first, this seems like a simple reversal of roles. The insiders become outsiders and vice versa. This in itself would already constitute a threat to the established community. The notion that outsiders could suddenly become insiders, that the distinction between the two could be applied in one direction or the other, serves to underscore the artibrary nature of the distinction and thereby undermines its effectiveness. It is no doubt this threat that Jesus' adversaries perceived in his message, and that led them to eliminate him.

But the reversal of the roles in favor of the outsiders is not the real point of the story. Jesus is not a revolutionary. He compares himself to a physician. His is a therapeutic approach, steering a narrow path between the sacrificial approach and the revolutionary approach. Both of the latter have in common that they presuppose and depend on the distinction between insiders and outsiders. Jesus, however, aims at abolishing the distinction altogether.

b. *Jesus and the woman caught in adultery* (John 8:1-11)

The abolition of the distinction as the purpose of Jesus' mission is made unmistakably clear in the passage in John 8. The woman is brought before Jesus in order to be stoned for her act of adultery. Stoning is one of the classical ancient modes of violent expulsion (Girard, 1982: 248) enabling the community to regain its unity through the unanimous act of choosing and eliminating a victim. The scribes and Pharisees bring the woman before Jesus in order to "test" him. Jesus is asked to uphold the community, to affirm its unity by consenting to the stoning of the woman.

Jesus refuses. His refusal first takes the form of silence. He does not actively oppose it; he does not want to be the ally of the woman or the adversary of the accusers. Active opposition would involve accusing the accusers, a form of counter-violence, even if it were only to accuse them of being too harsh. Any of these options would maintain the distinction between the woman and the community. The emphasis on Jesus' silence in the text seems to be an attempt to set all these options aside and to prepare the reader of the story for Jesus' eventual answer: "Let him who is without sin among you be the first to throw a stone at her." The answer reveals at once the fundamental ambiguity residing in the law to which the Pharisees had appealed. The announced purpose of the law is to combat sin, i.e. violence in the community and thus to maintain and unify it. But the law can never be applied "without sin," i.e. its application always involves counter-violence in one form or another. Thus the law that was to end the infernal cycle of violence ends up by continuing it. To "be without sin" would mean to have stepped outside the cycle, to be released of the need to find victims as scapegoats for maintaining the unity of the community. Obviously, in that case stoning would be excluded altogether, not just because it would be considered morally wrong or repulsive but simply because its futility and arbitrary nature, its destructive power and its utter uselessness for building up the community would have become obvious.

The immediate effect of Jesus' statement is that the Pharisees "went away, one by one, beginning with the eldest, and Jesus was left alone with the woman." This exodus contrasts sharply with the beginning of the story where the Scribes and Pharisees appear as one block, united in violence. Jesus' dissolving effect on the community he confronts, or which confronts him, finds here its graphic expression.

c. *Jesus and the community of the disciples*

The dissolving effect of Jesus' message on human communities is explicitly stated in some passages. Jesus predicts that "henceforth in one house they will be divided, father against son and son against father, mother against daughter and daughter against mother" (Lk. 12:49; Cf. also Lk. 18:29; Mt. 10:34-38). This effect even extends to the community of the disciples that formed around Jesus.

The formation of this community is reported in the Gospels in a series of stories about the "calling" of the disciples. What all these stories have in common is the abruptness with which the persons called are responding. This abruptness again indicates the disrupting effect of Jesus' message on the natural communities such as family and work teams. In the further portrayal of the disciples as they accompany Jesus there are hardly any features of community life. Rather, the disciples appear as an unstable group, torn and oscillating between different loyalties. Two passages can illustrate this behaviour.

Peter's confession of Jesus as the Messiah is in Matthew 16. This confession occurs in the course of a conversation during which Jesus is compared to a number of eminent figures in the Jewish past and present. The notion of comparison suggests rank and hence rivalry. In the popular mind that is evoked ("who do people say that the son of man is?") Elijah, Jeremiah and John the Baptist are rivals, rival heroes. And the disciples are reflecting the popular mind even though their answer is supposed to challenge that mind ("But who do you say that I am?"). Peter's answer on behalf of the rest of the disciples is different from the popular answer, but only in degree and not in kind. It is offered within the context of rival religious expectations. Within that context, Peter's "confession" is the attempt to outdo the popular religious expectations, to put Jesus at the top of the messianic totempole.

Despite the mimetic character of Peter's statement, Jesus calls him "blessed." The truth contained in the statement is not evident within the context in which it was made, the context that Jesus calls "flesh and blood." That context does not reveal anything because it is primarily concerned with hiding the truth underneath the rivalry. Within that context Jesus becomes one of the religious leaders who must compete with others. To claim Jesus as the Messiah within that context is to fuel religious competition.

But there is another context, revealed by the "Father who is in heaven." Within that context Peter's statement has indeed foundational quality and truth and will become the ground on which to build the new community. The revelation of that truth, however, will involve the dissolution even of the community in whose name Peter has just spoken. For, as the second part of the story shows, the disciples' community is not prepared to accept that revelation, not even in the form of Jesus' prediction of his passion. Peter is scandalized by this announcement, thus exposing his—and his co-disciples'—captivity to religious competition.

In the second passage we shall consider, Mark 10:35-45, the rivalry inherent in the disciples' community is coming out into the open and is explicitly addressed by Jesus. Two of the disciples request Jesus to grant them places of honor in the kingdom, thus provoking open antagonism on the part of the rest. Faced with open rivalry among his own disciples, Jesus spells out the principle, the foundation of a nonviolent, non-competitive community:

> You know that those who are supposed to rule over the Gentiles lord it over them, and their great men exercise authority over them. But it shall not be so among you; but whoever would be great among you must be your servant, and whoever would be first among you must be slave of all.

According to the Gospel account, this is the last time before his passion that Jesus speaks to the disciples about their community life. It is as if he were to provide a last chance for them before the final crisis to face the crisis within their own ranks and thus to be transformed into a true community.

The disciples are evidently not in a position to understand what Jesus is saying. Their rivalry is preventing them from understanding. Their community is too far advanced in its crisis and they, along with the other communities that are drawn into the Passion of Jesus, will have to experience the dissolution of their community in the revelation of the violence represented by the crucifixion.

II. Acts—The alternative community

Sharing the goods (Acts 2 and 4)

The new community emerging in the wake of the resurrection is one of the principal themes of the Book of Acts, especially the first part, chs. 1–5. What is the foundation of this community? The early chapters of Acts contain specific descriptions of the life of the early Christian community, especially in Acts 2:41–47 and 4:32ff. They are summary descriptions and hence do not provide many details. It is therefore all the more remarkable that they both insist on one detail in particular, the sharing of goods. In Acts 2 we hear that the members of the community "had all things in common; and they sold their possessions and goods and distributed them to all, as any had need." The text in Acts 4 is even more elaborate:

> There was not a needy person among them, for as many as were possessors of lands and houses sold them, and brought the proceeds of what was sold and laid it at the apostles' feet; and distribution was made to each as any had need. Thus Joseph who was surnamed by the apostles Barnabas (which means son of encouragement) a Levite, a native of Cyprus, sold a field which belonged to him, and brought the money and laid it at the Apostles' feet. (Acts 4:34–37)

Why this detailed emphasis on sharing? Because it represents the only logical alternative to the mimetic rivalry that pervades every other human community and which ultimately leads to its destruction. To say that none of the things one possesses are one's own is to totally reverse the process of mimetic appropriation in which each insists that what he/she possesses is his/her own. The traditional way of preventing mimetic rivalry from destroying the community was, and still is, to establish prohibitions against it or against its excesses. Prohibitions, however, always end up by creating an inside over-against outside and eventually produce the phenomenon of violent expulsion. A community that does not want to rely on prohibitions must, therefore, be able to reverse social relations. The two texts cited from Acts indicate the awareness of the need for such a total reversal, from a state of rivalry for the sake of appropriation of goods to the state of radical sharing of goods.

The nature of this reversal is starkly illustrated by the story of Ananias and Sapphira in Acts 5. The harsh fate befalling this couple as a result of their deception could lead us to conclude that the new experiment in community life had already broken down and that the apostles had been forced to re-introduce prohibitions. Such an interpretation, however, overlooks the fact that Peter's role is described in the story not as that of an executor of punishment. All Peter does is to reveal the lie involved in the deception. In the face of this revelation the lie cannot go on living. Since, as Peter says, Satan has "filled" their hearts to lie, Ananias and Sapphira are identical with the lie and can, therefore, not go on living either.

Inclusiveness (Acts 10–11, 15)

Another major preoccupation of the new community in Acts concerns its inclusiveness. The story of Pentecost shows the Apostles able to communicate to everybody in their language. In an obvious allusion to the story of the Tower of Babel that shows the destruction of the community, community here is re-established and given a new foundation. Moreover, it is open to everybody, it is universal by its very nature.

The story of Peter's mission to the house of Cornelius in Acts 10–11 offers a dramatic description of the major obstacles to be overcome in the process of the universalization of the human community.

First, Cornelius, a Roman officer and hence an enemy of the Jewish people, is portrayed as a man whose prayers are answered by the God of Israel. Next, Peter is told that the distinction between pure and impure, the main distinction for maintaining the unity and continuity of the Jewish community, is no longer valid. In fact, the text clearly indicates that the distinction cannot claim God as its author. It is the human community that has introduced and maintained these distinctions, using the divine sanction as a means to enforce them.

Upon arriving at Cornelius' house, Peter states a third obstacle to inclusiveness: "It is unlawful for a Jew to visit with anyone of another nation." But he states equally strongly that this obstacle is now overcome: "God shows no partiality" (10:34). No party line, however justified in the eyes of people, can claim to be sanctioned by God. Behind this abrogation of division is the notion that each dividing line requires an act of violence.

But God cannot be made responsible for any division and for any violence connected with such divisions. On the contrary, Peter continues, God sent Jesus to preach the "good news of peace" (10:36), the revelation that none of these dividing lines are really necessary.

The breakdown of the distinction between Jews and Gentiles predictably leads to a crisis in the Jewish community. The violence on which the distinction has been based is now revealed and hence released into the community. Peter is attacked by the "circumcision party" upon his return to Jerusalem and has to defend his action. The crisis is resolved—not by a new expulsion but by the community being moved to a higher level of inclusiveness: "To the Gentiles also God has granted repentance unto life" (11:18).

This movement toward greater inclusiveness reaches yet another stage in Ch. 15. Basically, the issue is the same, only here it is raised in a somewhat different form. The principle of inclusiveness is granted; Gentiles may become part of the Christian community; the community is open to everyone. But the request that they be circimcised before being baptized sets up a condition to their entry, the very condition that served to maintain the exclusiveness of the Jewish community. For circumcision in the context of that time symbolized exclusiveness, the very opposite from the inclusiveness sought by the gospel message.

The refusal to circumcise the new converts on the part of Paul and Barnabas threatened to throw the community into a new crisis and caused the convocation of the council in Jerusalem. There Peter once more makes his defense, based on his experience in the house of Cornelius. His arguments have gained in intensity. The abolition of the distinction between Jews and Gentiles is now directly attributed to God's initiative. Peter was merely God's "mouth to the Gentiles." Moreover, Peter now argues, maintaining the distinction will amount to putting God on trial, to expelling God from the community.

The Council of Jerusalem results in greater inclusiveness. Nobody is expelled. It might appear, however, that the Council's request to the Gentiles "to abstain from the pollutions of idols and from unchastity and from what is strangled and from blood" (v. 20), represents a relapse into prohibitions. Formally it is indeed a prohibition, but the abstention from pollution and blood means nothing else but the abstention from sacrificial practices. It is abstention from sacred violence, and it is the only distinction left, because it is the difference between violence and peace, between exclusiveness and inclusiveness.

III. *Unity, diversity and divisions* (1 Corinthians)

In the Pauline literature, and especially in 1 Corinthians, several important themes regarding the Christian community are touched on. Paul explicitly speaks about the foundation of the community. There is "no other Foundation," he says, that can be laid beside that in Christ (1 Cor. 3:11). The same theme is sounded in the letter to the Ephesians where the community is being defined as a house "built upon the foundation of the apostles and prophets, Christ Jesus himself being the cornerstone" (Eph. 2:20). In both instances the Greek term for foundation is *themmelion*, a term originating in the realm of architecture. It has no violent connotation and must, therefore, have been deliberately chosen in contrast to *katabole*, the term used throughout the New Testament, including the Pauline letters, when referring to the (violent) foundation of the world.

Paul's insistence on Christ as the peaceful foundation of the Christian community is part of his argument with the Corinthians about the split in their congregation. There are rival factions that have arisen— a Peter-party, an Apollos-party, and even a Christ-party. Here, rivalry has been re-introduced in the name of the very gospel that was proclaimed in order to reveal the violence behind it and thereby to bring the struggle to an end. Paul faces a situation similar to what Jesus faced among his disciples, whole-hearted and enthusiastic (too enthusiastic?) acceptance of the gospel message, a rushing to grab a hold of its truth—but all this within the context of mimetic desire. Instead of being the liberation from this desire, the gospel now becomes the fuel to feed the desire. Paul evokes this absurd state of affairs by asking the question, "Is Christ divided?" (1:13). A divided Christ, an amputated Christ is a Christ who has—once more—been used as a sacrifice in the interests of reciprocal violence. How does Paul deal with this situation? The difficulty for him is that along with others he has been cast into the role of a rival. Whatever he says, therfore, runs the risk of being understood as reinforcing his position within the context of rivalry.

Paul tries to deal with the situation in two ways. In the early part of the letter he strives to extricate himself from the rivalry by opposing the gospel to the wisdom and cleverness of the world. He specifically mentions that he did not preach the gospel with "eloquent wisdom" and later on he goes so far as to call himself a fool: "We are fools for Christ's sake, but you are wise in Christ. We are weak but you are strong. You are held in honor, but we are in disrepute" (4:10). There is deliberate irony in this play of words, also perhaps a deliberate ambiguity of meaning. Is Paul really commending the Corinthians for their wisdom, strength and honor, or is he ridiculing their claims to be wise, strong and honorable? It is up to the Corinthians to choose the answer, and their choice will determine whether they have stepped outside the circle of mimetic rivalry. Paul knows that he cannot force this liberation onto them. He can only open the gate, hoping that the Corinthians will become conscious of the irony of their situation and in that realization will grasp the absurdity of their division.

In the latter part of the letter Paul evokes the image of the body as a means to help the Corinthians to understand the nature of a non-competitive community. The image is introduced within the context of the discussion about spiritual gifts (12:1ff). The Corinthians had laid claim to a great variety of such gifts, and the claims had contributed to the divisions within the community. Spirituality itself had become a bone of contention, it had been seized by mimetic desire as the highest gift.

Paul reminds the Corinthians that the work of the Spirit is to maintain unity in the midst of diversity and thus to make diversity an instrument for the "manifestation of the common good" (12:9). Within the universe of mimetic desire such a combination of unity and diversity is totally unthinkable. In that universe diversity inevitably leads to rivalry, and unity is always achieved only at the height of the mimetic crisis when the various factions of the community can unify over-against a victim. Unity and diversity are two types of antagonism, and they are even antagonistic toward each other. The spirit of Christ opens up another universe in which unity and diversity help to build up the community. It is to describe this universe that Paul introduces the image of the body. In so far as the body functions organically, it functions cooperatively rather than competitively. Moreover, a body not only tolerates diversity, but it depends on diversity in order to function properly as a body. Paul brings out this point very clearly by endowing the physical members of the body with human voices,

> If the foot should say, "because I am not a hand, I do not belong to the body," that would not make it any less part of the body. And if the ear should say, "because I am not an eye, I do not belong to the body," that would not make it any less part of the body . . . The ear cannot say to the hand, "I have no need of you," nor again the head to the feet, "I have no need of you." (1 Cor. 12:15ff)

The absurdity of one member of the body wanting to separate itself from the body is clearly evident within the context of the fable. It serves to demonstrate that diversity and interdependence—the death-knell of a competitive community—are the lifeblood of an organic community. The notion of interdependence is further developed by Paul in the last part of ch. 12. By saying that the less honorable members of the body are invested with greater honor he seems to suggest an inverse process from that of scapegoating in which the inferior elements of the community will inevitably serve as potential victims. The interdependence even extends to suffering. In the case of a physical body Paul's statement that if one member suffers, all suffer together, is perfectly logical. However, as soon as this statement is applied to the members of a social body we can see that it implies a radical reversal of social relations.

IV *Unity and universality* (John 17)

Our examination of passages in Acts and Corinthians have shown a keen awareness on the part of New Testament authors of the need to describe the new alternative human community in terms that clearly oppose it to any community founded on violence. This awareness is especially pronounced in a text such as John 17, perhaps the most profound expression in the New Testament of the true unity of the community in the absence of violence. The chapter has long been hailed in Christian and especially in ecumenical circles as the classic text on Christian unity, but in spite of the attention that the text has received, or perhaps because of it, the extraordinary character of the language in which unity is described has remained hidden.

> "I do not pray for these only, but also for those who believe in me through their word, that they may all be one; even as you, Father, are in me, and I in you, that they may also be in us, so that the world may believe that you have sent me. The glory which you have given me I have given to them, that they may be one even as we are one, I in them and you in me, that they may become perfectly one, so that the world may know that you have sent me and have loved them even as you have loved me." (John 17:20–23)

Jesus and the Father are one. This affirmation is controversial, as is clear from another context in which it is made (cf. John 10:30ff). For it signals the abolition of all religious systems based on sacred violence that separates the divine from the human realm. Jesus came from the Father, he was sent by him, and he is going to the Father (v. 13). His crossing the line between the human and the divine realm means the abolition of the line on behalf of humanity, "that they may all be one." The unity—in the place of the enmity—of the human community with the Father is the fundamental good news that Jesus has come to bring to the world. Therefore he prays that the world may believe when this unity becomes visible in those who believe Jesus' word.

Two aspects in particular are worth considering in this description of unity. First, there is a surprising concentration of expressions of a comparative nature in the text. Three times two clauses are connected with the term "even as" indicating a comparison or imitation. Within the context of violence such imitative language would have to be interpreted as an expression of mimetic desire, a sign of a community in crisis. Obviously, this is not John's intention here in using this language. The unity of the human community can be modeled on the union existing between the Father and the son without placing the two into a position of rivalry. What passes between the two is not rivalry but "glory," the glory that Jesus has received from the Father. Within the context established by Jesus' word his relationship with the Father can become the model to be imitated as a sign of peace.

The reversal from rivalry to harmony is expressed in the curious language of "being in": "You, Father, are in me and I in you, that they may also be in us" (v. 21). Commentators usually see here a residue of Gnostic mysticism. Actually, this total interpretation of identities indicates the deepest level of peaceful existence; it is to be "at peace" with all, and that peacefulness is mutual.

Second, the fact that Jesus' unity with the Father creates the conditions for the unity within all humanity and of humanity with the Father, shows the universal dimension of this unity. It is unity in terms of total inclusiveness. To be sure the world of violence will hate those who enter into this unity but the hate will be one-sided, it will not be reciprocated. The cycle of violence will come to a stop again and again at the gate of this unity. But in order to be this counter-world to the world of violence, the unity must be truly universal, it must never close itself off over-against any part of humanity, it must be a unity without limits except the limits created by those who exclude themselves by wanting to exclude others. Unity in Christ, grounded in the unity of the Father and the son, can only be universal or else it falls back into the unity of violence based on exclusion and expulsion.

Some implications for the contemporary situation

The contemporary situation of the Christian community, embodied in a variety of churches and religious groups, is characterized by a double tendency towards unity and universality on the one hand, and towards institutional dissolution on the other. This apparently contradictory development should not surprise us in the light of the New Testament passages we have examined.

The pressure for unity and universalization is clearly a manifestation of the gospel message in our time. The affirmation of this message, however, can only be undertaken by the churches at the expense of their current institutional identity. For this universality and inclusiveness reveals that the churches' identity is founded on exclusion, or else there would be no division between the churches. The churches find themselves in the uncomfortable position of being at odds with the very message they proclaim. The message affirms unity, inclusiveness and universality, while the structures of the churches are based on rivalry, division and exclusion. Consequently, the more clearly the gospel is being spelled out through the work of the churches, the greater is the pressure on their structures, and the more deeply these structures will enter the institutional crisis.

A striking illustration for this dilemma is the story of the modern ecumenical movement of the last 60–80 years. The movement has successfully generated a pressure within the churches, first towards unity among them, but lately also towards inclusiveness of Christians and non-Christians. By welcoming this movement the churches have, at least implicitly, admitted the validity of the unity and universality of the new community founded in Christ, and hence acknowledged the arbitrary and violent nature of their divisions and the exclusiveness of their structures. By and large, however, the reason for the tension goes largely unrecognized, that is to say, the churches attribute the tension and the resulting institutional problems to things they are doing "wrong" (e.g. lack of commitment, inadequate training of clergy, etc.), rather than to what they are doing right, and so they are moving ever more deeply into the institutional crisis without ever understanding the reason for it. Calls for renewal and reform have multiplied, especially in the last 15–20 years. Whatever restructuring has been undertaken has inevitably never had the desired effect.

The inability to understand this situation has meant that the churches' relationship to the ecumenical movement, e.g. within the context of their membership in the World Council of Churches, has displayed all the signs of the oscillation we have observed in the disciples' community around Jesus as portrayed by the Gospels, alternating between profession of loyalty and being scandalized.

To be sure, the progressing institutional crisis is not limited in our time to the churches. The need for greater inclusiveness, for the participation of all without regard to race, sex, religion, etc. is being recognized ever more widely, revealing the arbitrary nature of the distinctions on which institutions are based. There is, however, a special factor involved in the churches' situation, in so far as their expressed and only *raison d'être* is to serve the revelation of the God of peace and thereby to reveal the foundational violence in all of our human communities. It is, therefore, to be expected that this revelation, like a lightning from heaven (Lk. 10:18), will strike closest to the churches, that the crisis begins with the "house of God" (1 Peter 4:17).

Throughout the history of Christianity there have been numerous attempts to create radical alternative communities in the name of true Christian unity and inclusiveness. All of them have eventually been trapped by a new form of exclusiveness. The price for exclusion in an age of dwindling distinctions is rapidly mounting, however. We are approaching the moment in history—and the ecumenical movement can be seen as a signal for this moment—when it becomes *inescapably* clear that the *oikumene*, the whole inhabited world, must provide room for all, or else it will face over-all destruction. In this sense the ecumenical movement can be said to be truly apocalyptic.

CHRISTIAN MORALITY AND THE PAULINE REVELATION

Eric Gans
University of California-Los Angeles

ABSTRACT

The essence of Jesus' message was the subordination of theology to morality, conceived for the first time as the potential basis for a concrete ethic. The keystone of morality is universal reciprocity; but the revealer of this universal reciprocity uniquely distinguishes himself from his fellows and thereby incurs their unanimous persecution. The lesson of Paul's revelatory experience on the route to Damascus was that his persecution of the moral doctrine espoused by Jesus' surviving disciples was tantamount to the persecution of Jesus' person, and that the latter form of persecution, by placing Jesus at the center, was indistinguishable from worship. This ineluctable persistence of Jesus is proof of his divinity; but this implied less the validity of his moral doctrine than the efficacity of his soteriological role. Hence the Pauline revelation was the essential moment in transforming Christianity from a sect concerned with awaiting the moral apocalypse into a universal religion of salvation.

The small group of Jesus' original disciples did not disperse at the death of its leader; on the contrary, it gained new adherents. The account of the Pentecost in Acts 2:1–41 describes the kind of experience that led to these early conversions. Peter's sermon contains the following passage:

"Men of Israel, hear these words: Jesus of Nazareth, a man attested to you by God with mighty works and wonders and signs which God did through him in your midst as you yourselves know—this Jesus, delivered up according to the definite plan and foreknowledge of God, you crucified and killed by the hands of lawless men" (2:22–24 [RSV])

This surprising accusation brought against an audience of potential converts gives a no doubt authentic illustration of the spirit of the early preaching. The resurrection, as confirmed by the glossolalic enthusiasm of the disciples, demonstrates the error of the Jews of Jerusalem, at the very least accomplices in the death of Jesus. This technique relied on the crowd's direct acquaintance with Jesus and on their feelings of remorse over his death in the face of the affirmation of his resurrection by the faithful. These two key elements—complicity in the persecution of Jesus and the vision of his resurrection—remain entirely separate. It is the crowd who is accused of the murder; the revelations to the apostles as described in the scene of the Ascension at the beginning of Acts (1:6–11) contain no trace of accusation. Yet all four versions of the Gospel narrative emphasize Jesus' solitude in his last moments, as well as his denial by this very same Peter whom we now see so willing to cast the blame on others. The two apparently dichotomous attitudes toward Jesus, faith and persecution, here unproblematically distinguished and attributed to different sets of persons, will later be presented as interdependent. It is our contention that the insight thus expressed is the founding intuition of Christianity as we know it, the source of the post-Mosaic theology that transformed a Jewish sect into a universal religion and that would lead three centuries later to the definitive formulation of the trinity credo.

Peter's sermon makes the vision of the resurrected Christ appear as the reward of untroubled faith. But we possess a text of Acts that shows this vision to be directly linked to, indeed, the product of persecution. This text recounts the last biblical appearance of Christ, his revelation to Saul/Paul on the road to Damascus. That this narrative appears three times in the book of Acts demonstrates its exceptional importance. The Epistle to the Galatians (1:11–17) authentificates the experience, if not its precise form. But as in the case of other narratives of revelation, the text is essentially self-confirming:

> But Saul, still breathing threats and murder against the disciples of the Lord, went to the high priest and asked him for letters to the synagogues at Damascus, so that if he found any belonging to the Way, men or women, he might bring them bound to Jerusalem. Now as he journeyed he approached Damascus, and suddenly a light from heaven flashed about him. And he fell to the ground and heard a voice saying to him, "Saul, Saul, why do you persecute me?" And he said, "Who are you, Lord *(kyrie)*?" And he said, "I am Jesus, whom you are persecuting; but rise and enter the city, and you will be told what you are to do." The men who were traveling with him stood speechless, hearing the voice but seeing no one. Saul arose from the ground; and when his eyes were opened, he could see nothing; so they led him by the hand and brought him into Damascus. And for three days he was without sight, and neither ate nor drank. (9:1–9)

This first and simplest version contains no doubt the authentic kernel of what would later be elaborated in the speeches of 22:3–11 and

26:4–18. The scene takes place only a few years after the crucifixion; Saul is a Pharisee and a persecutor of the Christians. He hears the voice of Jesus asking him why he persecutes him; it is this revelation that converts him to Christianity.

If Paul's conversion is recognized as a great moment of Christian history, its theological importance has been less remarked. It is nonetheless the sole revelatory experience of the New Testament that is both historically verifiable and the bearer of a theological intuition of comparable weight to that of Moses on Mount Sinai. The standard commentaries explain the persecution of Jesus as a metonymy of that which Saul exercised against the Christians (Haenchen: 322). But his experience is far more direct. The truth that Saul understands, the power of which is figured in the text by his blinding, is that it is the very persecution of Jesus that demonstrates his divinity. For the author of the text, this divinity is a given that has only to manifest itself; but it could only have convinced Saul if he grasped in an instant the essential connection between persecution and divinization. That the text fails to elaborate this truth, or that Paul's own writings only explore it indirectly, should hardly surprise us. The high point of a revelation is expressed in words that bear the mark of authority precisely because they cannot be explained. In this sense it may truly be said that "language speaks" through the human subject—it being understood, however, that it speaks in order to say something.

This text must be interpreted in the light of the Mosaic revelation, which is the model of all Biblical revelation scenes. The light in the sky is a revelatory sign become conventional and no longer requiring the natural etiology of the bush of Sinai. This formalization of experience is not a mark of inauthenticity; it reflects an openness to individual revelation that is a product of the prophetic tradition. A more immediate *rapprochement* can be made with the Ascension recounted at the opening of Acts (1:9–11), which makes the sky the abode of Jesus. The celestiality of the sacred is more clearly marked in the New Testament than in the Old, as if to assure by the opposition earth/heaven the reality of the passage from one to the other promised to the human soul in the Gospels. The physical occasion of the revelation becomes for this reason more abstract, and also more subjective: the sky that lights up for a single individual is not much more than a metaphor of a purely internal illumination. The Jews of Paul's era had long since forgotten the punctual, ritual centrality of the burning bush; revelation has become, in the etymological sense of the term, an apocalyptic phenomenon.

The most significant contrast with the experience of Moses is that the voice is shown to be of human origin. But Saul first addresses it with the term "Lord" *(kyrios)* normally used to address God. Nothing yet indicates to him that this voice is not that of the God of the Hebrews; it is only its answer to his question that will thus inform him. Dialogue is the essential form of revelation. What Saul first hears is the accusation of persecution. It is still the God of Moses who speaks, even if he expresses himself in a new fashion; Saul is only open to the word of his own God. His question "Who are you?" expresses the same interrogation of the divine substance as Moses's asking the name of God. Great revelations are not emanations of an immutable divinity; they involve a modification of its very substance. Saul, the persecutor of Christians, has just understood that in this persecution he persecuted God. But he can no longer recognize this God; he must ask his identity. It is then that he learns it is Jesus.

Paul's experience is more constrained, more conditioned by its context than that of Moses. Moses is concerned by the fate of his people under the Egyptian yoke, but the relationship between this and monotheistic religion is not immediately evident; its necessity appears only *ex post facto*. Paul, in contrast, is defined for others, and no doubt for himself, as a persecutor of Christians; persecution has become so to speak his profession. That this activity abruptly turns into its opposite is not surprising in itself. The conversion of an antagonistic fervor into the contrary passion is an aspect of even banal love stories; *odi et amo*, as Ovid put it. But if the revolutionary importance of the Pauline revelation cannot be grasped at the psychological level, it is because its theological and ethical truth is located at the metapsychological level. It is not the operation of conversion that is remarkable; it is rather the transformation of this operation into a source of theological insight. Paul's conversion is not so much unique as exemplary. The last in the long series of revelations of the resurrected Christ that he modestly summarizes in 1 Corinthians 15, it marks the end of the revelatory period of Christianity, and of Western civilization as a whole. Nor is its relatively minor place in Christian consciousness altogether undeserved. For it signals the exhaustion of the phenomenon of divine revelation as a means of access to anthropological truth.

Saul persecutes the Christians, even participating, according to legend, in the lapidation of St. Stephen. Those whom he persecutes have remained attached to one who preached the transcendence of the ethical Law by moral intuition in the awaiting of an imminent apocalypse. Saul, as a good Pharisee, reveres the Law, for it alone guarantees the survival of the Jewish community. But it no longer maintains the eminently ethical function that it had in the books of Moses. Phariseeism adapts the Mosaic precepts to modern conditions, but it multiplies secondary rules less in the aim of regulating social interaction than in that of guaranteeing, through an unending series of symbolic and commemoratory acts, the individual's membership in a community whose politico-economic functionality in the new world of "ecumenical" empires is increasingly dubious. To espouse the moral intuition expressed in the Sermon on the Mount is to abandon the Law for a radical prolongation of prophetic moralism, to abandon the ethical order of the Jewish community for an apocalyptic hope in the Kingdom of God.

The old pre-Mosaic theologies were born clothed in the ethical systems of which they were to serve as the foundations. The Mosaic revelation is revolutionary in that it clearly detaches theology from ethics, but it fails to reserve an independent place for morality, which remains only implicit. Hillel's aphorism that the "golden rule" of morality was "all the Law and the Prophets" reversed this relation, but it was left to Jesus to carry this reversal to its ultimate conclusion.

As Jewish skeptics have often remarked, there is nothing in Jesus' doctrine of moral reciprocity that is not already present in rabbinical reflection. And this should not surprise us. It is ethics that are complex and diverse; morality is one. If that of Jesus and that of Hillel are more or less the same, this is simply because there is no other. The difference lies in the radicality of Jesus' attachment to his moral intuition.

The heart of morality is reciprocity in human relations. It is with its exigency of reciprocity that morality becomes critical of ethics. Marxism tries to make of egalitarian morality the ethic of the proletariat, but it remains the same morality as ever. Morality has no history. What is historical is its formulation as a universal model of behavior independently of any particular ethic. The rabbis wanted to make of it the heart of an ethic; Jesus grasped the revelatory force of its constitution as an *autonomous* ethical model.

The origin of morality as of ethics is on the collective scene of representation. The concept of an originary scene of representation as the locus of the origin of man has been elaborated at some length in two works, *The Origin of Language* and *The End of Culture*. Although in both cases the presentation of the hypothesis is "atheistic," it suffices to consider the first word by which the newly-formed human community addresses the center as the name of God for the hypothesis to be reconciled with a theological perspective.

Very briefly, the originary hypothesis supposes that man, defined by his possession of language, emerges only when prelinguistic conflict-avoidance mechanisms prove inadequate, and that this occurs in a collective context when a group of hominids, perhaps following a hunt, are faced with an appetitive object (e.g., the carcass of a large game-animal) attractive enough to promote conflict within the group. Each member of the group makes a *gesture of appropriation* toward the object, but is held in check by the fear of reprisals from the other members. The gesture of appropriation is thus *aborted*, and becomes a *designation* of the object—the first "word." The object itself is understood to be the sacred, inaccessible source of the community's reconciliation, and its distribution in the feast that follows reveals the distinction between the "word" as the name of God and its temporary earthly incarnation.

The "scene of representation" thus formed by the protohuman community is reproduced in ritual and maintained in the essential symmetry of linguistic communication. The exchange of words on the periphery surrounding the sacred center provides the original model of perfect human reciprocity, of what we here call "morality."

The equality of men before representation is the original foundation of both their equality and their inequality in society. But it does not suffice to affirm that morality maintains equality whereas ethics justifies inequality. Ethics institutes the norms of communal interaction; its revelatory origin is the origin of an order. In the beginning, this order only comes to supplement, at a crucial moment, the preexistent animal order whose mechanisms have proven inadequate to their task. But there is nothing in the concept of order in itself that implies equality. The equalitarian foundation of humanity is not a proof of the superiority of primitive equality over the hierarchies that would replace it, but on the contrary an indication that all the resources of the scene of representation were not yet explored. The emergence of "big-men" of various kinds (Sahlins) would later show that the real center can be occupied by a man without disturbing the divine centrality of the scene of representation as such. Not even the most rigid hierarchy will ever attempt to suppress the fundamental equality of all before language; the deification of monarchs is nowhere total. The human scene of representation imposes on hierarchical inequality an implicit moral constraint.

The Mosaic revelation gave Judaic moral reflection a theological foundation whose absence would always be felt in the Greek philosophers' attempts to constitute, on the level of the polis or on that of personal relations, an ideal ethic. Theology is the living reminder of the scene of representation as the origin of man; we could only replace theology by ontology if the personality of the center could be understood conceptually, if it could reveal itself without speaking. The later stages of moral reflection concern less the elaboration of this revelatory content than its separation from concrete ethics. The Decalogue illustrates a stage in this process of separation. The uniqueness and the nonfigurality of God are linked to injunctions not to kill, not to covet the goods of one's neighbor. But this link is still abstract; the articulation is lacking. Mosaic theology constructs in the Decalogue a general ethic that we should certainly attribute to a moral intuition, but which does not yet constitute a morality in the strong sense of the term.

An ethic maintains a social order; morality, on the contrary, is indifferent to this order. What we call morality is a vision of human relations derived exclusively from the scene of representation. This vision is first intuitive, or in other words, imaginary. Moral reflection is an attempt at conceptualization that succeeds or fails according to the intellectual tools and talent of its formulator. But at the basis of every conceptual elaboration of morality is the same intuitive kernel, grasped with more or less intensity and clarity. The moral intuition of the Gospels, and no doubt that of Jesus himself, is more developed than that of Hillel, but the basis of the intuition is the same. The scene of representation gives the example of a perfect reciprocity of exchange that morality prolongs into real relations. Because these relations are indeed real there is no a priori frontier between the affirmations of morality and those of ethics, both of which derive from the same scene. But the place of this scene in the two fundamental intuitions is different. The ethical, like the moral, is normative: it proceeds not from empirical observation, but from an intuition of order. But the ethical intuition is directed at human relations not exclusively around the scene of representation but in real society, that not of exchanges of words, but of exchanges of things. The origin of the ethical doctrine of the Decalogue, far from contradicting this affirmation, on the contrary confirms it. Moses announces his legislation as dictated by a divine voice; never will Jesus use this procedure. Because the scene itself cannot suffice as the model for an ethic, it can only be the place where this ethic is dictated. In the Mosaic legislation, God is at the limit an arbitrary authority-figure. If certain animals are classed as impure, this characterization is not a consequence of the nature of God but of previously existing socio-economic and ritual conditions He is called upon to guarantee. Ethical intuition does not exclude moral intuition, but it must depart from it in an essential way in order to imagine how men should live together in the world.

When morality extrapolates from the scene toward reality, it imposes an order on human relations. But this order is no longer a social order, only an interpersonal one. The rules of morality are addressed to the individual as a person bearing the scene of representation in himself and who is required to regulate his relationships with others according to the model of equality and reciprocity furnished by that scene. Thus morality affirms this scene to be the originary essence of man. Rabbinical Jewish morality recognizes this ontological priority. But it allows itself nonetheless to be confined to a corner of the ethical edifice by a wisdom that understands the necessity of a worldly order so that human relations, moral or not, can have a material chance of existing. This wisdom is denied by the "folly to the Greeks, scandal to the Jews" that Jesus communicated to the first Christians.

We are far better informed about Jesus's morality than about his theology. The theology of the Gospels includes too many posterior accretions, mostly post-Pauline, for us to be able to distinguish the original layer of his teaching. What is striking is precisely the absence of any clear testimony to an unforgettable theological innovation. Instead of a theological revelation from which one would extract, at first implicitly and then explicitly, a moral doctrine, here it is the moral doctrine which precedes the theology. Jesus situated himself at the most radical point of prophetism, as a preacher of a moral apocalypse whose "Kingdom of God" is exclusively characterized by a new quality of interpersonal relations. This predication brings nothing new on the theological plane. God remains the same; it is human life that is going to change.

A phrase like "the first will be the last" informs us as to the probable experiential source of this moral vision. It was the sight of a Jewish society whose great families were forced to grovel before the Roman conquerors that must have provided Jesus with the intuition that no worldly hierarchy, however "ethical," can maintain itself uncorrupted. The punctilious piety of the Pharisees that makes of the individual the guardian of communal tradition exemplified the futility of all differential practices. The spectacle of difference in a colonialized Jewish society inspires a vision of a world beyond social difference, ruled by universal reciprocity. In this purely moral vision of human relations each individual must impose peace in his interactions with his fellows. Because the social center is no longer operative, it is for each individual to become his own center in recognizing at the same time the centrality of the other. Such a vision cannot be conceived as emerging in revelatory fashion from a unique center. On the contrary, he who makes of it the matter of his teaching should do whatever he can to efface even the formal sign of centrality that the privilege of discourse confers upon him. The "good news" must spread from mouth to mouth as quickly as possible; it would hardly be fitting that he who first announced it should present himself as the beneficiary of divine election.

With Jesus' doctrine, in sum, the phenomenon of revelation appears outmoded. In the imminence of the final apocalypse, the worldly order becomes transparent to its opposite, the moral order of the Kingdom, where the differential hierarchy of "first" and "last" will be inverted before being abolished. The universal fraternity will have its contingent of expelled; here, as with the prophets, social resentment presages reversal. And it is no doubt this aspect of Jesus' program that brought him to the cross. But for his disciples, the negative revelation of resentment was entirely subsumed within the moral apocalypse of the master. What Jesus had seen through the mediation of the worldly order, his disciples saw henceforth through him alone.

No discussion of the role of Jesus can ignore the notion of messianic hope. The Jews awaited a king who would deliver them from the Romans; Jesus spiritualizes, or more precisely, moralizes, this hope. But what this historical reference makes us forget is the paradox—and not the simple inversion—inherent in the role of the moral Messiah. He who comes to abolish difference arrogates to himself by that very act a difference absolute because situated on a higher logical level. Thus he who preaches the most radical fraternity is elevated after his death infinitely above the ranks of his brothers.

The divinization of Jesus is the paradoxical yet inevitable consequence of the "good news" he preached. In revealing his vision of moral decentralization, Jesus found, no doubt despite himself, the secret of absolute centrality. This paradox does not trivialize his moral doctrine, but it allows us to see its limitations. It is useless and even pernicious to curse the incapacity of men to accede to the fraternal kingdom, as if Jesus' vision constituted a total and definitive anthropological truth. Morality can only realize itself in the form of an ethic, and this realization passes, in the West, through the model of self-centralization furnished by the crucified Christ.

The four Gospels are one in affirming that Jesus predicted his execution. It is not inconceivable that he even desired it; martyrdom was a recognized sign of prophetic authenticity. The prophet's posthumous glory had always "recuperated" his martyrdom as a demonstration of fidelity to God in the face of the exigencies of the social order. But however moralistic it may have been, prophetic teaching was always aimed at worldly goals, as the popular vision of the prophet predicting the future suggests. Present society kills the prophet, but a future society will recognize his truth; his martyrdom does not find its full sense in itself. In the case of Jesus, however, any ethical compromise with the worldly order is rejected; his kingdom is not of this world. The only conceivable worldly content of his prophecy—which lends verisimilitude to the Gospel story—is precisely his death. But as a result his martyrdom is *wholly* recuperated; it leads not to mere human reverence but to divinization. Jesus could scarcely have predicted for himself such a fate. It is more probable that the apocalyptic hope still so visible in the Epistles to the Thessalonians (around 50 A.D.) is a reflection of his last thinking on the subject: in the Kingdom of God, divinization would apply to all without exception, each human being henceforth constituting an absolute center.

The first Christians—those before Paul—were Jews who believed in the moral apocalypse announced by Jesus. The content of their faith must be deduced less from what we know explicitly about Jesus' doctrine than from the reality of that faith itself. For we know a single historical fact about Jesus: that he was crucified. If his disciples had taken him for the Messiah in the traditional sense of the term, his worldly failure would have sufficed to turn them away from him. Because, on the contrary, they began to venerate him as a divine being, they must have been sensitive to the "recuperation" that we have just described. The execution of the bringer of the good news, proof that the human order is incapable of receiving it, implies both that this order, essentially immoral, is on the edge of the apocalypse and that Jesus was separated from it by an absolute difference.

In order for the disciples to continue to live in a world whose communal values have been discredited, they were obliged to create their own community around the moral doctrine of their master. Jesus preached an absolute reciprocity, but the only reciprocity practicable for the Christians was that mediated by his word. The promulgation of the moral apocalypse presupposed between Jesus and his adherents the same Mosaic, legislative distance that Matthew figures in the Sermon on the Mount. But once Jesus was dead, his word, instead of becoming the common property of all, became even more exclusively his. The Christian community could not found an ethic of reciprocity on this word without installing Jesus in its center as a universal mediator.

All this, it should be recalled, we must derive not from the doctrines of the first Christians, but from the mere fact of their existence. They are the proof that the moral revelation had "taken." And such is the radical simplicity of the founding anthropological truth of Christianity that we can deduce all its essential traits from this simple definition: a moral revelation that has "taken." But this "taking" only assumes its historical permanence from the conversion of Paul. It is the Pauline revelation that removes Christianity from its primitive state of an awaiting, mediated by the word of the master, of the imminent moral apocalypse.

Fidelity to Jesus signified the transcendence of the Law, but because Jesus had no doubt never taught its abandonment but only its "fulfillment," his followers did not believe they should separate this fulfillment from the Law itself. Their liberation was a passage through the Law to morality that did not annul, in principle at least, its practices, but which filled them with a moral sense. The moral revelation of Jesus, directed at the individual in his interactions with others, appeared no more to require the rejection of these observances than it required refusal to pay taxes to the Romans.

It was Paul who understood the essential opposition between the worship of Christ and any communal ethical practice. The rigor of the ethical Law makes man conscious of an inadequacy from which only Christ's mediation can save him. Paul understood as well that the interpersonal morality of Jesus, whose rigor was to that of the Law as the absolute to the relative, could not be enforced as such, that the decentralized reciprocity of human equals must be subordinated to the central equivalence between deity and victim.

The moral revelation decentralizes the scene of representation. "Love thy neighbor" defines the relations of men in such a way as to ignore the center, whose power dissolves as desire is turned from it. God plays in this system an essentially proleptic role; the promise of the Kingdom gives men the courage to realize it themselves on earth. What appears here for the first time is the ontological priority of the ethical, in its pure, moral, state, over the theological. The role of "God the Father" is not eliminated, but it is relegated to maintaining the promise of reciprocity in human relations. The revelation of the divine center, in other words, had only served to maintain men in relative peace so long as they did not yet know the "good news" that they could do without it. For in the Kingdom of God, all revelation would have already taken place; God will realize his promise by eliminating his external power over man. God will thus be no more than a memory; but this memory of the promise fulfilled will inhabit all men. For the apocalyptic leap will not eliminate past history; universal fraternity will always recall the divine guarantee without which it could never have constituted itself.

He who announces this word announces the existence of the revelatory center in all men, even if the word comes only from him. The promise of God announced by a man is proof that divinity is as much that of man as of God, for the sole function of God is henceforth to guarantee this promise. This guarantee will be provided not by a God external to man, but by a God who speaks within man. The divinization of Christ is the recognition that all revelation originates in an internalized scene of representation that defines both the absolutely human and the absolutely other constituted by its sacred center. The notion of moral revelation does not appear to carry with it all of Christian theology; but this is merely because in its abstraction the notion of "morality" dissimulates its anthropological foundation. The ideal of moral reciprocity is the telos of the history that begins with the originary scene of representation. And the revelation of this telos cannot be attributed to God revealing himself to man, but must come from a man who has understood in himself the promise that expressed itself in God.

For Paul Jesus is not the propounder of a moral doctrine, but the crucified Christ faith in whom will liberate us from sin. Must we say then that he understood nothing of Jesus' message? But his experience on the road to Damascus proves the contrary. Saul's conversion is a fact, just as is his revelatory experience. Even if the words exchanged between him and Jesus are an invention of the author, this fact resists criticism. Saul persecuted the Christians; his experience has transformed this persecution into a proof of the divinity of Christ. "Why do you persecute me?" is the very substance of this proof.

To persecute is to put oneself in the wrong. In refusing to admit the primacy of the moral, the Law puts itself in the wrong. Instead of nourishing itself wisely from morality, the Law shows itself to be irreconcilable with it. The persecutor's rage designates him as a sectarian struggling in vain to defend a partial revelation against a greater one. The greatness of the moral doctrine in the mouth of the living Jesus has been transformed among the early Christians into the presence of the dead Christ. That Jesus continues to appear to them is the result of his word; but this word is now understood as inseparable from his person, with which it is fused. The theology of the Word, which John will later formulate, is realized in fact in the first Christian church.

What Paul's revelation teaches him is that to combat this doctrine is to persecute a *person*. That this person comes to affirm this to him in a revelatory experience is certain proof of his divinity. But this personal divinity can henceforth be recognized as speaking in Paul himself, something that Moses could never have said of his God. Once the "external" revelation has taken place, every new revelation will come from within; revelatory experience proper will no longer be necessary. Inspired prophecy will play only a marginal role in the evolution of the Christian Church. The fathers of the church are more rabbis than prophets; they are the interpreters of a revelation already accomplished.

"Why do you persecute me?" is a leading question; it presupposes persecution without affirming it, as in the old routine where one man asks the other if he is still beating his wife. Jesus' question does not seek an answer, and it receives none in the text. Paul's confession is indirect, nonthematic; if the admission of guilt had not already been made within himself, the experience would never have taken place. What is revealed here is not the persecution itself, but the centrality of its victim. To persecute Jesus is to create the conditions for a dialogue with him. To desire to expel him is to insure his presence, and thereby to reveal that in persecuting him one in fact desired this presence. The centrality of the God-person is inexpugnable.

The answer to Paul's question "Who are you, Lord?" is "I am Jesus whom you are persecuting." God is he whom one refuses, whom one wishes to extirpate. With Paul, Jesus is converted definitively into Christ; the persecuted man becomes God, or rather already was God. Jesus preached the abolition of the unique center; but Paul saw that in an imperfect world this could only be accomplished in each individual through the mediation of this center. In Jesus' moral vision, each would be a sacred center for the other; for Paul, Christ alone maintains the link between humanity and divine centrality. This theological certitude is no denial of Jesus' moral doctrine; on the contrary, it is a necessary procondition for its elaboration in the Gospels. Christian morality is wholly contained in the equation of the sacred center with the Word, for it is with the Word—with language—that man came into being on the originary scene of representation.

IV
EVALUATIONS

CHRIST'S DEATH AND THE PROPHETIC CRITIQUE OF SACRIFICE

Raymond Schwager, S.J.
University of Innsbruck

ABSTRACT

René Girard has been criticized for misunderstanding the true nature of the sacrifice of the cross. But the concept of sacrifice has not been very clear either in theological tradition or in the exegetical discussions of today. Girard's thought on the other hand contributes greatly to clarifying this issue, because it agrees perfectly with a dramatic interpretation of revelation in Jesus Christ, as inspired by the "Theodramatik" of H. U. von Balthasar. Thus we gain a conception of sacrifice which incorporates the actions of men (liars, false judges, murderers), the behavior of Jesus himself (obedience towards the Father, non-violence towards the authors of violence, identification with the victims of violence) and the agency of the heavenly Father (abandonment of his Son to the action of men = divine wrath, and resurrection = final victory over lies and violence). Girard's thought helps us to discover the logic connecting isolated narratives.

Prophetic criticism often voices the accusation of idolatry, and it uncovers much latent violence in the chequered world of the various religions. Although René Girard does not intend to be a prophet, the issues of religious mass-deception and of violence play a decisive role in his thought. He interprets the sacrifices of archaic societies (i.e. societies without a centralized state authority) as the ritually concealed expulsion of a scapegoat. People hadn't mastered their aggressions through genuine reconciliation, but had transferred them onto chance objects which they sacralized (i.e. they made them into idols). This process was repeated regularly in sacrifices. The sacrificial rites had a positive function insofar as they contributed to the pacification of human society, but they were rooted nevertheless in a collective self-deception.

According to Girard, the hidden mechanism of sacrifice has been fully uncovered in one place only: in the fate of Jesus Christ. As in the sacrifices of primitive societies, the crucifixion of Jesus consisted in an expulsion, but this time it was no longer possible to conceal the truth of what had happened. For this reason, the Old Testament with its tendencies to criticize sacrifice, and especially the New Testament, are for Girard revelation in the proper sense, and he proposes a consistent "non-sacrificial interpretation" of the Gospel texts (1978a203–246). Since in the death of Christ, the hidden sacrificial mechanism was laid bare and thereby robbed of its power, any interpretation of Christianity as a religion of sacrifice would imply a regression to Old Testament or even pagan notions (246–285).

This understanding of the Gospels has met with sometimes firm resistance in theological circles.[1] Girard is accused of an intellectualist restriction of revelation (a new gnosticism), and of tending to reduce Christian faith to a knowledge of social process. Since he expressly believes in the true divinity and humanity of Christ, the working of the Holy Spirit in history, and even the virgin birth, and since he attributes central importance to Christ's cross and salvific activity, such broad-sweeping criticism rules itself out of court. More serious are the reservations of those who see his "non-sacrificial interpretation" of the Gospels as leading to a misunderstanding of the true dimensions of Christ's death. N. Hoffmann for instance maintains that the traditional faith of the Church that Christ died representatively for sinners, although not eliminated, is modified by Girard's abandonment of the idea of satisfaction. Representation no longer takes place "between the sinners and the God who is to be reconciled, but—consistent with the psychoanalytic idea of a collective transference of stored-up aggression onto an individual—between the sinners and the scapegoat (even if this is God himself in the last analysis)" (41). H. U. v. Balthasar, who finds a lot that is positive in Girard's thought, also criticizes the abandonment of the traditional understanding of Jesus' death as a sacrifice of atonement (1980b:288). For Balthasar, sins are not "ontic entities which can be simply transferred from one to another" (1980a:185), but acts of human freedom for which someone must answer before God, and this is what Christ has done representatively for us. A. Schenker's argument against Girard comes from a different standpoint, namely, from the Old Testament understanding of sacrifice. He maintains that Israel's sacrificial rites did not involve any transference of punishment onto sacrificial animals: the rite of the scapegoat mentioned in the Old Testament was not a sacrificial rite, and for this reason it does not provide a model for understanding the death of Christ (118f.).[2]

To consider these summarily presented objections, we will have to examine discussions within contemporary exegesis, since these objections rely partially on suppositions which are strongly questioned today. Influential voices within historical-critical exegesis are raised against some of the traditional theological interpretations of the death of Christ. They distinguish two doctrines of salvation or two soteriologies in the New Testament writings. Jesus himself promised his hearers the forgiveness of their sins through the message of the coming reign of God (eschatological soteriology). The doctrine of redemption whereby people's sins are forgiven only through the expiatory death on the cross (staurological soteriology) is to be distinguished from the former. "The opinion is widely held in contemporary critical exegesis that Jesus did not publicly proclaim such an expiatory doctrine of redemption before his Resurrection, and could hardly have thought in this manner. He himself had proclaimed a different type of salvation doctrine, an 'eschatological soteriology'" (Schurmann: 11). Once the problem is seen in this context, it becomes clear that the discussion of Girard's interpretation of the cross will have to begin from a broader basis, and so it is necessary to examine God's salvific activity in the whole life and fate of Jesus.

1.) The Gathering of the People and the Rival Gathering

Jesus proclaims the imminence of God's reign and even claims that this reign is emergent in his own proclamation and healing activity. His words present God and his activity in a new light and demand from the hearers a new way of behaving. He wants to lead them to love their enemies, instead of responding to them with violence (Mt 5:38–47); he justifies this exacting demand by saying: "You therefore must be perfect as your heavenly Father is perfect" (Mt 5:48). Through their rejection of violence and their love of their enemies, people are to become perfect as God is perfect, and thereby show him to be a God who rejects violence and loves even his own enemies.

Jesus makes God's loving attitude towards sinners markedly visible in his own behavior. He visits God's enemies, the tax-gatherers and sinners, he eats with them, and provokes the objections of the teachers of the law (Scribes). He defends himself against these objections with parables which tell how God seeks out the lost and the sinner. In this way, by mirroring God's attitude to sinners in his own behavior towards objectionable people (Jeremias, 1965: 132; Schweizer: 32), he reveals how God loves his enemies, how in his goodness and in his concern for their salvation, he goes out of his way to meet them. "Through his parables, Jesus wants his hearers to understand that this action of God's has taken place now and here for these sinners at the table, and that they, the hearers, are expected to share in the joy of reunion, to rejoice for the joy of God and so say their yes to Jesus' table fellowship with the lost, with whom he celebrates God's joy" (Linnemann: 78).

Jesus is able to speak and act in this way because he relates to

God in a new way and dares to address him as "Abba" (cf. Mk 14:36). This unique (Jeremias, 1966: 33–67) and intimate form of address reveals that God has come close to him as Father and has revealed everything to him (cf. Mt 3:13–17; 11:25–28). "Clearly the uniqueness of Jesus' message and practice has its source in the Abba-experience" (Schillebeeckx: 236). And for this reason, Jesus understands himself to be the true and legitimate interpreter and "exegete" of the divine will (cf. Jn 1:18).

According to his message, the forgiving Father dismisses the sinner's history of guilt as irrelevant from the start. "However a person stands before God, repentant or unrepentant, God forgives him unconditionally, *without presuppositions*" (Merklein: 204). His forgiveness *"precedes the repentance, both temporally and logically,"* as H. Merklein said in summarizing Jesus' proclamation. He "offers sinners salvation *before* they do penance" (Jeremias, 1971: 173). This doesn't mean that repentance is superfluous. It is no longer a condition which must precede God's willingness to forgive, but follows from it, as is clear from the parable of the merciless debtor (Mt 18:23–35). The debtor who cannot pay is released from the whole debt out of the sheer goodness of the master, and without having to meet any conditions. Linked to this gift however is the expectation that it would touch the heart of the released debtor and move him to treat his fellows in like manner. But when this expectation is disappointed, and the servant who received such a great favor does not himself act generously, he is called back and saddled again with the debt from which he had been absolved. The master's willingness to forgive is unconditional in the sense that it has no antecedent conditions; it does have a consequent condition: the favored servant is expected to behave in a new way.

Jesus addresses his message of God's love of his enemies and God's unlimited willingness to forgive not merely to individuals. He seeks the scattered and harrassed people (Mt 9:36) in order to gather them as the new people of God (Lk 11:23). His healings of the sick serve "to restore the people of God, among whom none can be sick in the eschatological time of salvation" (Lohfink, 1982b:23). His appointment of the twelve is a "prophetic sign-action" for the "gathering of Israel to the eschatological community of salvation" (20). As G. Lohfink clearly shows, the double petition of the Our Father that God's name be hallowed and his kingdom come is to be understood in the light of Ezk 36:22–24 as a petition for the new gathering. "'Hallowed be thy name'—that means nothing other than: 'gather and renew your people! Let it become again a true people of God'" (27).[3]

Jesus' message of the antecedent goodness of the heavenly Father, and his desire in his name to gather the scattered people to be the true people of God, these two elements set the frame of reference for understanding the subsequent events in the life and fate of the Son. They challenge all those interpretations of the cross which are derived from other assumptions on the basis of which it is claimed that the expiatory death was necessitated by the justice of God. Divine dignity is presumed to have required that a goodness be demonstrated which was consistent with the demands of justice. The concern to harmonize love with principles of justice (which ones?) was not part of Jesus' proclamation (cf. Mt 9:9–13; 12:1–8; 13:12, 1–8; 13:12; 20:1–16; Lk 15:1–32). Those exegetes who interpret his message of the kingdom as a genuine message of salvation (eschatological soteriology) are correct in this (Vögtle: 36–46; Fiedler). If his cross is nonetheless necessary, then it must be for a different reason.

Jesus' desire to arouse a similar goodness in people through his proclamation of God's goodness runs up against a radically contrary desire. Even the message of limitless love fails in the end to grasp the human heart. Looking back on his proclamation, he had to concede:

"O Jerusalem, Jerusalem, killing the prophets and stoning those who are sent to you! How often *would I* have *gathered* your children together as a hen gathers her brood under her wings, and *you would not!*" (Mt 23:37)

The desire to gather is frustrated by a contrary desire, and the efforts to unite people provoke a unification of a different kind. "We see how another diametrically opposed gathering takes place in opposition to Jesus' initiative in gathering Israel to be God's new society. All those who previously were divided among themselves unite to put an end to Jesus" (Lohfink, 1982a: 126).

2.) The Trial as a Scapegoat Mechanism

Jesus announces that the opposition to his message will be judged harshly, and he reveals that the unlimited goodness of the heavenly Father is no harmless or indifferent affair. People who do not open themselves to this message have no other possibility of salvation. They exclude themselves from the community of life and from his Father's kingdom. They condemn themselves to ultimate isolation and to hell. Before this judgment is realized, another curious one takes place. We see how he who so clearly proclaimed judgment is himself brought to judgment, faced with the most serious accusation, condemned and executed. What is taking place in this extraordinary trial where the one who claims to be the coming divine judge (Mk 14:62) is condemned by a religious authority acting in the name of God's law, and with the cooperation of the political authority is sent to a criminal's death? It is clear from the Easter experience that an innocent person, in fact the only truly innocent one, had been condemned. In that light, the whole trial appears as a fundamental lie. Behind the deceptive appearance of law a very different kind of process is at work. What kind of process is this?

Already during his public ministry, Jesus had subjected the opposition which had sabotaged his message to a searching diagnosis. According to John's Gospel, he radically challenges the self-interpretation of his opponents. They consider themselves to be Abraham's children, and want God alone to be their father (Jn 8:30–41). But on the evidence of their behavior Jesus discovers a very different ancestry:

> "You are of your father the *devil*, and your will is to do your father's desires. He was a *murderer* from the beginning, and has nothing to do with the truth, because there is no truth in him. When he lies, he speaks according to his own nature, for he is a *liar* and the father of lies." (Jn 8:44)

The persistent accusation which Jesus raises against his opponents has three distinct elements. Their self-interpretation is false, because 1) they have a satanic spirit, with its tendencies 2) to murder, and 3) to lie.[4]

Even if the actual words of the scathing speech of John's Gospel are not from the earthly Jesus, their content is consistent with the judgmental language of the synoptic Gospels. Jesus shows the Pharisees to be hypocrites (Mt 23:13, 15, 23, 25, 27, 29), and convicts them of being "sons of the murderers of the prophets," who complete the work of their ancestors, and so are faced with the threat of hell (Mt 23:29–33). His description of their attitude contains here also the three elements of the 1) lying, 2) murderous, 3) satanic spirit.

The most profound diagnosis of human hardening is found in the parable of the evil vine-growers (Mk 12:1–12). After his servants had been killed, the vineyard owner, out of an incomprehensible goodness, risks even his beloved son, and so corresponds exactly to God's love of his enemies as Jesus had proclaimed it. In contrast with the patience of the vineyard owner is the constant bad will of the vine-growers, who react with hostility, though without any apparent reason, to all the initiatives of their master. When the beloved son is sent, they finally betray the reason for their muderous action. All conspire together against him, and they say to one another:

> "This is the heir; come, let us kill him, and the inheritance will be ours." (Mk 12:7)

They reveal themselves to be the rivals of the vineyard owner and want to grab their master's property by murdering the son and heir. Since in this parable the owner is meant to be God himself, the vine-growers commit "the original sin of mimesis, of the desire to want to be like God, of enmity against God, which leads to violence (cf. Gen 3–4)" (Pesch: 106).

The synoptic Gospels make it quite clear in this parable that the unbelief confronting his proclamation of the kingdom does not arise from a mere lack of interest in God. A profound rivalry lies behind it. Jesus' opponents, the evil vine-growers, want to take for themselves what belongs to him as beloved son of the Father, and what he was even prepared to share with them. Here it is evident that the violence is ultimately not only directed against people. It is directed against the greatest rival, against God himself in his beloved Son (cf. Jn 8:58f; 10:30f., 38f) in the desire to appropriate what belongs to them both. The doers of violence no longer understand their life as gift, but want to possess it absolutely. They themselves want to be heirs, and so turn against the one who reminds them that they have to thank another for everything they have. Their murderous spirit has a truly satanic dimension and is identical with unbelief. The original sin of mimesis, of rivalry with God, is described under both these aspects.

The scathing diagnosis of the hardening of human hearts is validated in what happens to Jesus himself. He is accused of blasphemy (Mk 14:64) and according to John's Gospel, this accusation is meant in the most radical sense. Merely a man, he had made himself out to be God (Jn 10:33; 19:7), something which is an essential characteristic of Satan. Now all that is applied to him which he had uncovered in his opponents. He had shown their sin to be due to 1) their satanic spirit, 2) in lying, 3) and murder, and he himself is accused of 1) having a satanic spirit, 2) he is condemned by the lies of perjured witnesses, and 3) violently executed.

What then is the truth about the trial of Jesus? A confederacy of hostile groups emerges. At first the Pharisees (Scribes) appear as his opponents (Mk 2:6, 16, 24). The highpriests who are Sadducees, and the Elders (Mt 21:15) join them after the clearing of the temple. Herod, who is drawn into the affair by Pilate, mocks Jesus, but on this occasion becomes a friend of the Roman (Lk 23:6–12). Finally, the people (or a group of Zealots) demand the release of Barabbas, a Zealot, instead of Jesus. His own friends betray and abandon him, and Pilate gives in to public pressure out of political expediency. All allow themselves to be drawn in, and line up together against him. From the perspective of salvation-history, the New Testament writings interpret this procedure as a universal event, although concretely only a limited number of Jews and Gentiles are involved. The *whole* Council *in unison* condemns Jesus (Mk 15:1; Mt 17:11), and the *whole* people demands his crucifixion (Mt 27:22, 25). According to John's Gospel, no actual trial ever takes place, but everything occurs in the form of a great conspiracy into which all are drawn through contagion and fear of one another. Most explicit is the Acts of the Apostles, according to which the persecuted primitive community reflects on the fate of their Lord, and in the light of Psalm 2 and with reference to the new friendship between Herod and Pilate, endows it with the most universal meaning:

"Truly in this city there were *gathered together against* thy holy servant Jesus, whom thou didst anoint, both *Herod and Pontius Pilate, with the Gentiles and the peoples of Israel,* to do whatever thy hand and thy plan had predestined to take place." (Acs 4:27)

Christ's trial appears as a ganging together of all against one, as an alliance of the sinners against the sinless one, and as a rival movement to the gathering which Jesus wanted to initiate in the name of his heavenly Father. Exactly that which he had discovered in his opponents is done to him by this collusion: the conspiring sinners make him a victim of their *lies* and *violence,* and accuse him of being *satanic.*

Ultimately all those elements which Girard in his ethnological and anthropological analyses identified and summarized as the scapegoat mechanism are at play in the condemnation of Jesus (the ganging together of all against one, the violent discharge, self-deception, transference of guilt onto the victim of collective violence). The truth of that trial in which the beloved Son who had claimed to be judge is himself judged, can rightly be characterized as a scapegoat mechanism (Schwager, 1978: 189–205), whereby it must be noted as usual in theology, that the use of language is analogous. In contrast to the purely sociological mechanism, there is in what happens to Jesus a universal process at work, which is directed not against some accidental victim, but intentionally against one who proclaims a God of unconditional love of enemies, and against one who in a unique way understands himself as Son of this God and Father. As such he does not allow himself to be integrated into his opponents' system of lies and to be interiorly conquered by them. He can no longer be sacralized, but must be "satanized," and so is able to fully reveal his hidden truth at Easter.

3.) One for All

Does not the interpretation of the death of Jesus sketched here confirm the reservations of H. U. v. Balthasar and N. Hoffman, who maintain that Girard sees only a representation between Jesus and sinners, and that the salvation event between him and the Father is overlooked? According to O. Hofius, not only is this suspicion warranted, but the above mentioned must be understood differently on the basis of explicit Pauline statements. For Paul it is simply unthinkable that sinners could load their misdeeds onto another, for this would mean that they could distance themselves from their sins. The contrary is the case: "When Paul characterizes Jesus' death on the cross as the death of all, this presumes that identification had taken place. God had identified Christ with the sinner and the sinner with Christ" (39). Here it is not the people who have made Jesus to be sin and satan, there can be no mention here of a scapegoat mechanism, God himself has identified his Son with sinners.

The central idea that sinners alone cannot distance themselves from their misdeeds is fully correct. The synoptic Gospels which we have followed mostly up to now show very markedly in the case of Judas that one who betrays another and makes him a victim is in no way freed from his crime thereby. What he does to the other pursues him and falls back on his own head (cf. Ps 7). But does it follow from this that God had identified Christ with sinners? For a reliable answer we must orient ourselves on what in fact happens to Jesus, and not on isolated biblical passages, and investigate how he reacts to the hostility of the people.

Jesus does not respond with aggression to the violence of his opponents. He accepts interiorly, out of obedience to his Father, the difficult lot which falls to him. He acts in fidelity to his own message of the love of enemies, with the result that his proclamation does not remain an empty word, but becomes in him an historical act. Through his non-violent behavior in the face of hostile assault, he reveals with ultimate clarity that his Father is really a God of the love of enemies. In his name, he even rejects the more subtle forms of aggression:

> When he was reviled, he did not revile in return; when he suffered, he did not threaten; but he trusted to him who judges justly. He himself bore our sins in his body on the tree, that we might die to sin and live to righteousness. (1 Pt 2:22–24)

The First Letter of Peter expressly draws a connection between Christ's non-violent behavior, and his carrying of sins. In both he shows his fundamental decision, also in view of the perjurous human trial, to leave judgment in God's hands and not to seek justice for himself. But he does not remain passive. He appeals to his Father for these people (Jn 17:9–19; Heb 4:14–5:10). He prays for forgiveness for his deadly opponents out of love for his enemies (Lk 23:34), and in his intercession, he so identifies himself with them in their need for salvation that he draws them all to himself and gathers them anew from the cross:

> "And I, when I am lifted up from the earth, will draw all men to myself." (Jn 12:32)

The assertion of Jesus' identification with sinners, which for Hofius is central, is also acceptable from the perspective followed here, although it must be interpreted in a more differentiated manner. According to Girard, the Gospels say that "Christ is henceforth a victim in place of everyone else" (1982: 282). All ally themselves against him as the Lord's

Anointed, and make him a victim. It is precisely as victim that he intercedes for his enemies, and he identifies himself with them insofar as they are harmed by evil. As a result, people find themselves simultaneously in two camps. As *sinners* they turn against the crucified one, as *victims* of their own and others' misdeeds, they are accepted into a new community of prayer and hope before God, by him whom they have hurt. The cross effects a division within persons.

The critical difference from Hofius's position lies in the question whether one may say without distinction that God has identified sinners with the crucified Christ, or whether one does not more adequately express the truth of the situation by saying more precisely that Jesus on the cross identified himself as *victim* with all the others as *victims*. The reasons which clearly speak for this latter interpretation are briefly:

1.) In the parable of the evil vine-growers, the "beloved son" stands in line of succession to his father's servants who had been persecuted before him. He shares their fate, but in no way does he stand on the same side as his enemies, the evil vine-growers.

2.) The Old Testament figures who are taken to be prototypes of Christ are for the most part victims of others' misdeeds (Abel, the persecuted prophets and the righteous, the servant of God, the poor, the paschal lamb,[5] etc.). Christ's continuity with his "precursors" is understood from the point of view of their sufferings and their being victims (cf. Heb 11:36–12:3).

3.) The primitive community, which speaks in its prayer of the universal alliance of Jews and Gentiles against the Anointed of the Lord, sees the latter in the light of the persecuted of the Old Testament, and includes itself in the line of the persecuted (Acs 4:23–31). From this standpoint, it dares to make this generalization (*All* people against the Anointed one), and only in this context is the generalization intelligible. If it is true that the crucified Lord identifies himself with all victims, then anyone who injures another turns against Jesus himself. And since everyone is a sinner, all are against him; but he is always there where a person is a victim of injury.

4.) Saul, who rages "with threats and murder against the Lord's disciples," discovers on the way to Damascus that the glorified Lord identifies himself with his disciples. The one who speaks from heaven characterizes himself as persecuted, and so shows himself to be one with his disciples precisely in this respect (Acs 9:1–5).

5.) In the great judgment speech of Matthew's Gospel, the heavenly judge declares that whatever was done or not done to the "least," to the victims of others' deeds, was done or not done to him. But he will have nothing to do with the evil-doers as evil-doers, and he drives them from him (Mt 25:31–46) (Barthélemy: 212).

6.) On the cross, Jesus pleads to God to forgive his enemies and justifies his petition with the reason that "they know not what they do" (Lk 23:34). Since they don't know, they do not comprehend their criminal deed, and so are victims of their own crime. Jesus shows himself to be identified with them in this respect, and prays to God for them.

7.) If Christ had identified himself with sinners in every respect, then he would also have been at one with them in their sin. He would have been in solidarity with them in their rejection of his Father's message, and in their crime against himself. The difference between his sinlessness and their sinning would have disappeared. In a subtle way, through identification with their violence against him, he would even have crucified himself.

8.) It would remain unintelligible why sinners are still in need of conversion and faith in order to be saved by Christ, if God had already totally identified them with him at the crucifixion. The identity would have been already complete but it would have been the unity of a mixture of good and evil.

9.) The interpretation offered here is fully consistent with the Pauline statement on which Hofius relies for his global assertion: "One has died for all; therefore all have died"(2 Cor 5:14). Dead through crucifixion, Jesus is a victim of other's misdeeds. Those who have died with him, therefore, must also be understood as victims. This is exactly what Paul says when he talks about sin having killed him (Rm 7:11). All who kill Christ, sin, and so kill themselves. However, because Christ on the cross draws them to himself, they do not remain for ever in this state of self-destruction, but having died once and for all with him, they have found in him the hope of new life.[6]

The reasons indicated should show that the reality of the cross is adequately represented only if one speaks in a differentiated manner of Christ's identification with sinners, insofar as they are victims.[7] It follows that the analysis of the trial as a "scapegoat mechanism" outlined above remains valid. Also, those reservations are found to be unwarranted which would maintain that this interpretation ignores the salvation event between the crucified Jesus and his Father, since Jesus' obedience to his Father and his representation and intercession for sinners are decisive also in this interpretation. But what about Christ's sacrificial act? Does not Girard expressly reject a sacrificial interpretation of the Gospels, even though several biblical texts (especially in the Letter to the Hebrews) and the whole Christian tradition clearly understand Christ's death as sacrifice?

The Death on the Cross as Sacrifice

It is undeniable that Girard's first comments on the Letter to the Hebrews, and his sweeping criticism, laid the ground for several misunderstandings (1978a: 251–54). But in *Le Bouc émissaire* he is more differentiated in his assessment of this New Testament document and its theology of sacrifice (279), and further clarification is to be expected from him. But it is equally undeniable that very diverse images associated with the word "sacrifice" have become widespread in Christian tradition, and that these have sometimes led to almost perverse notions, as for instance in the post-Tridentine theories of the sacrifice of the Mass. Over-reactions are therefore very understandable. On the other hand, every undifferentiated appeal to tradition is faced with the question whether it remains bound up with very equivocal notions. It seems to me that theological clarification is required in this area, whereby the following aspects would have to be taken into consideration.

It was not because divine justice unconditionally demanded a sacrifice of atonement that Christ's death on the cross was necessary. For the salvation of men and women however it was unavoidable, because the message of incomprehensible goodness had foundered on hardened hearts, and because love which is not accepted cannot bring its healing and saving power into effect.

The rejection of Jesus necessitated some step beyond the proclamation of the Kingdom-message. In contrast to Vögtle and Fiedler (60-63; 277-80), it was not necessary that Jesus "revise" or even "disavow" his original message in order to reveal the necessity of his death. The beloved Son's representative death was the fruit of a divine consistency which despite human obduracy maintained the unconditional offer of salvation, and in fact realised it in a new way without doing violence to human freedom. It was precisely from the kernel of the Kingdom-proclamation, from the message of God's love of enemies, that Jesus responded to rejection and to the alliance of his enemies against him. These did not succeed in freeing themselves from their own sins by their collusion and by the transference of their own evil desires, but they did manage to draw the sinless one who offered no resistance on this level into their own dark world. He whom they wanted to get rid of entered fully into their own world, and there in the darkness, in that godless place, in the realm of hardened hearts, he obeyed, and through his obedience and his interceeding love opened anew the way to the Father out of the night of impenitence.

Christ's death is something very different from what Girard describes as sacrifice in the context of "primitive societies" (i.e. societies without centralized state authority), and to this extent, his non-sacrificial interpretation of the Gospels is justified. Christ's self-offering has nothing in common with that process whereby those sacrificing unconsciously offload their collective aggression onto some victim. What the opponents of Jesus did in ganging up on him, rejecting him, and in making him a victim by crucifying him, corresponds much more closely to this collective mechanism. In this sense, one would have to say that Christ's murderers had offered a sacrifice in killing him. The Christian Tradition never said any such thing however, but always characterized Christ's self-offering as a sacrifice. This manner of speaking presumes that "sacrifice" is to be understood as something very different from the mechanism which Girard analyses in "primitive" societies. The new meaning of sacrifice emerged above all because in the course of the Old Testament, the *notion* of sacrifice (not the hidden sacrifice-*mechanism*) was progressively linked to the idea of obedience (Gen 22:1–19; 1 Sam 15:22; Is 1:11–17; Am 5:22–25; Ps 40:7–9; 51:18f; 69:31f). On the basis of this new understanding, it is necessary to ask anew what precisely is meant when Christ's offering is called a sacrifice. The following elements will have to be considered:

1.) Jesus does not allow himself to be infected in the least by the aggression of his opponents, and so demonstrates his unique divine origin. In *obedience* to his Father and in *non-violent love*, he allows himself to be persecuted and to be drawn into the world of darkness without himself interiorly succumbing to it.

2.) He *identifies* himself with his enemies insofar as they themselves are *victims* of evil, with the result that they are no longer alone in their isolation and inner need of salvation. He joins them as a brother who suffers through the same or rather a deeper darkness, and he is able to help them because he remains obedient in the power of his divine mission, even in that godless place.

3.) Along with his own need, he includes in his *intercession* to God the need of all his enemies whom he wishes to make his brothers. For them as for himself, he begs for the life-giving Spirit, who in his death and resurrection breaks forth out of the dark human world and at the same time irrupts into it.

4.) The universal *sending* of the Spirit at Pentecost leads to the conversion of sinners. It becomes possible to distinguish one's own projections from God's action, to separate the true sacrifice from false notions of sacrifice, and to free the revelation of divine love from confusion with the all too human ideas of justice and retribution. It follows that Christ's death can be correctly called a sacrifice, if this is understood to mean an offering which includes the following elements: 1) obedience to the Father as willingness to be persecuted even to the point of death; 2) the identification with all persons who find themselves in similar situations and who are victims of evil; 3) intercession for his brothers and sisters before God, an intercession which is essentially linked to that obedience which led to being rejected and being killed. This free offering (sacrifice) calls to conversion, and within the history of salvation, the Holy Spirit who makes the conversion possible, flows from this self-offering.

This brings us finally to a conclusion. We did not find any falsification of the biblical message through the new theory of the scapegoat mechanism. Girard's magnificent attempt to bring the human sciences again into contact with the biblical writings does not demand "too high a price" as some maintain, but a real contribution is made to distinguishing the uniqueness of Christ's "sacrificial death" from other sacrifices. The new analyses help us to grasp the internal dramatic logic which lies behind the Gospel narratives. They contribute to resolving the apparent contradiction between the Kingdom message and the doctrine of redemption through the cross, and they urgently point to the great danger of projecting the darkness in one's own heart onto other people and ultimately onto God. In this way they aid the correct discernment between good and evil.

Translated by Patrick Riordan, S.J.

NOTES

1. P. Valadier, who is particularly hard in his criticism, concedes that Girard's interpretation of individual biblical stories is exceptionally good (260, n. 109).

2. A similar argumentation is to be found in K. Kornfeld, "QDS und Gottesrecht im Alten Testament." This criticism is based on the misunderstanding that according to Girard the transference takes place on the level of conscious *notions* of sacrifice. Foundational for his theory however is that the conscious notions of sacrifice are clearly distinguished from the hidden *mechanism* of sacrifice. For the debate with Schenker, cf. Schwager (1983).

3. cf. also R. Schwager (1978:125–129) and Jeremias: "We must point this out quite precisely: The only meaning of the entire efficacy of Jesus is in bringing together the finite (*endzeitlichen*) people of God" (1971:107).

4. These and similar words of the Gospels often served—mistakenly—as justification for Anti-semitism. According to John's Gospel, Satan is not merely father of the Jews but prince of the world. Paul, who also describes sin as lie and violence, strongly emphasizes that both Jews and Greeks are in its power (Rm 3:9–18). And so the accusation against the Jews serves to affirm that the chosen people are not any better than the others. As the chosen, Christians must therefore refer Jesus' accusations to themselves, and not judge others.

5. In reference to the paschal lamb, it must be noted: "Why does Israel, which is the victim, need a substitutive victim to escape the punishment which is going to strike its executioner. It is to make it clear to Israel that if it escapes this punishment, it does not do so as Israel, but as victim. The blood of the pascal lamb which marks its doors manifests its present situation as victim, which is what motivates its coming liberation" (Barthélemy, *Dieu et son image:* 212f.).

6. The statement "For our sake he (God) made him to be sin who knew no sin . . ." is an abbreviation. In Rm 1:18–32 Paul expressly says that God's anger is revealed in that sinners are *given over to (paradidonai)* the lusts of their own hearts, and so to their own judgment. And precisely in this sense are we to understand the formulation that God has made his Son to be sin. He made him to be sin in the same way in which he allows his anger to fall on people. He *handed him over (paradidonai*, Rm 8:32) to their evil will and to their judgment. This point of view is supported by the Old Testament notion of sin which Paul is thinking of here. "The root ḥt' is the fundamental idea in the widespread Old Testament terminology for sin' . . . The idea is used clearly in the framework of the dynamic understanding of existence ('fate-operating

sphere of action'), and indeed with regard to the unity of offense and judgement as well as to the relationship of the community and the individual." (Art.ḥṭ'.THAT I, 546). Accordingly we have to link Paul's statement that God has made Christ to be sin with the idea that he has delivered him over to the intrinsic dynamic of offence and judgement.

7. "The leaders of his (Jesus') people will assume, in the name of all of Adam's descendants, the role of executioner. Jesus will assume, in the name of his people who are unconscious of the mystery of his destiny, the role of victim. By thus realizing the vocation of the servant, Jesus does not monopolize it. It is in the name of Israel that he assumes the destiny of all victims in order to transform it. And if he assumes and transforms this destiny, it is in order to render it accessible to every executioner, Jewish or Gentile" (Barthélemy: 220f.).

RENÉ GIRARD ON JOB: THE QUESTION OF THE SCAPEGOAT

Baruch Levine
New York University

ABSTRACT

The book of Job must be studied within the context of biblical literature, culture and society, with attention to the role of languages in the interpretation of ancient classics, and to literary motifs in ancient Near Eastern perspective. Biblical applications of the scapegoat phenomenon to humans is quite different from what we find in Job, as we shall see with reference to Lev 16 and other "riddance" rites. The servant song of Is 52–53 tells how the human scapegoat was conceptualized in the early post-exilic period and shows how the scapegoat differed from other sufferers. There is no connection between the well-being of the community and the sufferings of Job, whose laments admit of a psychological explanation. His heroic dissidence is not a scapegoat phenomenon.

René Girard calls Job a scapegoat. He arrives at this definition through an analysis of several important poetic passages in the dialogues of Job in which our fallen hero bemoans his social isolation, his economic plight, and the rejection of his kinsfolk. He is *déclassé*. His position in society has suddenly plummeted, leaving him in a state of shock, angry and depressed. In Girard's view, it is not God who is Job's real enemy, the cause of his troubles, but rather his society. His community has made Job, the innocent victim, its scapegoat.

Girard's interest in the scapegoat is intense. He has devoted one work, *Le Bouc émissaire*, to this subject, and he utilizes the scapegoat theme to interpret ancient myths, to explain the role of society in ritual sacrifice, and to characterize social and political movements.

It is not my purpose to argue for or against Girard's many applications of the scapegoat phenomenon, a task surely beyond my competence. I'm reasonably sure I could agree with some of these applications. My question is whether Job can legitimately be called a scapegoat, in context. As much as usage undoubtedly changed from Leviticus, chapter 16, to Job, I do not think that one who speaks as Job does, or whose dialoguers confront him in the terms they do, can qualify as a scapegoat.

As I intend to show, we have biblical applications of the scapegoat phenomenon to humans. The conceptualization of the human scapegoat that emerges is quite different from what we find in Job. All innocent victims (or, to be more precise: all victims who claim to be innocent), share much in common, but the scapegoat differs in certain critical respects, at least within the context of biblical literature, culture, and society, to the extent that we know them. It is this context that must be clarified, and which must delimit our definition of the scapegoat, as it might or might not apply to Job.

In one matter, I agree with Girard quite definitely: The prose-tale of Job (the Prologue and Epilogue) is not integral to the book in literary terms. It is, indeed, an error to allow the more traditional tone of these chapters to determine the parameter of the dialogues themselves. Professor Avi Hurvitz has made a useful contribution to this problem by showing, through diachromic analysis of the language of the prose-tale, that it is probably later than the dialogues. In any event, I feel confident in regarding these chapters as a rubric, written expressly so as to interpret the startling dialectic of the dialogues in a manner more readily understandable to the ancient reader.

Girard focuses attention on social issues and has, at least for me, posed a question I had failed to confront in my own reading of the dialogues of Job: Why is it that societies react as they do to the victims of misfortune in their midst? How are we to understand the often-endorsed rationalization that such victims have only themselves to blame, that they are responsible for their own plight? To put it in the words of Job himself, who cites an ancient proverb:

> lappîd bûz le'aštût ša'ᵃnān
> nākôn lᵉmô'deî rāgel
> "Disaster strikes the despised—
>   so the reasoning of the complacent;
> It readily awaits stumblers!" (12:5)

I must, however, object to Girard's disdainful attitude toward the role of languages in the interpretation of ancient classics. Our present understanding of Job is admittedly inadequate, but it is also true that whatever progress has been made in the recent past has resulted from the careful study of the text of Job, with its strong Aramaic substratum, through an investigation of literary motifs in ancient Near Eastern perspective, and against the background of biblical literature itself.

I

In the first instance, the dialogues of Job should be studied within the context of biblical literature, culture, and society. But here we encounter a degree of uncertainty: The dialogues of Job are creations of the post-exilic period, perhaps of the fourth century B.C.E., or later. It is not entirely clear, however, for whom the dialogues speak. (The prose tale speaks for post-exilic Judaism, in a general sense.) Some doubt that the dialogues were written by Jews, or that they were composed within the Jewish society of their time. Ultimately, the book of Job was canonized by Jewish synods, not without resistance, because, at some later time, Jewish religious leadership responded positively to its message, as they understood it. Some Talmudic sages conceded that Job was not an historical person, but felt that his life experience could serve as a *māšāl*, an object lesson (Ginsberg, II:223-24, V:381, n. 3).

The authors of the dialogues were intimately familiar with earlier biblical literature, as was shown most incisively by M. Z. Segal in his study of the literary parallels in Job (Segal: 35–48). If we allow for the influx of non-Jewish ideas, there is no reason to doubt the Jewish provenience of the dialogues. In fact, they may well serve to indicate how broad was the post-exilic Jewish universe.

The scapegoat ritual of Leviticus, chapter 16, should be our starting point in any discussion of the scapegoat phenomenon. This is not to say that the question of Job's definition should be engaged within this context alone, but only to insist that it cannot be discussed without reference to the dynamics of the scapegoat ritual. Biblical phenomena never completely loose their moorings!

The ritual of Leviticus chapter 16 has many dimensions. Explicitly, the religious community acts to contain impurity by extracting it from places, objects and persons contaminated by it. Then the impurity is transferred to an animal—a goat—(Hebrew: *śā'îr*), who is promptly removed from the settlement, and whose return is prevented. By certain traditions, the goat meets its death in the wilderness.

Thus far the phenomenology is eminently clear: To eliminate dangerous impurity, we must localize it, pin-point it, thus reducing its area and volume, so that it can be eliminated without destroying everyone and everything in the process. We do this today when we grow viruses in laboratories, or try to contain the area of oil slicks, pumping the oil from a reduced area. This process is basic to rituals of "riddance," as they are called.

The goat was not a fortuitous choice, however. It represented the demonic powers of the wilderness, an idea suggested in Isaiah 13:21, and 14:14, both late passages which speak of *śe'îrîm* in the wilderness. From Leviticus 17:7 we learn that the Israelites had once worshipped such *śe'îrîm*, they continued to serve as the most frequent animal in sin-offerings.

These observations lead to the more implicit dimension of the scapegoat ritual: The sin-laden goat comes to be identified with sinfulness and impurity to start with, even before it was burdened. It is as if a goat had brought impurity into the community, initially, from the wilderness, its domain. The dispatch of the goat sent impurity back whence it had come! It is this sense of the scapegoat ritual that holds the most obvioius applications for the psycho-social phenomenon we call "scapegoating."

Caught between the alternatives of worshipping the powers of impurity or of combating them, the priests of ancient Israel opted for the latter course. This decision was understood by several Medieval Jewish sages and exegetes, including Nachmanides and Abraham Ibn-Ezra.

What is established by the above analysis is the nexus of riddance and the future well-being of the community. What is done to the scapegoat is explained by the belief that its disposition was essential, prerequisite to the well-being of the group. A cause and effect relationship between the two is pronounced. In the most basic sense, the scapegoat *substituted* for the group; it suffered what the entire community would have suffered had the goat not been laden with the collective impurity. It spared the group! This phenomenology is common to the rites of riddance found in the priestly codes of the Torah.

The most dramatic application of the scapegoat phenomenon to humans is expressed in the so-called "servant of the Lord" oracles, preserved in Isaiah, chapters 52-53. In themselves, these poems are cryptic, and have generated widely diverse interpretations throughout the centuries, since late antiquity. They have been associated with Christology in complex ways. For the purposes of our present discussion, they are most interesting because of what they have to say about different perceptions of suffering. I add my proposed translation to the many and worthy efforts already available:

A.

Is 52:13) Behold, My servant shall prosper;
He shall be uplifted, raised to great height!
14) Just as the public had been aghast at him,
So much had his human appearance deteriorated,
His form from that of human beings—
15) Just so shall he cast down nations;
Because of him, kings shall hold their speech.
What was not foretold to them, they shall see;
What they never heard, they shall observe!

B.

53:1) Who would have believed what we heard?
Upon whom was the Lord's arm thus revealed?
2) For he grew like a tree-crown in His presence,
Like a trunk from arid soil.

3) His form was not majestic that we would prefer him,
   No such appearance that we would want him.
4) He was despised and dehumanized,
   Suffering pain, experiencing sickness;
   One others turned away from,
   Despised, so that we gave him no heed.
   In fact, he was suffering the effects of our sickness;
   He was bearing the burden of our pain.
   Whereas we had regarded him as one stricken,
   Smitten by God and tortured—
5) He was, in fact, stabbed for our failures,
      Because of our errors.
   The chastisement [required] for our well-being
      was [laid] upon him;
   Through his wound we were healed!
6) All of us strayed like sheep,
   Each of us went his own way;
   While the Lord made him the target
      Of our collective punishment.
7) Though beaten, he remained submissive;
      He did not open his mouth.
   Like a lamb brought to the slaughter,
   Like a ewe dumb before its shearers,
      He did not open his mouth.
8) Through miscarriage of justice
      He was taken away;
   Who can describe his abode?
   For he was cut off from the land of the living;
   Because of the failure of My people,
      Who deserved to be smitten!
9) His grave was set among the wicked,
   With evildoers his funerary platform.
   Though he had done no violence,
   Had spoken no falsehood.
10) But the Lord chose to crush him with sickness!
    - - - - - - -
    Once his life *is declared* sacrosanct,
    He will see descendants,
    He will live a long life;
    So that the Lord's purpose may succeed through him!
11) Out of his torment he shall see [this],
    He shall enjoy [it] to the full,
       Out of his devotion.
    My Servant shall bring vindication to the public
    By bearing the punishment for their error.

12) Therefore, I will allow him to share with the public;
With the multitudes share in the spoils;
In return for exposing himself to death,
For being numbered among the sinful.
For he bore the penalty for the public's offense,
He substituted as a target for the sinful.[1]

These passages tell us how a human scapegoat was conceptualized in the early, post-exilic period, and they highlight the difference between the scapegoat and other sufferers. They are clearly related in diction and concept to the scapegoat ritual of Leviticus 16, and to other riddance rituals. The priestly vocabulary is represented by the terms for sinfulness, *ʿawôn* and *pešaʿ*, and by forms of the verb *nāgaʿ*, literally: "to touch," connoting the disabling touch of the gods. The formulas *nāśāʾ ḥēṭʾ* "to bear the punishment for transgression" in 53:12, and *sābal ʿawôn* "to bear the burden of error" in 53:11 recall the priestly formula: *nāśāʾ ʿawôn* "to bear the punishment for error." Most telling is the clause: *kî nigzar mēʾereṣ ḥaîm* "For he was cut off from the land of the living," which recalls: *ʾel ʾereṣ gᵉzērāh* "to the land cut off," in Leviticus 16:22, the destination of the scapegoat. Finally, we have the term *ʾāšām* in 53:10, usually rendered in one of two ways: "guilt," a state, or "guilt offering."

I sense a different connotation in Isaiah 53:10, however. God had crushed the servant with sickness. Then—the turning point: The servant's life is declared sacrosanct! Here, Hebrew *ʾāšām* possesses a positive rather than a negative connotation, known from II Chronicles 28:10 where we have the masculine plural: *ʾašāmôt* in the sense of "devoted persons." There we read that the Ephraimites, who had defeated the Judeans in battle, thus arousing God's wrath, were told that they dare not take Judean captives as slaves. They were protected by God, sacrosanct!

This interpretation of the passage in II Chronicles was discussed elsewhere (Levine:130). Its application to the special meaning of *ʾāšām* in Isaiah 53:10 did not occur to me until later. In our verse, the rescue of the servant is signaled. He is saved at the brink of death. In some way, his suffering symbolizes that of the Judean exiles in Babylonia, who speak of themselves as being "cut off" (Ezekiel 37:11; Lamentations 3:54).

In terms of our present discussion, the most significant subtlety comes in Isaiah 53:4-5. The people recognize that they had been mistaken about the sufferings of the servant. They had regarded him as one being punished for his own sins, and they consequently paid him no heed. The descriptions of his deteriorated form belong with this perception of him, and they are the ones which remind us of Job. The servant was: *nāgûʿa mukkēh ʾelōhîm ûmᵉʿunneh* "stricken, smitten by God and tortured." Similarly Job (19:21) states: "For the hand of God struck at me (*nāgeʿāh bî*)."

As it turns out, the servant of Isaiah, chapters 52–53 is a different type of victim. He suffers for the sins of others, truly a human scapegoat! (The goat has become a lamb, however.) The rescue of the scapegoat was a most unusual occurrence. How many human scapegoats have actually been rescued? Even more remarkable is the compassion shown him by his own people, or at least by some of them. They recognize their debt to him. Most often, a society seeks to banish or destroy what it cruelly and incorrectly identifies as the carrier of impurity, the cause of its troubles!

There is not a single indication in the speeches of Job, or in those of his dialoguers, of a connection between the suffering of Job and the wellbeing of the community. The authors of the dialogues were simply not thinking in such terms, either compassionately or cruelly. Otherwise, the argumentation would have been very different.

III

In the dialogues of Job we find a challenge to the doctrine that the unfortunate must have offended God, who is just and does not punish the innocent. We also find lengthy, almost tiresome laments. In ancient Near Eastern literature other similar laments have come to light. The best known is that of the so-called "Babylonian Job".[2] The main difference between Job's laments and those of the Babylonian sufferers is in the terms of the complaint. The Babylonian sufferer appeals from his cultic piety, his munificence in contributing sacrifices, his participation in public celebration. Why was someone so pious treated so cruelly, in a manner which only the impious deserve?

Job doesn't mention any such factors. He cites his uprightness, his goodness to others, his innocence of any injustice. In the late biblical tradition a sufferer who claimed cultic piety as his foremost virtue would be open to the challenge that such was not sufficient in God's eyes. In a sense, the prose-tale places Job's sufferings in a more popular perspective. There, Job's piety is highlighted, a theme which continues in the post-biblical Jewish tradition.

Job persists in his hope that God will redeem him by vindicating him. In his respect, he more closely resembles the speaker in one of the earlier servant passages of Isaiah (50: 4 f.); if, indeed, that speaker is to be associated at all with the servant of chapters 52–53. In chapter 50 we have a first-person statement by a leader who is repudiated by his people, but who is confident nevertheless of his eventual vindication:

Is 50:5) The Lord-God has opened my ears;
    I did not rebel, nor did I retreat!

6) My back I offered to floggers,
   My cheeck to pluckers;
   I did not turn way
   From shaming and spittle.
7) For the Lord-God will come to my aid.
   For this reason I am not shamed;
   For this reason I made my face strong as flint!
   For I know I shall not be disgraced.
8) My vindicator is near;
   Who dares to dispute with me?
   Let us appear together!
   Whosoever would be my antagonist—
   Let him approach me!
9) Behold, the Lord-God comes to my aid—
   Who can convict me?
   May they all wear thin like a garment;
   Be consumed by moths!

The authors of the dialogues of Job may well have taken their cue from this passage. Sylvia Scholnick, a former student of mine, has stressed the importance of the legal language we find in the dialogues of Job. She has investigated the *rîb*, the legal dispute, and specific connotations of the verb *šāpaṭ* "to judge," and *ṣādaq* in the sense of "vindication." These locutions are common to Isaiah, chapter 50 and to the dialogues of Job. The speaker of Isaiah chapter 50 claims God as his defense attorney, who will plead his case in court. Job would have settled for an appearance in court by God, to answer for His treatment of one of His creatures!

God is very real in the dialogues of Job. For the sake of argument I am prepared, however, to accept a humanistic equation: God = reality, fate, the human condition, etc. Let's assume that all that Job charges God with—indifference, injustice,—is an ancient way of saying that one's community, family, or the impersonal realities of one's life are the cause. Even in such terms, we do not have a scapegoat in Job. What we find is the rationalization that the "loser" has only himself to blame. People tend to shun losers. This attitude can best be explained psychologically: The loser makes us uneasy, even frightens us by identification. What happened to him may happen to us! I have often observed wealthy persons, in particular, who are morbidly fascinated by tales of those of their group who suddenly lost their fortunes!

Job is shunned because of *what had already become of him*, and what had become of him did not result from any effort to eliminate him from society, initially, so that society would be spared through his riddance.

IV

René Girard extracts from the dialogues of Job those passages which epitomize his own concerns: How do the many treat the few, the mob the individual, the strong the weak? I insist, however, that Job is no scapegoat. He is an heroic dissident! God's answer to Job may be a hard pill to swallow, but Job exacted an answer nonetheless, showing that God is reachable if we don't despair of the effort to communicate with Him. Leaving God out of the picture, we learn from the dialogues of Job that consensus is not truth. In this I find much common ground with René Girard.

NOTES

1. My translation is influenced by that of *The Prophets*, the Jewish Publication Society of America, Philadelphia, Second Edition, 1978. It is, however, an independent translation, for which I am responsible. The only emendation reflected in it that is crucial for our discussion (translations based on emendations are underlined), is in 53:10, where Masoretic *táśim* "You shall place, make" in revocalized: *tussām* "shall be made, declared." No change of consonants is required. The subject of the passive verb, as now vocalized, is *nepeš* "life," a feminine noun.

2. See Robert D. Biggs, translator, "I Will Praise the Lord of Wisdom," and "The Babylonian Theodicy," in J. B. Pritchard, ed., *Ancient Near Eastern Texts relating to the Old Testament*, Third Edition, Princeton, 1969, 596–604.

THE INNOCENT TRANSGRESSOR: JESUS IN EARLY CHRISTIAN MYTH AND HISTORY

Burton L. Mack
Claremont, California

ABSTRACT

Girard's challenge to New Testament scholars is just that he approaches the gospels with a new hermeneutic informed by a fully rationalized theory of religion. His approach may be compared formally with Bultmann's program of demythologizing the kerygma on the basis of then current views of the history of religions. But the new views on religion from a human sciences perspective are quite different. And Girard's theory, won in conversation with these, introduces a reading of the gospels for which New Testament scholars may not be prepared. The essay offers an analysis of Girard's readings of the gospels, presents a contrastive reading more in line with the canons of historical-literary criticism, and offers a reflection upon the disparities. Girard's reading of the gospels is resisted. But his theory of religion is nevertheless found to be poignantly apropos to early Christian social formation.

In *Le Bouc émissaire* René Girard offers the most startling reading of early Christian texts since Bultmann's announcement of a program for their demythologization. Bultmann accepted the theory of myth current at that time in the history of religions, and regarded the language world of early Christian discourse largely as mythological. As an enlightenment intellectual he was unable to accept such a world view, and he sought ways to overcome the "objectifying" nature of its mythic expression. But as a Christian theologian he was concerned to salvage the core of the kerygma with its indication of a momentous event. This event called for replication, as he understood it, in the faith event of the individual Christian. He proposed, therefore, a translation of early Christian mythology into the language of existentialism, reducing "world" to "self-understanding," and interpreting the kerygma as a word event which called for decision. But the objectifying *form* of the kerygma, with its curious mixture of myth and history, Bultmann left unexplored. And Bultmann's kerygma has remained unexplored in the scholarship since his time, biblical scholarship which still refers to "Easter" or the "Christ

Event" by using capital letters, reticent as it has been to investigate the mythology of the momentous event, or the moment of its mythologization. Girard has not been so reticent.

Bultmann's work did, in effect, open up early Christian history and literature to the full range of the human sciences and humanities for its elucidation. His anthropological perspective, given with his program of existential interpretation, was the invitation for that. But this secularizing approach could flourish only after the sharp emphasis upon existential interpretation had subsided, discharged mainly in a spurt of philosophical reflection called the "New Hermeneutic," then merged with the New Criticism in such a way as to legitimize discourse, finally, with literary critics outside the field. Criticism then superceded existentialism as the extra-theological discipline brought to bear upon biblical texts in the post-Bultmannian era, especially in America. More recently sociology entered the arena, and more recently still a few attempts informed by general notions from cultural anthropology have surfaced. But critical conversation with the history of religions, that discipline which phrased the question Bultmann was to put to early Christian discourse, has not been actively pursued within the guild in relation to biblical texts for over fifty years. What has ridden under the rubric of the history of religions in the mainstream of biblical scholarship is actually a search for historically contiguous analogues to religious phenomena reflected in the biblical texts, much on the model of the philological disciplines. Apparently the guild has been satisfied with theories of religion coined by the older eras of the history of religions. Perhaps it has felt in the case of New Testament studies, that Bultmann's program answered the questions about myth and ritual. At least this much is so, that the problem of myth has become passé, and the question of ritual has scarcely been asked. Enter Girard.

Girard takes up the gospel texts as a literary critic with a fully fledged theory of religion and culture based upon his own recent work on myth, ritual, and social formation. This theory breaks with the older tradition of the history of religions, thus taking its place among other, also recent explorations of social formation as the matrix within which both ritual and myth are generated. It takes its place uneasily, however, mainly because it derives its insights about ritual and social formation not directly from the empirical sciences as others are beginning to do, but from texts via a criticism forged on the anvil of recent French thought. Thus Girard begins with literature as cultural artifact. But in the analyses to which his texts are subjected, theories are formed and readings won which engage the full range of the human sciences as the French understand them, and which drive toward the disclosure of human relational equations and dynamics fundamental to human conflict and social formation. Thus his theory of religion and culture is comprehensive, his methodology axiomatic, and his reading of a text radical.

He does not come to the New Testament unprepared to tackle its enigmatic texts. The signposts of his intellectual quest can be charted for us in the sequence of publications which runs from *Mensonge romantique et vérité romanesque* (1961) through *La Violence et le sacré* (1972) and *Des Choses cachées depuis la fondation du monde* (1978) to *Le Bouc émissaire* (1982). That he finally comes to a reading of the New Testament may not appear to be surprising now, in retrospect upon this trajectory. But still, one could not have been completely prepared for what he is able to do with the gospel texts. It is explosive. What he has achieved in half a book is nothing less than an invasion of the field of biblical scholarship. Biblical scholars will have to take note, and scurry for arms. Winged words will no longer do.

Many biblical scholars will be troubled by Girard's theory of ritual, and reticent to relocate the center of concern in early Christian studies from semiotics (myth) to social formation (ritual). But none will be able to deny that Girard has touched the nerve of early Christian imagination, nor avoid his challenge to take up the issues of social conflict and violence. For those are the issues around which our debate about early Christian speech (literature) and practice (social formation) must revolve—unless of course the guild is willing to forfeit its claim to respectability in the academy. If it does that in favor of protecting some privileged notions about the efficacy of hermeneutics to disclose the divine meaning of early Christian discourse on graciousness and the peaceable kingdom, its tell-tail will be showing. It will have turned out to have been an effort in theological quest and apologetic all along.

This essay is an attempt to take up Girard's challenge, to offer a substantive evaluation and critique, particularly with respect to his treatment of New Testament texts and Christian origins. My critique will be that, far from defusing the mechanism of the scapegoat by disclosure, as Girard argues, the gospels make the mechanism constitutive for early Christian social formation by means of a double deception. Thus we have a debate on our hands of some significance.

I. Girard's Many Texts

It was the English edition of Girard's *Violence and the Sacred* in 1977 which sent shock-waves through the American academy. In it Girard proposed a theory about "sacrificial crisis" and its resolution in the collective killing of a surrogate victim which, he said, was a mechanism basic for all human social formation and the generator of religion and culture. If one reads this book first, as many have in their encounter with Girard, one is left stunned, as if in the presence of the primal scene itself. That is because the theory appears to burst upon the scope of academic discourse fully clothed and armed in the manner of Athena's birthing leap from the head of Zeus.

Turning back to his earlier work, *Deceit, Desire and the Novel*, we are able to discern Girard's point of departure from traditional notions about two motivational phenomena: desire and rivalry. These he found it possible to relate to one another in a single equation of human intercourse by seeing both as functions of yet another relational category: mimesis. Putting the notion of mimesis together with the notion of desire a construct is given: mimetic desire. One *learns* to desire an object mimetically, by imitating some other one who seems to value the object already. Thus desire is derivative. The mimetic relation is primary. And in the novels Girard has chosen for study, the mimetic desire can be shown not only to provide the fundamental dynamic for plot development, but also to generate a series of encounters which escalate the intensity of desire to the breaking point. This point is dramatic. It is the point where the positive regard of the imitator, thought to determine the mimetic relationship with the model, turns to rivalry and conflict. Having worked out this "mechanism" of mimetic desire, a theory about the fundamental plot of the human drama was now in place. Girard could go on to explore its incidence in the larger world of cultural history.

In *La Violence et le sacré*, the construct of mimetic desire was socialized, i.e., explored as to its function for groups, societies. Facilitating this move may have been the dislocation of the Freudian family drama from its oedipal linkage, its correlation with the proverbial "French triangle," and its usage as equation in the theories of other French intellectuals of the time who were also seeking a general theory of socialization based on Freud. Girard discusses his indebtedness to Freud in chapter seven of *Violence and the Sacred*, and also gives there his critique of Freud. The discussion makes it clear that it is Girard's theory of mimetic desire which is at stake. We may conclude that this theory not only determined Girard's reading of Freud, but that it also was the contribution which Girard brought to the French interpretations of Freud in the interest of social theory.

The relation between mimesis and rivalry was also explored. The theory was expanded to suggest that, while mimesis had as its project the overcoming of difference between imitator and model, it was precisely the eventual recognition of similarity which precipitated the switch from regard to rivalry. And rivalry is now explored as to its dramatic telos. That telos was found to be violence, the elimination of the model in the desire to assume the model's identity, but claim it as that which could distinguish the imitator now as different from the other.

Once violence as the elimination of the rival was introduced, the range of human behavioral and cultural phenomena available for evidence could be garnered for the theory. And Girard put in the sickle.

Murder became definitional for the primal human act, the inevitable end of the escalation of mimetic desire, the threat to human social formation, and the problematic actuality which called for resolution if society was to function. And now the vast collection of texts from the history of religions could be mined. The myths of violence and the rituals of killing could now be stacked around their common axis, and read as texts related to the drama of mimetic desire. If the construct of mimetic desire traced out the tragic drama of the ever present possibility for rivalry to run its course, religious texts could be seen as attempts to write another script, addressing the problem of mimetic desire, but inverting the significance of its momentous event from a negative to a positive sign. Sacrifice became for Girard the constitutively religious act, an act of violence which, because of its retrospective view on the mimetic drama, could shift its focus from the moment of rivalry to the moment of resolution. The challenge now for Girard was to account for the mythic notion of sacrifice as a saving event, and understand how a ritual killing could possibly work to effect social constraints on the primary mechanism of mimetic desire. This challenge he accepted in *La Violence et le sacré*.

Girard's theory of religion is outlined in bold, definitive strokes in the first ten pages of this book, fleshed out to a working hypothesis in the next three chapters, then refined as he broadens its scope of application to the full range of religious phenomena in vigorous debate with scholarly traditions. According to Girard, humans have no braking mechanism against intra-specific aggression. This means that rivalries and conflicts, once unleashed, cannot stop short of manslaughter. Because of the mechanism of mimetic desire, violence therefore is endemic. Since the only answer to murder on the level of social or shared concerns is another murder, cycles of reciprocal retaliation create unending series of revenge killings. To bring the series to an end, a "final" killing is necessary.

The final killing is achieved, according to Girard, in the mechanism of the surrogate victim. It is this mechanism which can confound the unending actualizations of the mechanism of mimetic desire. From within the group, or from it borders, one is separated out as victim. The selection is arbitrary, though there are requisites. The victim must be recognizable as surrogate for those caught up in the crisis of violence, those from whom further violence may be suspected or feared, ultimately for the group as a whole. It must be vulnerable, unable to unleash retaliation, i.e., without champions to continue the vengeance. And there must be unanimity within the group that it is the one at fault. The process by which this unanimity is achieved is the social manifestation of the mechanism of mimetic desire itself, now raised to the level of group hysteria. When this unanimity is achieved, when a victim becomes the "monstrous double" for the group as a whole, it is treated as a criminal, just as the model turned rival, then expelled and killed. This, Girard says, brings the violence to an end. The group has directed its aggressions upon the single victim which has thus released them. Now there is peace, the possibility to begin anew, to cooperate. And the group comes to consider the victim as the source of its well-being.

The fiction of the victim as saviour erases the memory of the preceding violence and determines that the mythic notion of surrogate become the necessary illusion for the rationalization of cultural well-being. Now the mechanism of "substitution" is in place, and rituals can be performed in the place of the originary event itself. And thus it is that sacrifice is invented to recall, however darkly, re-enact, however mythically, and re-experience, however vicariously, the moment of "generative violence" which constitutes human society. Thus primitive religion is rooted in a profound self-deception. But it is a necessary self-deception, the price society must pay for its sense of well-being. If the illusion were to be disclosed, actual violence would again errupt.

Thus the study of *La Violence* leaves the reader to struggle with two very serious questions. In his discussion of primitive societies Girard points out that the myth is necessary, for without the fictive illusion of surrogate salvation society would be faced with the horrible truth about its generation, plunged into the chaos of "sacrificial crisis," and unable to control the violence which would ensue. But as Girard describes the function of the critic, it is just the exposure of the mechanisms at work in social history which is called for. The questions thus are: 1) What are the manifestations of the originary surrogate victim mechanism at the level of social history? and 2) How can their exposure by the critic be achieved, and to what end? I.e., how can the disclosure of these mechanisms guarantee peace instead of instigating renewed violence?

In *Des Choses cachées depuis la fondation du monde* and *Le Bouc émissaire* we are given Girard's answers to these questions. The scriptures of the Judaeo-Christian tradition turn out to be yet another type of literature. In them human conflict is narrated without recourse to mythic mentality. The primary way in which this is achieved in the Hebrew scriptures is by resisting resolution which depends upon seeing the victim as totally guilty and the victor as totally innocent. There are some fine interpretations of Hebrew narratives in *Des Choses*, which show that a script other than that of the surrogate victim is definitional. Girard sees this strange, new literature against the background of the universality of the surrogate victim myth, and concludes that the Hebrew scriptures are a special case, doing the work of criticism. But now it is clear, as well, that there will be a special relationship between Girard's ideal critic and the Judaeo-Christian scriptures. And that which is to be exposed now has another name. It is the mechanism of the scapegoat—a phenomenon which brings the originary moment right up to date, and very close to the surface of observation. It might even be thought to be the case that, as a phenomenon well understood by those who have been its victims, scapegoating should be difficult to deny as an explanation for violence and injustice at all levels of human history.

The rub is that, as Girard explains in *Le Bouc émissaire*, scapegoating by definition cannot be recognized by the persecutors, just as the surrogate victim mechanism could not be recognized by religions of sacrifice. But the critic can see it at work even and especially in texts about an event of conflict written from the persecutor's point of view. The things to look for are at first the marks of the surrogate victim in its description as culprit (stranger, maimed, vulnerable, etc.). Then, however, another step may be taken. Knowing how the mechanism works, one can make the move from text to history. Girard shows how this can be done with a passage from "The Judgment of the King of Navarre" written by Guillaume de Machaut in the fourteenth century. The passage tells of the horrible plague, the divine manifestations of displeasure with the Jews, and the resulting violence of the French as they put them to death. Girard's point is that, in spite of the mythic exaggerations in the description of the event, or rather just because of them, we can know that the violence actually occurred. That is because the mechanism of the surrogate victim has left its mark—concealment of the truth about the victimization from those who victimized.

The first half of *Le Bouc* looks at many texts from many cultures in order to establish this hermeneutical theory. But Girard is no longer talking about an originary event, nor reading a literary text against the background of the myths and rituals of violence. He wants to move now from text to history, showing that his theory of collective murder and the surrogate victim, possible only by the delusion of the persecutors, can be used to read the texts of violence another way—as documents of the human history of violence. With this in place, a veritable hermeneutic of myth and history, based on the concealment of violence which myth achieves, Girard is ready for a reading of the gospels.

II. The Gospel as Sacred Text

Roughly one half way through *Le Bouc émissaire* the reader is confronted with a caesura of some significance. This occurs in the space between chapter eight on "The Sciences of Myths" and chapter nine on "Les maîtres mots de la passion évangélique." With this title Girard announces a new theme. He acknowledges this immediately in the first four paragraphs: 1) The reader may have concluded on the basis of the preceding analyses that the costly dissimulation involved in scapegoating is endemic to society and that our own culture also is not only plagued by the threat of violence in this form, but doomed to its chaos. 2) The reader should be reminded, however, that the capacity to decode the signs of persecution also belongs to our culture, and that this capacity is already antidotal. 3) This capacity to decipher the signs of persecution is closely related to a powerful constraint in Western culture which counters the tendency toward conceit, deceit and falsehood. And we all know this second cultural force is operant. 4) It is the force of the biblical tradition, more especially that of the Gospels of the New Testament.

The Gospel text takes up the age old plot of the sacrificial crisis and the collective murder. Mimetic desire and its escalation to hysteria and violence are depicted. And the process is described by which the unanimous consent of all parties involved occurs. But instead of casting the victim as guilty, this account makes clear that Jesus was innocent. This shift in perspective, which Girard describes as taking the victim's point of view, positions this text against all other mythic accounts which are always written from the persecutors' point of view. Thus the illusion of the victim's guilt, constitutive for all mythic accounts of a scapegoat event, as well as for the surrogate victim mechanism itself, is disclosed for what it is—self-deception which conceals the persecutors' participation in the ordeal of mimetic desire. This disclosure is nothing less than the event of revelation in human history.

There is, however, need for the critic's work still. This is because the full significance of the gospel has not always been seen by those who have cherished it as foundational text. Girard does not deny that the text can be misread, and that misreadings can play into the hands of those who would use it against itself to reconstitute and legitimize a scapegoat mentality. It is, as Girard has said, a "text in travail," at work in Western culture, seeking its proper telos—the full disclosure of the mechanisms of human desire and deceit. Girard's purpose in *Le Bouc* is to give that proper telos a chance by means of a critical reading of the text. He will show the text subverts every aspect of the scapegoat mechanism.

There are two "masterful statements" which Girard has in mind to discuss in chapter nine. The first is the citation of Psalm 35:19 in John 15:25: "They hated me without cause." He argues against taking this as a rhetorical ploy, i.e., a Christian usage of a Jewish text against the Jews, choosing instead to see both the Psalm and its citation in John as intentional definitions of the situation of persecution. As descriptions of what actually occurs in victimization, both the persecutors referred to in the Psalms as well as the crowds depicted in the passion narrative are seen as acting without a (real) cause. The purpose of the citation is to align the demythologization of the scapegoat mechanism already at work in the Old Testament with the radical demystification of it in the Gospel. That aspect of the scapegoat mechanism which is challenged by these factual statements is what Girard has called in previous studies on other texts the arbitrariness of the trumped up charges which the persecutors unanimously agree upon.

In order to support this reading of the Psalm citation in John (with reference as well to Luke 22:37, "He was counted among the transgressors."), Girard notes the way in which the passion accounts describe the formation of the unanimous agreement to have Jesus crucified. We normally think of this process as instigated by the religious leaders, then decided by the political leaders, only finally to involve the crowd. But Girard turns this upside down, arguing that Pilate's "weakness," for instance, as well as the denial of Peter, are calculated to emphasize the pressure toward unanimity which builds until all succumb to its power. And as for the "reasons" for this coalition against Jesus, they are groundless. Note, Girard says, that the accusations of the trial are vague, that the witnesses cannot agree, that the Gospel describes the hatred of the crowd as "without cause."

The second "masterful statement" is also a word spoken by Jesus: "Father forgive them, for they do not know what they are doing" (Luke 23:34). According to Girard this is not to be taken as a magnanimous gesture intended to excuse the crowd, but as another factual description of the situation. It is in fact "the first definition in human history of the unconscious" (1982:161). Not only does the crowd, mobilized against a victim, not have a cause, it does not know that it does not have a cause. And so it is that the passion narratives of the gospels not only describe accurately a scapegoat event, but also disclose in the description of that event the mechanism for what it really is—arbitrary, unanimous, unconscious persecution of an innocent victim.

In chapter ten, "that a single man die . . ." (John 11:50), Girard takes up the role played by Caiaphas the high priest. Caiaphas' statement is, of course, a succinct rationalization of a surrogate victim sacrifice and its vicarious effectiveness. Girard notes that this sacrificial interpretation of the scapegoat event is curiously appropriate in the mouth of a high priest, sacrificer par excellence. But he struggles with what it would mean, were we actually to regard Caiaphas in this case as a sacrificer who knew what he was doing. He concludes that in the mouth of Caiaphas, the statement functions merely to "mobilize" the essentially mythological mechanism of victimization by declaring its political rationale. In the context of the gospel, however, it functions as a bald disclosure that the passion as a whole is to be understood precisely *as* mechanism. Because the "lamb of God" is innocent, the gospels differ qualitatively from all other texts, even those in which the *pharmakos* theme is recognized as to its social function. The gospels do not treat scapegoating as a *theme*, but as a structural mechanism. They name it, and thereby disclose it.

We need not belabor the details of argumentation given in the next six chapters. In chapter eleven on "The Beheading of St. John the Baptist" Girard takes up the Markan text. Its function in the gospel is to reveal mimetic desire as the real cause of violence. The discussion of

"Peter's Denial," chapter twelve, argues that in the case of Jesus mimetic desire was not aroused! This prepares the reader for a consideration of the unique quality of Jesus' miracles. The story of "The Demons of Gerasa" is interpreted in chapter thirteen to show that the Gerasenes represent a society held together by a scapegoat, and that Jesus confounds that social structuration. The saying about the kingdom divided is discussed in chapter fourteen to show that Jesus' purpose as a prophet-teacher was to expose the demonic in scapegoat structures. And the concluding chapter on "History and the Paraclete" returns to the theme of the revelatory force unleashed in Western culture by the gospels. The Christian gospel is the unacknowledged revelation that has enabled the critical spirit to arise, even if it has not achieved its full purpose—to be recognized as the source for the capacity to see scapegoating in others, and accepted as the power to see it in ourselves.

Girard intends his earlier studies to have established his views on mimetic desire, endemic violence, and the mechanism of the surrogate victim as a general theory of social formation. In the first half of *Le Bouc émissaire* this claim is supported by means of two additional considerations. The first is that "persecution texts," though replete with mythological description, betray actual events of violence. They are mythological accounts because they are written from the persecutors' point of view, a point of view which, according to Girard's theses, necessarily involves self-deception and dissimulation. But once we know that this concealment of the motivational matrix for persecution must be involved, we can read even the mythological swerves in an account of persecution as hard evidence for the actuality of the social occurrence. This is Girard's way of resolving the problem of myth and history.

The second consideration, given as an additional argument for the universality of the surrogate victim mechanism, is that the mythologies from exceedingly diverse cultures outside of the Western cultural tradition also turn out to be "persecution texts." It may be a bit more difficult to read myths this way, because the linguistic mode of historical report has not yet emerged. But knowing about the mechanisms, and having learned the hermeneutical method appropriate to persecution texts, myths which feature a killing can now be analyzed to show that a collective killing of a surrogate victim actually must have occurred as the occasion from which they arose. The myths amenable to such a reading extend from ancient Greece, pagan Scandanavia, and the Aztecs to primitive cultures and all human mythologies. This is Girard's answer to the question òf imagination and social experience. He has, as he says, "a certain confidence in language" (1977:316). At first he took mythic language seriously in order to derive from myths his theory of the surrogate victim; now he can read them in the light of his theory to establish the universal occurrence of the social event as actual. He has moved away from his earlier insistence on a single originary event at the dawn of human history. It was the discovery of the "persecution texts" in the Western tradition with their linkage to actual historical events which allowed Girard to make this important shift.

With these considerations in place, Girard could now take up the Christian gospel as a text which also focuses upon a killing. Voilà. It differs markedly from all the other texts. That is because, though reporting an event of persecution, the gospel does not mythologize. Instead, it actually demystifies the mythology of persecution by exposing to the light of day the mechanisms of the surrogate victim which are always involved. This amounts to a radical critique of the universally operant mechanisms of social formation, and establishes the gospel as revelatory. It is a unique text, a text on persecution written for the first time for the victim's point of view. The victim is innocent.

This would seem to mean that Girard must regard the account as historically accurate. He does not discuss this problem fully. But he does say that whatever inaccurate nuances in the account may be charged to later conflict between church and synagogue, they only amount to "certain details" which cannot destroy the veracity of the report as such (1982:293). And he remarks on the way in which he imagines the "earliest Christians" to have perceived the events and transmitted an account of them to the evangelists who are our sources. Peter's denial shows us that even the disciples were fallible and thus incapable of perceiving clearly what was happening. But that does not destroy the veracity of the gospel accounts; it merely enhances their value as texts which have not been fabricated. He speaks of a "superior knowledge which dominated the disciples and their writings," a knowledge which cannot be accounted for as generated from within the circle of those around Jesus. Both the disciples and the evangelists are in a sense passive intermediaries of this superior knowledge which must originate with Jesus. This means that the gospel accounts cannot be regarded strictly as accurate historical descriptions. But because of the superior insight on the meaning of the event which they transmit, an insight available even to us who read them as the "festival of light," we can say that it is not possible that they have "falsified anything essential" (1982:231–232).

So the gospels are unique texts. They are not myths because myths by definition conceal the mechanism of mimetic desire. Neither are they persecution texts, because persecution texts are written from the persecutors' point of view. They are not great literature because literature merely probes and explores aspects of the mechanisms involved in victimization, not structures. And they are not history, strictly speaking, because historical observation alone is incapable of documenting the mechanisms at work at the level of the unconscious. They are revelatory texts, gospels, which narrate that which no other text has ever narrated—

the drama of the surrogate victim *mechanism* itself, which serves as plot for an historical event of collective killing. By telling *that* story, the gospels disclose the truth about human history and its deceits.

This can only mean that the antidote to human dissimulation and its horrible consequences is to be found in a certain reading of the Christian gospels. One might conclude from this that Girard is recommending a Christian answer to the problems of the world. That would be true. But it is not true that Girard is therefore to be seen as espousing any actually recognizable form of Christianity or Christian culture as the answer. He intends his view of the gospels to cut as deeply against the grain of institutionalized forms of Christianity as against the traditions of the academy, both of which resist a radical exploration of the source of human violence. His concern is, rather, a social and political one. He is abhorred by the victimization of the oppressed which he notes at every turn and level of social conflict. And he has discovered what appears to him to be the problem. It is the inability of the oppressor to acknowledge that victimization is actually taking place. The Christian gospel can expose this conceit. It is not, according to Girard, a comforting word of forgiveness and salvation as most Christians understand it. This gospel is radically secular in its view of culture, religion, history, and society. The "sacred" is still violence for Girard. But violence has to go, and thus the sacred as well. The gospels show that that is so, and destroy thereby any mystique which religion including Christianity may attribute to sacrifice.

So we are left with a text and a critic on our hands. And we are put in the position of wondering how, indeed, both have managed to work their ways into the wilderness together as they have, now to join in a concerted call for enlightenment. The challenge to accept this enlightenment, this criticism, this gospel, is presented as a scientific theory which should be persuasive in terms of its own empirical and rational logics. But it strikes the conventional scholar strangely, as Girard himself knows it will, and it demands in the last analysis decision rather than consent. The decision it demands, moreover, is a willingness to radicalize one's desire to read the future history of Western and world culture from the innocent victim's point of view. To satisfy that passionate concern for social justice by secularizing a central Christian construct as a challenge to the intellectual integrity of our times will be a very attractive proposition to many Christians in the academy. But upon what basis can one believe that the exposure of mimetic desire which this gospel intends will have as its consequence the peaceable kingdom? And what are we to make of the continuing possibility that even this gospel be misused in an ever more subtle process of self-deception and violence, i.e., "innocence" at the expense of others? Girard wants to wrest the gospel from the hands of Christians who do misuse it, and relocate it as a force within Western culture working for social justice. Thus he knows its dangers. He wants to avoid contaminating the vision of innocence made possible by the gospel, and see it as a power for good alone. Thus he has touched the nerve of Christian concerns for redemption. The question is whether, by means of this abstraction, history can any longer be accounted for, or even held accountable.

III. Violence in the Texture of the Gospel

A. Setting Out

Girard's work should be taken seriously by New Testament scholars for two reasons. The first is that he has brought critical thought to bear upon the significance of Jesus' crucifixion for early Christian social formation and the composition of its literatures. That Jesus' death was of some significance for early Christianity would be acknowledged immediately by most biblical scholars, to be sure. None would disagree with Girard's statement that the gospels gravitate around the event of the crucifixion (1982:148), nor that some interpretation of Jesus' death is involved in all of the varieties of early Christian movements available to us for study. Certainly it is the case that Jesus' death, interpreted in various ways, took its place early on as the central symbol which Christian myth, ritual, piety, and ethics were understood to articulate. But how it could have been that a civil execution came to be regarded as a saving event in the first place, a central symbol for a new religion, is a question which New Testament scholarship has not been prepared to ask or answer. What Girard has done is to force this question. He at least has proposed a theory by which to explain why the "power" of the "Christ-event" is unleashed by means of a crucifixion. It is true that he has had recourse to an assumption of Jesus' special knowledge and innocence in order to carry out his reading. This we will have to challenge as a mythological *deus ex machina* in Girard's purportedly scientific essay. But if we cannot accept Girard's explanation, we are forced to come up with some other. That is because, to date, we really do not have one. Is it because, merely to ask the question straight is to risk the danger of exposing a mystery we do not want to destroy?

The second reason Girard should be taken seriously is because he brings to bear a theory won in the rough and tumble of a cultural anthropological approach to the history of religions. This is a challenge indeed. Most New Testament scholars will have to scramble to catch up. Theory of ritual and myth is involved and, in the circles with which Girard is in debate, the older notions of the irreducibility of the Sacred as prior to any human myth-ritual response have been given up. Social labor, social conflict, social formation—these are the matrices being explored as generators of religion. Girard's reading of the gospels amounts to an invasion of the field of biblical studies by the human sciences of religion. No one can claim foul. The texts are there is to be read by anyone who wishes to do so. Biblical scholars do not own them. So if we wish to keep our standing in the arena of academic discourse, we are required now to respond on the basis of what we do know, on the basis of what we hold to have been won by historical-literary criticism, and venture in the direction of open dialogue once more with others in the academy who study religion.

What New Testament scholars will know is that Girard's reading of the gospels frustrates two hundred years of research aimed at getting the history of this literature and its social-historical setting established. From the point of view of traditional scholarship Girard's reading is most idiosyncratic. He apparently has made a selection of gospel texts mainly with a view to demonstrating his theory. That in and of itself cannot immediately be criticized. But the principle of selection is not given except in terms of the theory, and the selection itself turns out to be a most uncongruous mixture. Then he has handled all these texts as if they belonged to a single level of literary discourse about a single level of (unique) historical event. One wonders what to do with all the other texts, all the historical data so laboriously reconstructed, and all the criticisms which have been developed in order to be precise about the forms, settings, histories and redactional compositions of early Christian literature. Literary history has been erased in Girard's reading. And social history has been effaced as well, in spite of his concerns for both—i.e., the actuality of historical events behind myths and persecution texts, and the social formation component of his theory. Girard has given us his answer as to why this is so. The Gospel-event is unique. Presumably this means that the truth of the matter cannot be gotten at by conventional historical-literary criticism. Girard has said as much in a polemic against Germanic biblical scholarship (1982:159). But what if one were to take seriously Girard's theory in general about the surrogate victim, and use it to read the gospels not as unique texts, but as myths generated by social conflict, just as Girard has done with all his other extra biblical texts? Then our competence as historians of biblical literature could come into play in order to test aspects of Girard's theory itself. In the process of dialogue we might even see how serious Girard is about social history as the arena within which both the mechanism of the scapegoat and the revelation of the Gospel make a difference, i.e., actualize.

We can focus the issue quite simply. For biblical scholars the gospels present the *problem* of the relation of myth and history; for Girard they offer the solution to that problem. If he is right biblical scholars may have been wasting their time. If we have not been doing so, what we have learned should be brought to bear upon the issues Girard raises. This should be done if for no other reason than to offer an alternative account of the same gospel-event for debate. We shall try to keep Girard's theory of sacrifice and social formation in mind as that which is under discussion.

Succinctly put, biblical scholars understand the history of the Jesus movement and its literature as follows. The historical Jesus was a Jew who performed generally "prophetic" functions. Those functions would have been recognized by his contemporaries in terms of traditional and currently active social roles. These prophetic activities of Jesus instigated a movement which included socially marginal persons, if it did not consist primarily of such persons, a movement which was perceived by the Romans and their appointed Jewish high priest as a threat to law and order. Things apparently got out of hand in Jerusalem. Jesus was caught and crucified.

But the movement Jesus started did not cease. Instead, some individuals continued to replicate the prophetic message of Jesus, became wandering preachers, and understood themselves to be "prophets" in his line and mold. The evidence for this is the synoptic sayings-source called "Q." Others formed small groups of Jesus people who met together in homes for the purpose of keeping alive what they came to understand to be the purpose of Jesus' activity. It was this phenomenon which gave rise to a variety of social formations distinguished from one another by notions of sub-cultural identity, diverse practices, competing leadership roles, understandings of purpose, mythological rationales, and the generation of ritual identifiers. All of the literature available to us in the New Testament was produced in the matrix of these processes of social formation. And the earliest literature extant, the letters of Paul, shows that the function of this literature was intended to facilitate social formation itself, i.e., it was addressed to groups by leaders seeking to structure these groups according to certain patterns of authority by using mythological rationales.

Two shifts of some significance took place in this period. One was that Jesus was "identified," as New Testament scholars say, with various mythological figures (eschatological prophet, Son of Man, Christ, Lord, Son of God, and so forth). The other was that the sub-cultural identity of these groups came to be marked by boundaries which separated them both from other social forms of Judaism as well as from other sub-cultural social formations current in the Greco-Roman world at large. For both of these shifts interpretations of the crucifixion played an important role. The Gospels are literary forms which presuppose these shifts and addressed their "communities" precisely as groups for whom these shifts have proven to be constitutive. They take up the earliest symbolic produce of the process of social formation in order to re-cast it once again with the questions of authority and boundaries still very much in mind.

B. Severance from the Past

Keeping this historical sketch in mind we may now identify and elaborate upon several points which pertain directly to the issue under consideration. The first is that, if we are to keep our conscience as historians, the historical Jesus cannot be pictured as an innocent victim by any stretch of the imagination, much less one whose innocence is such that his death may be taken as a founding event for a new social order as early Christian literature has it. It is quite true that New Testament scholars have not yet satisfied their minds about the precise nature of Jesus' activity as it related to the complex society which he addressed. The options under debate range from 1) charismatic compassion for the socially disenfranchised, through 2) espousal of an essentially Cynic-like rejection of social conventions in general, and 3) prophetic critique of Jewish social institutions, to 4) apocalyptic pronouncements and revolutionary posturing against Roman rule. The rub has always been the more generous the construction as to Jesus' "innocence" with respect to law and order, the less plausible his crucifixion by the Romans becomes. And *that* is the firm datum for which a historian must give an account.

The picture the gospels portray of the trial and crucifixion are just plain historically implausible. Neither prophetic critique of Jewish society, nor espousal of a "new teaching," to say nothing of delusions of messianic grandeur, are plausible as grounds for his being killed by his own people. Messianic pretenders, we should remember (supposing we entertained the favorite view about the historical Jesus), were heralded by the Jews, killed by the Romans. Responsible students of the development of the passion narrative tradition acknowledge that the trial before the Sanhedrin, for instance, is a replica of the earlier story of the trial before Pilate, one clear literary evidence among many for the general tendency to shift the blame from the Romans onto the Jews as the stories were told and retold. So however we imagine the reasons for the crucifixion of Jesus, they cannot have been those insinuated by the gospels. To understand the reasons given in the gospel accounts we must explore not the social crisis occasioned by the historical Jesus which led to his crucifixion, but the social formation of the Jesus movement as it led away from the crucifixion. One need not offer any apologies for the social orders within which Jesus was killed in order to admit his transgression of them. One need only acknowledge that he was not killed as the innocent victim which later Christian interpretation claimed him to have been.

All of the literature produced by the early Christian movements does, of course, assume that Jesus was innocent in one way or another, a *dikaios* at least, if not something divine. If as historians we cannot concur, not being able to imagine by what standard Jesus could have been so assessed by his contemporaries (if judged righteous by Torah then Jesus would not have been crucified by the Jews; if by *lex* then not by the Romans; if by *nomos* then not by the polis; and if by *physis* then not at all—for who would have known it except his followers?), we must ask how it was that early Christians came upon the notion.

The answer lies in what we know about the social history of early Christianity. The story is one of quest for social identity and of vociferous conflicts both within the several Christian groups, as well as among them and their leaders, and especially between all of them taken together and the forms of Judaism they were leaving behind. Two points can be made about this extremely fluid and complex period, points with which all New Testament scholars must agree. The first is that self identification was made difficult because of the mixture of people who were attracted to the new movement. The second is that, precisely because of the mixture, it became increasingly difficult to justify the movement in terms of Jewish models, even as a reform movement. The usual reconstruction is to imagine that Jesus himself had broken open the conventional codes of social acceptance and thus unleashed the "mission to the Gentiles" based on some ideology of a universalized Judaism, a Judaism without borders. This is most probably an exaggeration. But it does catch up the issues of self-identification faced by the early Christian groups. They wanted to claim ownership of the legacy of Judaism for a new social formation which did not include only Jews. The battles which ensued, though fought along many lines, at diverse times, and with various results, did produce the general recognition very early on that the Christian movement was quite different from the Judaism which gave it birth. Marking out the borders which clarified that difference was one way social identification took place. As the lines were drawn, separation occurred and hostility resulted. The process is one of the movement from the espousal of commonality (similarity to Judaism) to the recognition of difference. The bitter battles were fought after the difference was recognized, even though the hostility may be understood by us as historians actually to have had its roots in the continuation of the confusing similarity between the two social groups which would not go away.

The problem faced by early Christian groups seeking social identification may be clarified by the following simplication. Born of an ideology which espoused the breaking down of social barriers and border markers, in order to expand inclusively for any and all to enter in, it now found itself describing borders of difference against those who would not join them. Within the group this problem was experienced in yet another way. If, as Paul said, there was neither Jew nor Greek, slave nor free, male nor female in the new community, recognizing the basis upon which fellow Christians took their place and belonged to the same social group would have been difficult indeed. The only thing everyone shared in common was that each had crossed a border between their old social arena of identity and the new social movement. This experience was conceptualized radically as the rupture between the "old" and the "new," and it was fastened upon early on as definitional for membership in the new group. Thus, by definition, Christians were those who experienced conversion, transformation, separation from their old social identities in order to belong to the new community.

This essay cannot be the place to fill in the picture of all the ins and outs of early Christian social formation even from this point of view. But New Testament scholars will know full well the impossible tensions which arose as soon as a border experience ("transformation") was made definitional, i.e., placed at the center of the group's life, thought, and ethics as the model by which the community sought to structure its social behavior. All of the Pauline letters can be read as an attempt to work this out in a certain way, i.e., an address to just this issue. And, judging from his letters, the ways in which the community sought to work out its social markers by using images of transformation are very important for the purposes of this essay.

Whether we consider its emerging ritualization of the meal time which constituted the community gathered, or the emerging mythology of Jesus as the founder and authority of the community, the symbolism by which Christians recognized their commonality was the same, single event—Jesus' crucifixion. Biblical scholars have frequently thought to find the "origin" of the Christian movement in the "resurrection" of Jesus, to be sure. Such a reading of the early history is quite convenient for those who prefer to leave the "mystery" of the Christian event and gospel unexposed. But the notion of the resurrection is merely one of the many ways in which Jesus' death could be rationalized (as "vindication" of a righteous one!), and it is not essential to the meaning of the Jesus' death which was crucial for early Christian social identity. That meaning, it can now be said, was given with the interpretation of Jesus' death as a martyrdom. Sam Williams's study of the pre-Pauline tradition in Romans 3:25-26, as well as works by Dormeyer, Gubler, and others on the passion narratives, show that this is so. And even that understanding of the death would not have happened immediately after the crucifixion. Prophets, philosophers, revolutionaries all were known to suffer their own kinds of violent deaths. The sayings source (Q) shows that Jesus' death could be accepted by his followers solely on the model of the (probably Deuteronomistic) notion of the killing of the prophets. Neither scandal nor glory need be attached to any of a variety of ways in which the death could have been accepted and understood at first. Only with the continuation of the Jesus movement in the process of social formation would a particular interpretation of the death of Jesus have served to make clear a specific relationship between Jesus as founder and the group as founded by him. And the particular interpretation which served as a firm foundation for all subsequent, mythological embellishments was that of Jesus as martyr, i.e., one who died for that cause which now his followers imagined themselves to represent.

It is important now to emphasize two points. The first is that the interpretation of Jesus' death as a martyrdom did not require entertaining notions of Jesus' special status as a divine being or person of superior power. Thoughts such as these could, however, arise once the death as martyrdom was grasped in a certain way. The second point to be made is that the interpretation of Jesus' death as a martyrdom was just that—an *interpretation*. Sam Williams has helped us imagine the crisis-occasion in early Christian social formation to which Jesus' death as a martyrdom answered. It was the point at which the community had to justify its composition as a mixture of Jew and Gentile, exactly that problem which occasioned the great severence of Christianity from Judaism! Jesus' death as martyrdom was important because it could be imagined as the violent event which actually severed the new from the old. Gentiles, moreover, could understand its function "for the community" (read "polis") on the model of their own noble death tradition. And Jews could understand it as a mark of Jesus' integrity (read "righteousness"), his refusal to bend before the Roman tyrant on the model of the Maccabees. Both Gentile and Jew could see in such an event, as well, ways to rationalize acceptance of one another in a new social grouping. They could do this by elaborating various aspects of the noble death schema. That for which Jesus stood firm could now be identified—it was his "cause," his vision, his intention which, from the point of view of early Christians, was the social formation early Christian groups were actualizing. And the "nomos" basic to any social formation, as well as to any notion of martyrological integrity, could now be imagined—it was Jesus' "teaching" or "message" itself. We might find it curious to imagine Jesus' teaching, that which we can reconstruct of it, as the constitutional basis for social life. It is hardly adequate for such a purpose, as the long history of debates over the "interim ethic" has demonstrated. Paul also found it difficult to imagine, and Mark, and John and the other writers of early Christian literature. Nevertheless they all accepted the basic premise that Jesus had inaugurated a (strongly non-legal) "law" of some kind as "constitution" for the new movement. The notion is both demanded and enabled by the view of Jesus' death as a martyrdom. Accidental, isolated, deserved executions cannot be martyrdoms. The martyr must die for a polis, land, people, cause, idea, law,—i.e., for a social formation which can become the standard for making a judgment as to his integrity, his "rightness," his representation of an ideal even unto death. But these are Christian *interpretations* of the event, read back into the founding history, rationalizing their own situation by mythologizing their past.

Once that notion was in place marvelous theologies (of divine judgment, approbation, and active intervention), christologies (of vindication, exaltation, lordship), and soteriologies (of justification, regeneration, transformation) could burst forth from the explosive imagination in firey display against the dark night sky, as in fact occurred. Jewish Christians saw the death as a vindication both of Jesus and of God, and thus of the Gentiles as well, who had recognized it as the supreme martyrdom for the sake of the unsurpassable social order. Gentile Christians celebrated the "freedom" such a victory of "transcendence" over the worn out (read "actual") social orders demonstrated. The meal time could be changed symbolically as a re-collection of the founder's "death for" the new society-being-actualized. And so forth. Amidst the conflict of social formation the need to determine the grounds upon which shared experience could be rationalized and recognized as fundamental became critical. A movement which lacked at first the markers necessary for social ordering fixed upon the violent death of Jesus as a foundational event. And it generated the most amazing set of mythologies and rituals—a Christ crucifial as saving event; a Son of God sent to give his life as a ransom; a meal in which those who dared to receive such a gift gave thanks for it.

C. In Retrospect

All of the Jesus traditions taken up into the synoptic gospels presuppose the momentous shifts in perspective created by early Christian rationalizations. These rationalizations were called for by the need to determine the group's foundations as a society. Jesus is now always and only seen as the one who was vindicated because he was right—i.e., God's true prophet, messiah, or even son. And the communities which continued to live out of their memories of Jesus' activity as the prophet-king who was crucified, do so only and always from the perspective of the new order, looking back across the gap which separates the Christians from the Jews.

Parable studies have shown what happens even to a plausibly "authentic" story by the historical Jesus when it is retold in the context of the new social order. As historians we work very hard to place such parables in their "original" setting in order to hear them as if for the first time. Hearing many of them for the first time in this way we think we are able to understand something of the nature of Jesus' prophetic stance. Like many prophets gone before he appealed to the best in his hearers, evoking the major themes of Jewish narrative traditions, and affirming the highest ideals of Jewish aspiration and Jewish ideologies of social justice. But he brought these ideals to bear with forceful, parabolic critique upon the actual social circumstances of the day. And thus we leave it there, satisfied that the critique was justified, and thinking that it justifies the usual Christian reading of that history. That reading usually assumes that Jesus was pure, innocent, fully justified in making his critique. But what we also know is that none of these stories got into our texts except by a "second hearing." And in that second hearing the shifts in perspective which concern us in this essay took place. They make all the difference in the world. One already knew that, in the story of the Good Samaritan, the Samaritan was "good" and how the story would end. For a later Christian to imagine that story being told by Jesus (whom the Christian knows to be the Christ) to his first audience (whom the Christian knows to be under the sign of the old, the past, the outside, those not right) determines that the second hearing can easily be voyeuristic and smug. One can "watch" Jesus address the Jews outside, knowing what the outcome will be.

The same is true for all of the story types upon which the gospels are built. The "pronouncement stories" case Jesus as the champion for the peculiar discursive formation of early Christians. He is seen speaking their language against their detractors and winning. The miracle stories imagine him as the divine man whose entrance into the world literally explodes all constraints, even the boundaries between the sane and the demonic. Naturally those who wish to hinder this activity are the intransigent, old order Jews. And the passion narratives cast him as the crucified king, the sacrificed saviour. The Jews are those who plot to kill him and succeed. The gospels are *not* history. We have known that, or should have known that for fifty years now. They are myths claiming to be history. They are products of the christological and sociological shifts which marked out the boundaries by which the early Christian movement defined itself as new over against its own past, and as distinct against its contemporary rivals. The boundaries were, moreover, lines of battle raging both behind and on its flanks. The retrospective view, back to the time before the crucifixion, which the gospels allow us to imagine, should not fool us. We dare not read them as history. They presuppose both the ruptures which have occurred, and the mythic solutions to those ruptures which have been fastened upon and refined. We need to read them as accounts, not of the time of Jesus, but of the time of the early Christian communities which produced them. The history which we need to get straight is precisely that of early Christianity.

Girard says that the gospels are written from the victim's point of view. It is this perspective which makes of them a unique literature, distinguished from all other myths and persecution texts—all of which are written from the persecutor's point of view. Because Jesus, the victim, is innocent, the guilt of the persecutors is disclosed. The gospels thus do not allow for the age old self-deception of those who victimize "without a cause." They are revelatory, working against all attempts to conceal the horrible truth about the surrogate victim mechanism in social formation. Girard is wrong.

The gospels are written from the point of view of early Christians. Jesus is portrayed as an innocent victim, but this is false as an historical assertion. It is true only for those who have inverted the valencies from unrighteous to righteous, violence to vicarious gift, in the interest of justifying a social rupture. And those cast as the ones who killed Jesus? They are now the Jews instead of the Romans, thus reflecting the actual rivalries forced by the new social formation. By casting their myth of the vindicated martyr as a history of those events which founded the new social order, early Christians kept their distance from those events and erased the signs of their own responsibility for thinking the daring thoughts which could transform another's violence into their own grace. This erasure is none other than the concealment of the truth about the innocence of the victim which Girard has documented for his persecution texts. So who are the persecutors writing the gospels? They are Christians. And who are the victims? They are the Jews. And what is unique about the Gospels? That the victims are cast as persecutors of an innocent victim.

It is the lag between the two "periods" of history, the time of Jesus and the time of the Gospels, which Girard does not account for. It is the separation which has occurred between Christianity and Judaism which he does not see. And it is the Christian claim involved in the absolute innocence of Jesus which he wrongly takes as the historical truth. Girard makes these mistakes innocently enough, perhaps, because the nature of the gospel accounts invites such a reading. They cover their tracks, bridge the chasm of the great divide most cleverly. They do this by collapsing myth and history, giving those on the inside a revelatory disclosure of the wisdom at work among those from whom it is hidden. The result is devastating. The real persecutors are not in the picture, not at work during the sacrificial crisis as it were. They were privileged to be spectators from afar, looking out from within the borders which separate those who are right from those who are wrong, out and onto the scene of darkness from which, by means of the violent event to be perpetrated by others, the origination of their grace could be seen. The Jews killed Jesus, the innocent son of God; God raised him up, and demonstrated rightness; Christians receive the benefits. Thus it runs expressly in Peter's sermon in Acts (2:22–36).

This means that the gospels are "persecution texts" after all. They are peculiar texts, to be sure. One reason is that they are not written from the point of view of the dominant strata in a culture. They are written by a small sub-cultural group under duress, making extravagant claims to superiority over all other extant social orders. Christianity's special rival, however, is not the dominant culture as oppressive, but just that social order from which it emerged, itself a minority culture in the great ecumene. Were one able to see the squabble contained within the family, a marvelous debate, if not beneficial self-critical principle, might be imagined to have emerged. But with the break made definitive, difference could no longer be held in tension with commonalities, and the "sacrificial crisis" was on.

This essay is not the place to work out all of the marks of Girard's sacrificial crisis as they occur in the Christian-Jewish conflict of the first century. But they are there. They are there, in fact, as in no other text Girard has given us to illustrate his thesis. Mimetic desire, rivalry, the emergence of the monstrous double (surely we don't need the references to remind us), the hysteria of ecstatic experience, and the violence done to history, tradition, texts, and reputations as the "guilty" victim is obliterated in the attempt to possess its true being for oneself. The double deceit which makes *this* sacrifice of the surrogate victim especially dangerous is that, not only is the scapegoat mechanism fully in operation, it is carried through under the sign of innocence. Thus there is no peace resulting from *this* sacrifice. Girard's paradigm calls for the plague to recede from the crowd whose hands have done violence. But the Jews are the ones depicted in the gospels to have done the deed, and they are not said to be blessed here. And the Christians who wait for the kingdom of peace have guaranteed that it will not come. Using Girard's own categories, the gospels are documents of Christians seeking justification at the expense of the Jews. If the notion of the innocence of the victim is to be seen as a momentous revelation to Christians, they have turned it to scapegoat advantage, using it now to "wash their hands," so to speak, of the whole horrible affair. In *Violence and the Sacred*, Girard emphasized that the surrogate victim mechanism is very costly in terms of human self-deception. Using his own paradigm, the gospels actually double the cost. Deceptions now are involved both in one's view of those outside, as well as one's view of those inside the Christian borders. Not only is peace between Christians and Jews made impossible by construing the crucifixion mythically as a sacrifice, a sacrifice in which the Jews by definition must be imagined to have performed the deed which determines Christian freedom. Inside the Christian circle as well the mythic mentality which conceals the truth about the arbitrariness of the victimization is compounded now by the claim of one's own innocence of justification. That is salvation at some cost.

A Biblical Scholar's Response

Perhaps I have exaggerated the demonic at work in the Christian gospels. If so, I have done so to counter Girard's attributions to them of a singularly divine and revelatory nature. I have done so with a reading as pointed as his, and on his own terms. It remains now to ease off a bit, reflect on the reasons for such an impasse, and assess if we can where we are.

We started out with the observation that it might be helpful for New Testament scholars to compare Girard's program with that of Bultmann. The overriding issue in both cases continues to be the relation of myth and history to the crucial event which Christianity reifies. Bultmann wanted to dispense with myth because of its "objectifying" language, and proposed a translation of the Christian kerygma into existentialist categories. His description of the crisis in self-understanding which the Christian proclamation occasions is well known. The crisis calls for transformation—a leap of faith, radical obedience, freedom from the past, and so forth. Once this program was in place Bultmann could demonstrate its hermeneutical possibilities for a variety of discourses found in the New Testament—especially the message of Jesus, the eschatology of Paul, and the mythology of John. But the program itself was dependent upon a certain privilege granted to the kerygma itself. Bultmann was quite eager to demythologize the gospels' portrayal of Jesus as divine, the world views of early Christianity, whether apocalyptic or gnostic, and the cosmic destiny christologies which they generated. But he refused to separate history and myth in this way in the case of the kerygmatic event itself. For Bultmann the kerygmatic event was the proclamation of the death *of Christ*, and it included the resurrection as the indicator of transformation. This event he demythologized only in the sense of saying what it called for existentially in the transformation of the believer, *not* by means of rigorous distinction between the history and myth of the event proclaimed itself.

This failure of Bultmann turns out now, in the light of issues Girard has raised, to have been his genius. By refusing the gospel accounts as the primary articulation of the Christian myth or message, Bultmann escaped the horrendous problem they create for Christian imagination. He reduced the entire pre-crucifixion "history" of the Christ to the *dass* of Jesus. And he erased all of the mythic markers of post-resurrection destinies as well. These moves concentrated the conjunction of myth and history upon the single event of death-resurrection, the "Christ-event." That it happened was important, but its historicity was actually also only a *dass*, i.e., an event dislocated conveniently from its salient social-historical context. Such a studied naivete about the actuality of social history can be regarded as an attempt to protect from exposure the mysterious ground for the Christian desire for radical transformation. But he did see that Christianity could not be deprived of its symbol of crisis without destroying it. And he understood as well that a critical hermeneutic was required in order to translate that symbol of crisis into categories appropriate to post-enlightenment mentality. Thus Bultmann's notion of the Christian kerygma is analogous to Girard's notion of the gospel as a "text in travail." But Bultmann's kerygma is a more innocent "text" or logos, precisely because it does not allow for contamination by considerations of its generation and influence within the real world of social conflict. It remains mythic, and Bultmann applied it only to the individual Christian within the boundaries of an existential crisis which contains violence within a moment of self-critique. It does not appear to feed upon, or generate, a scapegoat mechanism, because the "sacrifice" has been internalized, and the vicariousness of a prior event has been all but erased in the elevation of that event to the level of proclamation-with-reference.

Girard has called Bultmann's hand, in effect, by taking up the gospel accounts instead of the Pauline kerygma, placing the "Christ-event" squarely in the midst of salient social history, and arguing that the gospel explicitly addresses the problem of myth and history in a specific way. Because the problem of human history is the replication of victimization, and myth by definition is the concealment of that horrible truth, a logos is required which can *expose* mythic thinking, not translate it into symbolic, conceptual, or even existential categories. Girard does not discuss the Pauline kerygma, nor Bultmann's interpretation of it. But it is quite clear that, given Girard's thesis about the problem Christianity addresses, the kergymatic form of the Christian logos would not easily do the job which needs to be done. The gospels can do it, according to Girard, by re-writing the script of the scapegoat myth as a fully fledged account of a sacrificial crisis in which, however, the victim is innocent.

So Girard has challenged a pietistic understanding of Christianity and its comfortability with a kerygma which can be internalized as a principle of self-critique and personal transformation. (Protestant theologians would talk about the experience of "judgment" and "grace".) He has done so by working out the mechanisms which actually may undergird the mythic aspects of the kergyma as the proclamation of an objective, prior, and vicarious event. These mechanisms are, according to Girard, equations of social dynamics, and they have to do with crises in social history, not personal salvation. It is true that Girard's anthropology is different from that of Bultmann. His view of religion and society is different. And his notion of the intention of the Christian gospel is different. But his challenge still stands, whether one agrees with his particular views on social formation or not. That is because neither Bultmann nor the scholarship in his wake have discussed the issues Girard raises, much less adequately addressed them. They have not demythologized "Christ-crucified" in terms of social history; and they have not discussed the social function of the gospels as a hermeneutical issue with the same kind of energy invested in the kerygma.

But now we must note that to take Girard's challenge seriously will not rescue us from the storms of hermeneutical debate. It will in fact plunge us back into very heavy seas indeed. I have argued that Girard made a fatal error in accepting the gospels as accounts which disclose the reality of the event of Jesus' crucifixion instead of as myths which conceal the social conflict in early Christianity. But my own reading of that history of early Christianity as a sacrificial crisis was a Girardian reading. By using Girard's theory of social formation I was able to expose the self-deception involved in the particular construction Christians put upon that event as a violence which brought Christianity into being. I read Girard against Girard merely by shifting the historical location of the event addressed by the text, and re-introducing the mythic aspects of the gospel. I did not have to re-define Girard's definitions of myth and social conflict in order to do this. But I did violate his hermeneutic.

That hermeneutic which I violated needs now to be discussed. According to Girard my reading of the gospels fails to take note of what he calls the critical spirit they have unleashed in Western culture. I have read them cynically so to speak, noticing only the surface phenomena of (early) Christian social history, but not noticing my indebtedness to the gospels as the source of my critical posture to begin with. Girard knows that Christian history is messy, and that the gospels can be read as charter documents for persecution. But this does not get at their genius. Their genius is their capacity to evoke, enable, and withstand a radically critical reading of their own misreadings as texts which ultimately cannot justify persecution. So the issue at stake is hermeneutical with respect to two fundamental questions. The first has to do with the social function of the text in Western history. The second has to do with the social function of the critic. Both are related to Girard's notion of the critical spirit of the enlightenment.

For Girard, the hermeneutical circle runs from the gospels, through the enlightenment, and back to the gospels. The "travail" of the gospels as texts is that, while they have succeeded in awakening a critical spirit in Western culture, they have not succeeded in being recognized by critics as the source of that spirit, nor have they succeeded in bringing the enlightenment scholar to the point of self-criticism with regard to involvement in scapegoat mechanisms himself. Girard's program is to point that out. On the one hand he wants to claim all Western manifestations of the critique of myth (such as the end of witch-burning) for the Christian gospel. On the other, he wants those who share the critical spirit of the enlightenment to go further. To see that it is the *gospel* which has given birth to the critical spirit is the next step. And this would be to acknowledge as well the mechanisms of the scapegoat at work even at the level of intellectual labor. If the circle came full, the critical spirit would become truly critical, i.e., self-critical.

So Girard's criticism turns out to be curiously similar to Bultmann's own after all. A superior position of privilege is granted to a specific form of early Christian articulation of the Christ-event. For both, the history of the church's readings of this text is most problematic, suffering mainly from a mythic mentality. The enlightenment calls this mythic mentality into question and provides the critical spirit to exegete the text correctly. The exegete then turns apologist—Bultmann calling for the internalization of the crucial "Christ-event"; Girard calling for an intellectual conversion in keeping with the gospel's disclosure of mimetic desire. Both involve the reader in a hermeneutical catch twenty-two, but Girard's net is the broader because of his claim that the (self-)critical spirit is precisely the gospel's legacy and intention. Only be reading the gospel this way can one claim to have been truly enlightened. And only true enlightenment can save Western culture from sacrificial crisis.

To counter this claim as claim would be to rethink the entire history of the manifestations of the rational critical spirit. That we cannot do here, although it is important to indicate that I would have to disagree with Girard, even while granting that Christianity has strongly sensitized Western thought to the problem of motivation in rational reflection. But we can suggest that, on Girard's own terms, he has done precisely what he said his program can do—exegete the gospel in terms of its own intentionality, then use its lens to interpret critically all of the mythic manifestations of human cultures in general. Notice the categories: originary, unique, revelatory. Notice the level of significant event: either unconscious mechanism or superior knowledge. And the event is sacrificial. And the perspective is that of the innocent one(s). And the desire is for a peaceable kingdom without oppression, victimization, i.e., without misuse of power. Taken as a set, these categories and concerns are strongly suggestive of Christian mythic mentality.

It may be extremely difficult, therefore, for many Christian scholars to withstand a persuasion evoking such desires. I have tried to withstand it on the basis of knowledge which has been won by historical-literary criticism. From a Girardian point of view my own reading of the gospels can only and already be laid to the account of a criticism not sufficiently enlightened, I suppose. My ploy has been therefore to read Girard against Girard by appealing to such enlightenment as the guild of biblical studies has thought it had. What has happened in the doing of that may now be stated. Four issues emerge for us.

1) At issue: The Hermeneutical Circle. What I suspect Girard has done is a reading of the gospels as the church has understood them, i.e., as they were intended to be taken by those who wrote them, filtered by two thousand years of category formation in keeping with the myth of innocence. It may be the case, that is, that the myth of innocence (as I read them) or the disclosure of persecution (as Girard reads them) is

actually what the gospels achieve, and that this particular poignancy in the script is a peculiarly Christian creation and vision. If so, Girard's entire program is an exegesis of Christian mentality, not a disclosure of the mechanisms at work generally in all human social formation. But then, what are we to make of all the other texts Girard has read in order to establish his general theories of violence and the sacred? From his point of view he read them first, and he has read them correctly, only to discover, perhaps later on, that the gospels share the script, but invert the valencies. From my point of view the hermeneutical categories given with the gospels *may* have been in place all along, there in the set of assumptions about what is important which gave the twist to Girard's own earlier work. That would mean that the other texts, used first to establish the theories, then for contrast and comparison, have been used mainly as a foil to reiterate again the "uniqueness" of the Christian text, and on its own terms. It would mean that the "dark side" of the gospels as I have read them (i.e., as texts of persecution) may not have been so completely "concealed" in the history of their readings in Western culture as Girard's theory of concealment in persecution texts posits. But of course that way of reading them can't have been front and center, or the "grace" could not have shone forth. So repressed, but known or sensed in some troubling way, the dark reading was there, and may have provided Girard with his theories of the scapegoat and the sacrificial victim. The sequence of discoveries then would be: from the (unacknowledged) dark reading of the gospel, through explorations of Western literary texts, to the myths of all cultures, and back again to the gospels now read as "light," via the Hebrew scriptures. The suggestion is seriously made, and it raises a serious issue. If it is right, we need to rethink Girard's claim to a universal theory of social formation. And we need to ponder the familiar hermeneutical circle.

Biblical scholars may have trouble identifying the problem with such a procedure, and evaluating its results. The distinction between eisegesis and exegesis won't do in this case. And neither will a facile appeal to the old hermeneutical circle make it all right. Girard has played the game fairly in comparison with much of the history of biblical hermeneutics. He has not done much differently, for instance, than Bultmann, whose set of existential categories breathed the atmosphere of Lutheran piety from the beginning. But now we see that Girard has made an argument for legitimation out of the hermeneutical circle itself, and has used it to interpret not only Western texts, but texts from any and all human societies. What is being challenged in its procedure is our sense of gaining some critical distance and perspective on our texts as scholars. We've assumed that translations into other systems of academic discourse could provide us with that perspective. Now we cannot be so sure. Category formation is at stake and the ethnocentric issue is upon us. Biblical scholars have recognized this problem whenever the interpretive categories begin to look like theological statements, putting quotes around the big words in the biblical texts. But we have scarcely been aware of the ethnocentric issue outside our field, in the disciplines we use to do our "criticisms." What if they really are, as Girard claims, enlightenment versions of the Christian gospel? Is it possible to learn anything new, to break the hermeneutical circle without destroying it, to see our own things from another's point of view? Something seems to have gone wrong here with the method of comparison and contrast. Similarity and difference have been valorized radically in different directions by Girard. Dialogue, diairesis, and debate have no more room for play. Degrees of difference don't count any longer. It's all or nothing, wrong or right, guilty or innocent. Girard's challenge is challenge indeed. We will need to argue for every step "outside" the field, that it gains for us some critical distance, and that that distance makes a difference.

2) At issue: Historical Reconstruction. Biblical scholars practice "historical-literary criticism." There is no guarantee that the distance won from the text by means of historical criticism will make a critical difference in how we understand its meaning. That has been demonstrated over and over again. But it does appear to be a very important way to create some gaps in the hermeneutical circle, across which the scholarly imagination can play while seeking sets of categories for filling in the picture. I have appealed to this tradition in the guild, relying on its findings as I understand them, in order to challenge Girard. Girard is aware of this historical scholarship. But he has not taken it into account. He has read the text at the level of the history of ideas. As for social history, it has become a *dass* for him.

The difference it makes when one does place the text in its social-historical context should be clear by now, however. Using Girard's own categories, the text becomes a persecution text, just like all the others. It is curious and troubling that Girard has seen this mechanism at work behind all of his other texts where collective killings may be imagined, but fails to see it in the case of the gospels. The issue is now very serious, as I see it. That is because, if one reads the gospels this way, i.e., as texts which reify the crucifixion as violence against innocence in the interest of the self-justification of the author-readers at the expense of others, the charges against the putative persecutors storied in the mythic history are not adjudicable. So is that what we have for a text on our hands, or is Girard's theory wrong? Surface level social history does become a kind of test, it seems, even for theories of the history of ideas. We need to insist on this placement of texts in their social historical contexts, I think, or else the claim to be doing criticism is in danger. Notice that, in the case of the gospels alone, Girard does not go on to describe the social-historical effect of the actual event reported, as he does with his other texts. The effectiveness of the gospels is now discussed only at the level of intellectual history. So it makes some difference whether we place our Christian texts in the order of private transformations (as Bultmann does), or in the order of the history of ideas (as Girard ultimately does), or in the order of salient social history (as I have tried to do). After Girard, we can no longer be complacent about the difference it actually makes.

3) At issue: Social Formation. We should not lose sight of the fact that Girard's reading of the gospels is based upon a theory of social formation through conflict resolution. I have countered Girard's reading by relocating the text in a salient history of conflict. But that merely inverted the valencies of the scapegoat mechanism. It did not offer a critique of the mechanism itself. In order to do that an alternate theory of social formation would be required. We have none. We have operated mainly with the assumption that ideas lead the way. Thus we may find it difficult to counter Girard's sociology on the one hand, and withstand his notion of the powerful influence of the gospel as text on the other. Recent attempts at social description or sociologies of early Christianity are therefore to be applauded. But working with models and structural correlations has not provided a way to ask about the effective relation of myths and social behavior. Nor has it produced a theory of social formation itself, other than those which presuppose the power of symbols as systems. Girard's challenge is therefore most unnerving. If he's wrong about the gospel, but right about the mechanisms, what then? Clearly we have work to do.

4) At issue: The Academy. Girard has found a way to work with texts both as critic and as a prophet of sorts. His concerns for social justice often break the surface as he writes his books. Biblical scholars will have a difficult time faulting Girard for this. That is because his concerns, and the way in which he bridges from criticism to social commentary, may well be attitudes shared by many. And though the field of biblical scholarship seldom takes up the question of the Bible's place in the living traditions of Judaism and Christianity, most scholars are aware of this other tradition of readings of the same texts. If we judge by the nature of published discourse, moreover, many biblical scholars assume that their work as scholars has, or should have something to do with the way in which the Bible is read outside the field. That assumption could very well be wrong. But the more interesting observation is that we do not know whether it is. So our inability to address the question of the social function of our texts in their early historical contexts is matched by our inability to say very much about the function of texts and text critics in our own time.

Girard's challenge to us is to think these matters through. I have countered Girard on a single issue only—his misreading of early Christian history. But his proposals involve theses about religion and culture, literature and society, and he asserts that the gospel has been at work throughout our cultural history enabling the rise of the critical spirit. What are we to do with that? His foray into the field of New Testament scholarship brings all of that along. Is it enough to debate with him the composition of the text? Since I have done that, and have come to another reading of it, what then? My reading also might be "documented" in the subsequent history—up and until Jonestown, and the moral majority, and the policies of the Reagan administration in Central America, and the state of the churches in southern California—all "readings" of the gospel as a persecution text by self-righteous innocents. Or are they? Girard would say they very well may be readings of the gospel as a charter for persecution, but that my own ability to see that they are is also a gospel legacy. Does that constitute a call to social service?

Thus the issue of biblical criticism! The issue is real, and Girard may prove too much for us to handle, serious about our work as we are, and prone to dramatics. He has certainly caught us off guard, and ill-prepared to respond. So some may be tempted to join him in his program of enlightenment. But my own view is that we should not do that. We have more and other work to do. We have not yet paid our dues to the critical spirit of the "old" enlightenment. And we should do that. The academy does not need the gospel. But we, together with our texts, do need the academy. And, who knows? If we ever learn to differ and defer instead of always to be calling for conversion, we might see *that* mechanism at work in the world as well. That would give us quite an attractive option to the scapegoat gospel to be sure. We might even be able to tell, eventually, which one has, or should be given, its chances for survival.

BIBLIOGRAPHICAL NOTE

Books by René Girard

1961   *Mensonge romantique et vérité romanesque.* Paris: Grasset. (rpt. Livre de Poche, Coll. Pluriel, 1978)
(1966) ET: *Deceit, Desire and the Novel: Self and Other in Literary Structure.* Baltimore: Johns Hopkins UP. (rpt. 1969, 1976)
1963   *Dostoievski: Du double à l'unité.* Paris: Plon.
1972   *La Violence et le sacré.* Paris: Grasset. (rpt. Livre de Poche, Coll. Pluriel, 1980)
(1977) ET: *Violence and the Sacred.* Baltimore: Johns Hopkins UP. (rpt. 1979)
1976   *Critique dans un souterrain.* Lausanne: L'Age d'homme. (rpt. Livre de Poche, Coll. Biblio-essais, 1983)
1978a   *Des Choses cachées depuis la fondation du monde:* Recherches avec Jean-Michel Oughourlian et Guy Lefort. Paris: Grasset. (rpt. Livre de Poche, Coll. Biblio-essais, 1983; trans. forthcoming with Athlone and Stanford UP).
1978b   *"To Double Business Bound": Essays on Literature, Myth, Mimesis, and Anthropology.* Baltimore: Johns Hopkins UP.
1982   *Le Bouc émissaire.* Paris: Grasset. (rpt. Livre de Poche, Coll. Biblio-essais, 1985; trans. forthcoming with Johns Hopkins UP).
1985   *La Route Antique des hommes pervers: Essais sur Job.* Paris: Grasset. (trans. forthcoming with Athlone and Stanford UP).

A translation of excerpts from *Des Choses cachées* can be found in "Interdividual Psychology," *Denver Quarterly* 14, No. 3 (Fall 1979), 3–19. Trans. of excerpts from *Le Bouc émissaire:* "Peter's Denial and the Question of Mimesis," *Notre Dame English Journal* 14, No. 3 (Summer 1982), 177–89; "History and the Paraclete," *The Ecumenical Review,* Jan. 1, 1983, 3–16; "Scandal and the Dance: Salome in the Gospel of Mark," *New Literary History* 15 (Winter 1984), 311–24; "Generative Violence and the Extinction of Social Order," *Salmagundi,* Nos. 63–64 (Spring–Summer 1984), 204–237.

A complete bibliography of books by Girard, and of essays by and about him through 1983, is to be found in the volume of essays edited by Michel Deguy and Jean-Pierre Dupuy, *René Girard et le problème du mal* (Paris: Grasset, 1983). A still more up to date listing can be found in the volume of essays, *To Honor René Girard,* Stanford French and Italian Studies 54 (Palo Alto: Anma Libri, 1985). Further references to critical discussion of Girard's work among Biblical Scholars, mostly European, can be found in the essay by Robert North S.J., "Violence and the Bible: The Girard Connection," *Catholic Biblical Quarterly* 47, No. 1 (1985), 1–27. The recently appeared proceedings of the Colloque de Cérisy on Girard, *Violence et liberté*, ed. Paul Dumouchel (Paris: Grasset, 1985), contains essays from a broad spectrum of disciplines.

WORKS CONSULTED

Balthasar, H.U.v.
1980a "Die neue Theorie von Jesus als 'Südenbock.'" *Intern. Kath. Zeitschrift* 9.
1980b *Theodramatik, Bd. III. Die Handlung.* Einsiedeln: Johannes.

Barrett, C. K.
1968 *A Commentary on the First Epistle to the Corinthians.* New York: Harper & Row.
1973 *A Commentary on the Second Epistle to the Corinthians.* New York: Harper & Row.

Barthélemy, D.
1964 *Dieu et son image: Ebauche d'une théologie biblique.* Paris.

Bauer,
1957 *Theological Dictionary of the New Testament and other Early Christian Literature.* Tr. Arndt & Gingrich. Chicago: Univ. of Chicago Press.

Betz, H. D.
1967 *Nachfolge und Nachahmung Jesu Christi in Neuen Testament.* Tuebingen: J. C. B. Mohr. (Paul Siebeck).
1979 *Galatians, A Commentary on the First Epistle to the Churches in Galatia.* Philadelphia: Fortress Press.

Bultmann, R.
1948 "Neues Testament und Mythologie," *Kerygma und Myth.* herausgegeben von H. W. Bartsch, 15–53. Hamburg: Reich und Heidrich. (Tr. "New Testament and Mythology." *Kerygma and Myth.* Ed. H. W. Bartsch, tr. R. H. Fuller, 1–44. London: SPKC).

Burke, K.
1966 *Language as Symbolic Action: Essays on Life, Literature and Myth.* Berkeley: Univ. of California Press.

Burkert, W.
1983 *Homo Necans: The Anthropology of Ancient Greek Sacrificial Ritual and Myth.* Tr. Peter Bing. Berkeley: Univ. of California Press.

Conzelmann, H.
1975 *Corinthians, A Commentary on the First Epistle to the Corinthians.* Philadelphia: Fortress Press.

Dormeyer, D.
1974 *Die Passion Jesu als Verhaltensmodell.* Muenster: Aschendorff.

Dumouchel, P. & Dupuy, J.-P.
1979 *L'Enfer des choses: René Girard et la logique de l'économie.* Paris: Seuil.

Dupuy, J.-P.
1982 *Ordres et désordres: Enquête sur un nouveau paradigme.* Paris: Seuil.

Fiedler, P.
1976 *Jesus und die Sünder.* Frankfort.

Fishbane, M.
1985 *Biblical Interpretation in Ancient Israel.* London: Oxford.

Furnish, V. P.
1968 *Theology and Ethics in Paul.* Nashville: Abingdon.

Gans, E.
1981
1985 *The Origin of Language: A Formal Theory of Representation.* Berkeley: Univ. of California Press.

Gaster, T.
1971 *Festivals of the Jewish Year.* New York: William Morrow.

Gerhardsson, B.
1966 *The Testing of God's Son (Matt 4:1–11 & Par): An Analysis of an Early Christian Midrash.* Lund: CWK Gleerup.

Ginsberg, L.
1910, 1925 *Legends of the Jews.* vols. II, V. Philadelphia.

Goodhart, S.
1985 "'I am Joseph': René Girard and the Prophetic Law." *To Honor René Girard.* Stanford French and Italian Studies 54. Palo Alto: Anma Libri.

Gubler, M.-L.
1977 *Die Frühesten Deutungen des Todes Jesu.* Göttingen: Vandenhoeck und Ruprecht.

Haenchen, E.
1971 *The Acts of the Apostle Paul: A Commentary.* 14th Ed. Oxford: Blackwell.

Hertz, J. H.
1978 *The Pentateuch and Haftorahs.* London: Soncino.

Heschel, A.
1971 *The Prophets*, II. New York: Harper & Row.

Hoffman, N.
1982 *Kreuz und Trinität, Sur Theologie des Sühne.* Einsiedeln.

Hofius, O.
1983 "Sühne und Versohnung. Zum paulinischen Verständnis des Kreuzestodes Jesu." *Versuche das Leiden und Sterben Jesu zu verstehen.* Ed. W. Maas. München.

Hurvitz, A.
1974   "The Date of the Prose Tale of Job Linguistically Reconsidered." *Harvard Theological Review* 67: 17–34.

Jeremias, J.
1965   *Die Gleichnisse Jesu*. Göttingen.
1966   *Abba*. Göttingen.
1971   *Neutestamentliche Theologie* I. Gütersloh.

Jewett, R.
1982   *The Captain America Complex: The Dilemna of Zealous Nationalism*. Santa Fe: Bear and Co.

Kornfeld, K.
1981   "QDS und Gottesrecht im Alten Testament." *Congress Volume, Vienna 1980* (VTSup 32). Ed. J. A. Emerton. Leiden: Brill.

Levi-Strauss, Cl.
1964   *Le Cru et le cuit: Mythologiques*. Paris: Plon.

Levine, B.
1974   *In the Presence of the Lord*. Leiden.

Linnemann, A.
1964   *Gleichnisse Jesu*. Göttingen.

Lohfink, G.
1982a   *Kirchenträume*. Freiburg. i. Br.
1982b   *Wie hat Jesus Gemeinde gewollt?* Freiburg. i. Br.

Lohse. E.
1971   *Colossians and Philemon: A Commentary on the Epistles to the Colossians and to Philemon*. Philadelphia: Fortress Press.

Merklein, H.
1978   *Die Gottesherrschaft als Handlungsprinzip*. Wurzburg.

Otto, R.
1970   *The Idea of the Holy*. New York: Oxford.

Pesch, R.
1978   *Das Abendmahl und Jesu Todesverständnis*. Freiburg. i. Br.

Pritchard, J. B. ed.
1969   *Ancient Near Eastern Texts Relating to the Old Testament*. 3rd. ed. Princeton.

Radkowski, G.-H.
1980   *Les Jeux du désir: De la technique à l'économie*. Paris: P.U.F.

Ricoeur, P.
1970   *Freud and Philosophy: An Essay on Interpretation*. New Haven: Yale University Press.

Sahlins, M.
1972   *Stone Age Economics*. Chicago: Aldine.

Bibliographical Note, Works Consulted 171

Sampley, J. P.
1980 *Pauline Partnership in Christ: Christian Community in Light of Roman Law.* Philadelphia: Fortress Press.

Schenker, A.
1981 *Versöhnung und Sühne.* Freiburg/Schweiz:Kath. Bibelwerk.

Schillebeeckx, E.
1976 *Jesus: Die Geschichte von einem Lebendem.* Freiburg. i. Br.

Schmithals, W.
1972 *Paul and the Gnostics.* Nashville: Abingdon Press.

Scholnick, S.
1982 "The Meaning of Mišpāṭ in the Book of Job." *Journal of Biblical Literature* 101: 521–529.

Schürmann, H.
1983 *Gottes Reich—Jesu Geschick.* Freiburg i. Br.

Schwager, R.
1978 *Brauchen wir einen Sündenbock? Gewalt und Erlösung in den biblischen Schriften.* München: Koesel-Verlag.
1983 "Versöhnung und Sühne." *ThPh* 58: 217–225.

Schweizer, E.
1968 *Jesus Christus in vielfältigen Zeugnis des Neuen Testaments.* München.

Segal, M. Z.
1949–50 "The Parallels in the Book of Job." (Hebrew). *Tarbiz.* 20.5709: 35–48.

Serres, M.
1977 *La Naissance de la Physique dans le texte de Lucrèce: Fleuves et turbulences.* Paris: Grasset.

Valadier, P.
1982 "Bouc émissaire et Révélation chrétienne." *Etudes* 257:251–260.

Vögtle, A.
1977 "Der verkündignede un verkündigte Jesus 'Christus.'" *Wer ist Jesus Christus?* Ed. J. Sauer. Freiburg i. Br.

Weissman, M.
1980 *The Midrash Says.* Brooklyn: Benei Yakov Publications.

Williams, S. K.
1975 *Jesus' Death as Saving Event.* Missoula, Mt.: Scholars.

Zlotowitz, M. ed.
1978 *Yonah / Jonah.* Brooklyn: Mesorah Publications.

www.ingramcontent.com/pod-product-compliance
Lightning Source LLC
Chambersburg PA
CBHW032256150426
43195CB00008BA/476